WHEN SATURDAY MATTERED MOST

WHEN SATURDAY MATTERED MOST

The Last
Golden Season
of Army Football

Mark Beech

THOMAS DUNNE BOOKS
ST. MARTIN'S PRESS ≋ NEW YORK

THOMAS DUNNE BOOKS.
An imprint of St. Martin's Press.

www.thomasdunnebooks.com
www.stmartins.com

Design by Steven Seighman

ISBN 978-0-312-54818-6 (hardcover)
ISBN 978-1-250-01356-9 (e-book)

First Edition: September 2012

10 9 8 7 6 5 4 3 2 1

To Allison

CONTENTS

WHEN SATURDAY MATTERED MOST

INTRODUCTION

THERE WAS A TIME when Saturday mattered most. Football got its start in America as a college game, and for the better part of one hundred years, from the first contest between Princeton and Rutgers in 1869 through the 1940s, that's pretty much the way it stayed. The sport's brightest stars were campus men, all-American boys who played for little more than school pride. Professional football, far from being the most popular spectator sport in the United States, was more of a Sunday afternoon sideshow—one that lacked the distinction of noble amateurism. That distinction was in many cases a sham, of course—corrupt recruiting practices and academic dissimulation are almost as old as college football, but the fact remained that the chance to play professionally was almost never the reason a young man played in college.

That all changed forever on December 28, 1958, when Johnny Unitas and the Baltimore Colts beat Frank Gifford and the New York Giants in overtime—and on national television—to win the National Football League championship. Commonly referred to as "the Greatest Game Ever Played," the Colts' sudden-death victory over the Giants drew an unheard-of forty-five million viewers to CBS and is widely credited with launching the NFL to the enormous popularity it enjoys today. While professional football's fast-paced, high-scoring action had already begun to attract new fans in the years after World War II, the Baltimore–New York clash was like a doorway between two eras, the first of blue-collar grit and the latter of gilt-edged glory.

It's no coincidence that the predawn of the NFL marked a golden age of service academy football. Army and Navy were regularly two of the top teams in the country, and their annual classics in Philadelphia were the focus of intense media hype. Long before anybody had ever heard of the BCS, Army-Navy was as big as any bowl game. Indeed, it was in some ways the Super Bowl of its day, a national concern complete with its own entire week of pageantry and hoopla. In a sport that prized its nonprofessional status, the Cadets and Midshipmen who played at West Point and Annapolis were the pinnacles of gridiron purity. World War II and the Korean War were still fresh in the American memory, and most people were close to somebody who had served in one or both. Far from being controversial, the profession of arms enjoyed widespread acceptance and admiration. The nation was then fully invested in winning the space race (the Soviet Union had launched Sputnik I in October 1957), and the war in Vietnam, where the United States had been sending military advisers since 1955 to aid the non-Communist forces of the South, was still far from being a painfully divisive domestic issue. In 1956, in fact, CBS had debuted a television series called *The West Point Story*, which depicted an idealized version of both cadets and the academy—and which featured a raft of young actors who would go on to greater fame, including Clint Eastwood, Barbara Eden, and Leonard Nimoy.

It was an age, in other words, in which duty and honor and commitment counted for more than a professional signing bonus, and nothing prevented Army and Navy—both of which then required three years of military service after graduation—from competing against other powerhouse programs for the best talent in the country. But within a few years, as the fledgling American Football League began to bid against the NFL for collegiate stars, the country's best players began to spurn the military schools. Three years was just too long to wait for fame and fortune. The Cadets' 8–0–1 campaign in 1958 remains the last undefeated season Army or Navy ever had, and the two weeks in mid-October that the men from West Point spent atop the college football rankings were the last time any service academy team ever reached number one.

Fittingly, the members of that team were more than just football stars. They were archetypes. No player better exemplified this than Pete Dawkins, who enjoyed a senior season unmatched in the annals of college football, winning gridiron and academic honors with remarkable finesse. And as Army's iconic Lonely End, Bill Carpenter cut a hauntingly romantic figure on the field, a solitary sentry held aloof from the mayhem of the game. Towering over everything was Red Blaik, the Hall of Fame coach who unexpectedly chose to make the 1958 season his last. In twenty-five years on the sideline at West Point, he had established himself as a titan of college football. He was a prodigious winner—from 1941 to '49, his teams won or shared three national championships and finished undefeated five times. He was also a coach of coaches, populating his staff with some of the most influential minds in football, including Sid Gillman and Vince Lombardi, both of whom would play major roles in the transformation of the NFL. All told, twenty-two men who worked for Blaik would go on to be head coaches at either the collegiate or professional level. And the triumphant twist with which he capped his glorious career, a mysterious offense that both devastated opponents and captured the public's imagination, remains a singular achievement in the annals of the sport.

By 1958, Army had been one of college football's marquee teams for nearly two decades. And when the final gun sounded at the end of the Cadets' 22–6 defeat of Navy on November 29, there seemed little reason to think things would ever change. What happened that season is the story of the end of an era. It's the story of a particular time and place—of a truly unique moment in college football history, one with an impact that still resonates. It's the story of one team's, and one man's, finest hour.

Chapter 1

LINING UP IN THE SNOW

START WITH THE MAN and go from there. In January 1958, Earl Henry Blaik was a month away from celebrating his sixty-first birthday. But at six feet two inches tall, the figure he cut still recalled his form from nearly four decades before, when he had been a sleek 182-pound end on the Army football team. He had kept his body fit through a lifelong aversion to both drinking and smoking, as well as adherence to a diet that was as bland as it was meager—his good friend Stanley Woodward, the urbane sports editor of the *Newark Star-Ledger*, often referred to Blaik as "strictly a Shredded Wheat man." A long nose and deep-set blue eyes accentuated his angular, patrician face. And the thatch of auburn hair he kept neatly parted to the side, a provision of his Scottish heritage, as well as the inspiration for the nickname "Red," which he would carry throughout his life, was almost as thick as it had been the day he played fifty-eight and a half minutes of a 6–0 loss to Navy in 1919. He had been coaching football for over twenty-four years, the last seventeen of them at West Point, but he looked nothing like a man in the waning days of his career.

In addition to being a teetotaler, Blaik was also something of a prude. The closest he typically came to vulgarity was the starchy phrase "Jeebers Katy!" Only rarely "Jesus Katy!" But such exclamations were infrequent. Publicly, he hardly ever betrayed emotion or raised his voice, save to issue one of his crisp commands on the practice field. Though he despised being described in the press as "austere" or "aloof," Blaik carefully cultivated his manner of dignified cool. He stood apart at practice and remained mostly mute throughout each ninety-minute session. Indeed, he almost never spoke to players. And rather than fly into a rage when he saw someone make a mistake, it was instead his habit to summon the wayward cadet to his side, where he would dispense a quiet, private correction. His command presence was overwhelming. Despite having been off active duty for nearly forty years, Blaik was known to just about everybody at West Point, including his civilian assistants, as "the Colonel," and they addressed him that way. They did it not just out of deference to the rank he'd held at retirement—he'd been recommissioned in the reserves in the early days of World War II—but also out of respect for his authority.

Blaik's dominance over his program was total. To his players, most of whom were old enough to remember Army's storied, unbeaten national-championship teams of 1944 and '45, their distant and imperturbable coach was not so much a mentor as a living, breathing artifact of Americana. They held him in awe and accorded him the respect usually reserved in the army for general officers. To his civilian assistants Blaik was a powerful executive. Instead of dictating policy, he set agendas and left it to them to formulate solutions. He encouraged vigorous debate, and it was only after he had heard everybody out on a matter that he would render his decision, at which point all discussion came to an end. So compelling was the force of Blaik's personality that it had once brought to heel the man who was soon to become football's most famous authoritarian—Vince Lombardi, who when 1958 began was just a year away from becoming the head coach of the Green Bay Packers. As Army's line coach for five seasons beginning in 1949, the unpolished and volatile Lombardi could become surprisingly meek in Blaik's chilly presence. Indeed, Lombardi came to see his boss as both a mentor and a father figure. Years later, after he turned Green Bay into Titletown, U.S.A., he rarely missed an opportunity to say that all he knew about organizing and preparing a team to win he'd learned from Red Blaik.

The Blaik persona was the result of the nearly four decades he had spent emulating Douglas MacArthur, his idol, whom he had met as a First Class, or senior, cadet in 1919. That was the year the then-thirty-nine-year-old brigadier general, who had risen to national prominence as the second-most-decorated officer of the First World War, had become the youngest superintendent in the history of the academy. Behind Blaik's desk in his office on the top floor of the cadet gymnasium's south tower hung an enormous portrait of MacArthur rendering a salute, and any visitor who climbed the steps to the coach's aerie could not help but notice the physical resemblance between the two men. It was no coincidence. Blaik had been devoted to MacArthur since their first encounter at West Point, when at a formal reception for members of the First Class the superintendent had made a simple gesture of goodwill. Ignoring academy protocol, he greeted the star-struck Blaik and a handful of his classmates, all of them decked out in their full-dress uniforms, with an informal handshake and a pat on the arm. He then offered them their choice of cigarettes—Fatimas or Melachrinos. Never mind that smoking was strictly forbidden for West Point cadets, or that Blaik, then twenty-two, didn't smoke. It was MacArthur's effort to put his guests at ease that won him over. From that moment forward, as far as Blaik was concerned, the general could do no wrong.

The two men saw each other frequently that first year. On New Year's Day 1919, Blaik had been among the first cadets to discover the body of Fourth Class cadet Stephen M. Bird, who had shot himself in the chest with a Springfield rifle. The shooting was obviously intentional; the freshman had tied one end of several feet of string to the trigger and wrapped the other around the butt-end of the rifle, giving himself the necessary leverage to fire the weapon. Bird was apparently distraught over a hazing session from the night before, which began after several upperclassmen had discovered him writing poetry in his room.* Public outcry over the suicide had persisted through the spring and became especially intense in the halls of

---

* Wrote Blaik years later, "That this had disturbed him and that he was probably morose by nature was indicated by the poetry itself."

Congress. When MacArthur assumed command at West Point in June 1919, the issue of hazing was at the top of his agenda. He appointed seven cadets, including Blaik, to a Fourth Class Customs Committee and tasked them with spotlighting areas of abuse in the treatment of plebes. Among the recommendations made by the committee—of which Blaik was chairman—were that upperclassmen should not be permitted to "lay hands" on fourth classmen and that plebes should not be denied food. MacArthur, who two decades before had been the subject of some particularly brutal hazing sessions as a Fourth Class cadet, threw his weight behind Blaik's committee, adopting a number of its recommendations.

The relationship between Blaik and MacArthur grew even closer as a result of the superintendent's obsession with Army football. Two decades earlier, accompanied by his doting mother, Pinky—who would reside in a room at a nearby hotel for the next four years—MacArthur had arrived at West Point a gawky teenager, standing five foot eleven and weighing just over 130 pounds. MacArthur had grown up in the army. His father, Lieutenant General Arthur MacArthur, had been awarded the Congressional Medal of Honor in the Civil War, and Douglas, the youngest of his three sons, always liked to claim that his first memory had been "the sound of bugles." Driven by his family legacy, MacArthur would go on to graduate in 1903 as the most decorated cadet in academy history, becoming both the top student in his class and the highest-ranking member of the Corps of Cadets. But for all his academic and military accomplishments, "Dauntless Doug" had never been able to achieve the success in athletics that he craved. As a scrappy, light-hitting right fielder on the baseball team, the highlight of his three-year career had come in 1901, during a 4–3 loss at Annapolis in the inaugural Army-Navy game. MacArthur, notorious for his inability to hit a curveball, went hitless in three at-bats but also walked, stole a base, and scored a run. The closest he had come to playing football was in the autumn of 1902, when he had served as the team's manager.

Upon his return to West Point as superintendent, MacArthur quickly set about establishing himself as Army's number-one football fan. Whenever he could make time in his official schedule, he liked to summon Lieutenant Elmer Oliphant to headquarters for a visit. Oliphant was then a young Army assistant coach, but just a few years before, as a member of the Cadets' backfield, he'd been perhaps the finest fullback in the country, twice named All-America. The office visits were mutually beneficial: MacArthur got an inside perspective on the team, while Oliphant received weekend passes to travel to upstate New York, where he earned as much as two hundred dollars a game playing Sunday football for the Buffalo All-Americans.

Even more than talking about the Army team with Oliphant, however, MacArthur loved to see it up close. On fall afternoons, it was not uncommon for him to leave his office early to walk over to the Plain—the academy's vast parade ground doubled as a practice field—so he could watch as the coaches put the squad through its paces. There he would walk the sidelines holding his signature riding crop, the same one he'd so famously carried in lieu of a sidearm across the battlefields of France just the year before. He made himself conspicuous, and his presence did not go unnoticed by Blaik, already the general's committed disciple, who was Army's star right end.

During the war, MacArthur had been profoundly impressed by how well athletes among the army's officer corps had performed in combat compared to nonathletes, and he also took note of how greatly enlisted soldiers tended to admire accomplished sportsmen. His love of football sprang from his conviction that the game provided a nearly perfect metaphor for warfare. In this he was hardly alone. Walter Camp, the venerable Yale coach so influential as a framer of the game, often referred to teams as "armies" and the kicking game as "artillery work." MacArthur took things even further, formalizing the academy's intramural program at the same time he was broadening and upgrading its academic curriculum, and proclaiming that every cadet would be an athlete, and every athlete would be a cadet. He also vigorously promoted varsity sports, with the goal of raising the academy's national profile. No longer would Army leave West Point only to play Navy. MacArthur sent his teams out into the world. In 1921 the Cadets made their first trip away from West Point, traveling to New Haven, Connecticut, where they fell 14–7 to mighty Yale in the Yale Bowl. The ambitious young general harbored dreams of luring the nation's gridiron superpowers to the banks of the Hudson and had plans drawn up for a hundred-thousand-seat football stadium that would sit on the river's western shore, hard against the rocky bluffs on which the academy stood.* It was during this time that MacArthur uttered one of his most oft-quoted lines, of which he was so fond that he ordered it carved into the stone portals of the cadet gymnasium:

UPON THE FIELDS OF FRIENDLY STRIFE
ARE SOWN THE SEEDS THAT
UPON OTHER FIELDS, ON OTHER DAYS
WILL BEAR THE FRUITS OF VICTORY

The young Blaik believed every word. In MacArthur, he saw a man—a great man, in his estimation—who not only loved football but who had also articulated precisely why it was the best game a young man could play, especially if that young man was a soldier. The affinity Blaik felt toward the general was reciprocated, in part because Blaik, never the total cadet that MacArthur had been, was named the best athlete in the Class of 1920—an honor that certainly impressed the superintendent. When Blaik was laid up in the hospital over Christmas after his final game against Navy (an ungentlemanly Midshipman had stuck a finger into his right eye, causing a corneal ulcer), MacArthur sent his personal aide to visit him daily, and even arranged with the academic board to excuse Blaik from his first-semester examinations, a special exception made for a special cadet.

When MacArthur's tour at West Point came to an end in 1922 and he was reassigned to the Philippines, he wrote to Blaik and invited him to become his aide de camp. The young lieutenant was

---

* MacArthur's stadium was never built. In 1924, two years after his tour at West Point came to an end, the academy opened Michie Stadium, a sixteen-thousand-seat structure that sits on a high bluff overlooking the river valley.

then galloping horses in the 1st Cavalry Division at dusty Fort Bliss, Texas, where he found himself less than enthralled with the lack of opportunity presented by a peacetime army. In a twist that Blaik would rue for the rest of his life, MacArthur's letter arrived at his Fort Bliss address the very day his resignation from the army had been accepted by the War Department. By the time the message finally reached him at home in Dayton, Ohio, it was too late to go back. Nevertheless, the general's invitation initiated a regular correspondence that the two men would continue for the next forty-two years, until MacArthur's death in 1964. Their letters covered a wide variety of topics, including war and politics, and were at times intimately personal. But always they returned to Army football. In 1924, MacArthur wrote to Blaik from the Philippines to comment on the team, then coming off a 12–0 win over Navy: "I agree personally with what you say that the system of play at West Pont is antiquated, too involved and totally lacking in flexibility and adaptiveness. Had I stayed at West Point, I intended introducing new blood into our coaching staff. Rockne of Notre Dame was the man I had in mind."

That MacArthur was so well versed in the deficiencies of the Army team from more than eight thousand miles away is a testament to the thoroughness of Blaik's correspondence, as well as to his abiding passion for the game of football. Immediately upon returning to Dayton, Blaik had gone into business for himself selling real estate and insurance. Within the first year, he had dumped the insurance racket to partner with his father, William, in the elder Blaik's long-established real estate and home-building concern. But Earl craved the sort of action that the business world couldn't provide, and neither games of squash nor rounds of golf were enough to satisfy his hunger. Blaik was so bored and restless that he would often borrow his father's car on autumn Saturdays to drive up to Oxford and watch games at Miami University—where he had played football and earned a bachelor's degree before entering West Point in the final months of World War I—or he would strike out for Columbus to see Ohio State play in its new sixty-six-thousand-seat stadium on the banks of the Olentangy River. In December of 1923, he and his bride, Merle, spent their honeymoon at the Polo Grounds in New York City watching Army and Navy play to a scoreless tie. The next autumn, he began volunteering as a part-time ends coach at Miami. More coaching jobs followed, first a temporary job at Wisconsin and then a permanent one at West Point. By 1934, when Dartmouth hired him away from Army to become the Indians' head football coach, his course through life was set.

The game consumed Blaik. He'd been infatuated with it since his days at Dayton's Hawthorne grammar school, when as a fourth-grader he had formed a neighborhood team, the Riverdale Rovers, and appointed himself its coach, captain, and quarterback. Now that football was his profession, he rarely thought, or spoke, of anything else. It was a labor of love, and Blaik—never a social creature—enjoyed few things more than drawing up game plans or breaking down film, play by play and position by position. He had been one of the first coaches in the country to make extensive use of film study, and his enthusiasm was so great that, even in the off-season, he had been known to phone up assistants after the workday had ended and order them to meet him at the gym so that they could brainstorm with him late into the evening.

In January 1958, nobody in college football had been a head coach as long as Red Blaik. Such titans of the game as Amos Alonzo Stagg and Pop Warner, whose careers stretched back into the nineteenth century, were still active when he had landed his first job at Dartmouth in 1934. And the men alongside whom he had dominated the game in the following decade—Michigan's Fritz Crisler and Notre Dame's Frank Leahy—had long since departed the arena. A new generation whose legends were still to be written, including Woody Hayes at Ohio State, Bud Wilkinson at Oklahoma, and Bear Bryant, then making preparations for his first season at Alabama, had taken their place. None of them was more than forty-four years old, but Hayes and Wilkinson had already combined to win three of the last four national titles. Blaik had not won an outright championship at Army in more than twelve years, and his teams hadn't won more than seven games in a season since 1950. Football, it seemed, might finally be passing him by.

Tom Harp was intimately familiar with Red Blaik's abiding passion for detail. Two years earlier, in 1956, Blaik had hired him away from his post as the head football coach at Ohio powerhouse Massillon High to coach Army's offensive backfield. The job was Harp's first on the collegiate level, and he spent his opening season performing his duties like a good soldier, carrying out Blaik's orders. But as Army began spring practice the next year, Harp asserted himself, suggesting to Blaik that he change the way his halfbacks blocked defensive ends on sweep plays. Blaik preferred his backs to throw a shoulder-roll block to either the outside, if the play was going off-tackle, or to the inside, if it was going around the end. Harp, concerned that defenders could read the play by watching the blocker's approach, wanted the backs to employ a simple bull block, charging straight at the end and standing him up before moving in either direction.

Like Blaik, Harp was an Ohio native who had played football at Miami, where he enrolled in June 1945. That fall, he lined up as a defensive back and a fullback for coach Sid Gillman—who would go on to coach Army's line for Blaik in 1948—before entering the navy in December.* At the end of Harp's two-year tour of duty, he enrolled at Muskingum College in New Concord, Ohio, where his former backfield coach at Miami, Ed Sherman, was the head coach. After graduating from Muskingum in 1951, Harp landed a job as the head football coach at Carrollton (Ohio) High. He took to coaching as if he'd been born to it, winning twenty of twenty-seven games in three years before moving on to Massillon, where he led the Tigers to a state championship in 1954 and a runner-up finish in '55. His fullback's build, open face, and easygoing manner combined with all the victories to make him an extremely popular local figure, and Blaik's contacts in his home state sent word that Harp was a young man worth keeping an eye on. Blaik hired him at the first opportunity, telling Harp he needed a young coach capable of

---

* President Harry Truman ended the World War II draft by allowing the Selective Training and Service Act to expire on March 31, 1947.

both tutoring running backs and recruiting in the state of Ohio. Harp was all of twenty-eight when he took the job—the youngest coach on the Army staff—with a wife and two little girls, and he arrived at West Point full of ambition. The job was an important step in his career: Seventeen of Blaik's assistants at Army had already gone on to become college or professional head coaches. The joke in coaching circles was that a two-year stint on the Army staff was one that most assistants would gladly do for free.

Harp's halfback-blocking proposal prompted just the sort of argument over the details of the game that Blaik relished, and in the staff meeting room located one floor below his office, he subjected his young assistant to a withering cross-examination in front of his colleagues. At one point, Harp, who had quickly come to see the dispute as a chance to make his mark, became so defensive that he blurted out, "Colonel, I don't think the roll block is worth a darn! At least if we do it my way the defensive end doesn't know whether he's going to be blocked out or blocked in." Blaik pressed, noting that the ultimate benefit of the roll block was that it put the defender on the ground. Harp dug in his heels. Gathering himself to restate his case, he began, "Colonel, I don't want to be obnoxious about this, but—"

Blaik cut him off. "The word is obstinate," he said with a gentle smile. "You mean you don't want to be obstinate, Harp. You're obnoxious all the time." The room erupted in laughter, and even though Blaik ultimately rejected Harp's proposal, the young coach had made the impression he'd hoped for. He soon became one of Blaik's most trusted lieutenants.

Along with the rest of the Army coaching staff, Harp had begun preparing for the 1958 season on January 1. Blaik absolutely refused to concede that any team in the country would ever outplan, outscheme, or outwork his own, and to drive this point home it was his standard procedure to meet with his assistants at eight in the morning every New Year's Day. Sitting around the long table in the conference room on that holiday morning with Harp were Dale Hall, the top scout and defensive backfield coach, who had been a halfback on Blaik's first national championship team at West Point in

1944; Chuck Gottfried, the ends coach, who had been All–Big Ten as a guard at Illinois in 1948; and Frank Lauterbur, the defensive line coach, who two years before in the same role for the Baltimore Colts had been working with NFL standouts Art Donovan and Eugene "Big Daddy" Lipscomb. The off-season had amounted to little more than a few days, from Christmas to New Year's Eve, because each assistant had spent the three weeks following Army's 14–0 loss to Navy on November 30 driving around the country, scouting talent and visiting recruits.

Blaik had used those three weeks to recharge, traveling with Merle to Key Biscayne, Florida, for his first vacation in a decade. He'd gone as much for his health as for the chance to relax in the surf. The raw winters of New York's lower Hudson Valley had in recent years begun to leave him at the end of each season with a chest cold and a deep, bronchial cough. But even the revivifying effects of the sun and the sand could not keep his mind from wandering back to football and to the problem that was plaguing his team.

The loss to Navy was the fourth for Army in the last seven years, the worst stretch of Blaik's career. Defeat was intolerable to Blaik, who liked to say that there was "a vast difference between a good sport and a good loser," but it had lately become all the more galling because he felt he was being made to compete with a team chronically short of manpower. The Corps of Cadets in the latter half of the 1950s numbered about 2,500, one of the smallest enrollments of any school with a football team annually ranked among the nation's best.* Even the Naval Academy was over 3,800 strong. And where Blaik brought in roughly 25 new football players every fall, his greatest rival regularly welcomed more than 120. As a consequence, Army's teams rarely went much deeper than their best eleven players—a serious disadvantage in the days of iron-man football, when players lined up on both offense and defense.† In the

---

* Enrollment in the fall of 1958 at Notre Dame: 6,000; at Oklahoma: 12,000; at Ohio State: 22,750.

† Before FDR ended the practice in 1938, Army got around its chronic manpower shortage by beefing up its roster with players who had already played from one to three seasons at other colleges. The academy justified this tactic, known as open recruiting, by

season just concluded, during which Blaik's squad went 7–2, seven of the eleven Army starters had averaged more than fifty-three minutes a game. The Cadets had started fast, overwhelming Nebraska 42–0 in their opener and then downing Penn State 27–13. But after a 23–21 loss to Notre Dame in Philadelphia and a 29–13 victory over a strong and deep Pittsburgh club, they were spent. Army had to come from behind to win three of its next four games, against inferior teams from Virginia, Utah, and Tulane, before being beaten decisively by the Midshipmen. "We expended a year's supply of football energy in the first four games," Blaik told *Sports Illustrated*.

On the sands of Key Biscayne, he obsessed over how to spare his team the punishment inherent in, as he called it, "impact football." Blaik's greatest success at Army had come running the ball out of a Power T formation, which he had installed at West Point in 1943 after two years of running the single wing. He favored a tightly packed T—a seven-man front, the quarterback under center and the running backs lined up three abreast (a fullback flanked by halfbacks to the left and right) about five yards behind—not only because it allowed ball carriers to hit their holes at top speed, but also because it greatly reduced the need for a single dominant back and still provided opportunities for offensive deception, for ball fakes and option plays (though not as many as did the single wing). Army was the era's preeminent three-yards-and-a-cloud-of-dust team. The defensive counter to the T was to position as many players as possible within five yards of the line of scrimmage in order to stop the run. By the latter half of the 1950s, most teams accomplished this with either a 5-2 or a 5-4 defensive alignment, with five down linemen and anywhere from two to four linebackers. The 5-4 was com-

---

citing the extra time required to train the men to become officers. Blaik insisted it was also necessary in order for the Cadets to meet opponents, especially Navy, on even terms. Some of Army's greatest stars from this era had first lettered at other schools, including Charles Daly (Harvard, Class of 1901), Elmer Oliphant (Purdue, '14), Chris Cagle (Louisiana-Lafayette, '26) and, of course, Earl Blaik (Miami, '18). Open recruiting was reinstated during World War II, during which time Blaik cherry-picked collegiate stars who had been drafted into the armed services. By attending West Point, players were able to delay their active-duty commitments.

monly known as the Oklahoma Defense, made popular by Bud Wilkinson and the Sooners, and its third and fourth linebackers were actually rolled-up cornerbacks who played off the outside hips of the defensive ends to present opposing running backs with a nine-man front. Blaik knew from hard experience that a team lacking depth would wear down quickly if it insisted on running the ball headlong into such a wall. To defeat the Oklahoma Defense, he decided that he first had to "dislocate" it, especially the rolled-up cornerbacks on the ends, who made it so hard for his backs to bounce their runs to the outside.

Blaik admired the version of the T run by Michigan State coach Duffy Daugherty, who within two years of taking over from Clarence L. "Biggie" Munn in East Lansing, had led the Spartans to a victory in the 1956 Rose Bowl. Daugherty, widely respected as an offensive innovator, ran the Power T but augmented it with variations that featured unbalanced lines—a guard, two tackles, and an end on one side of the center; a guard and an end on the other—as well as wide receivers and slot backs. Such sets were hardly new. Wide receivers, especially, were almost as old as football itself. But as Blaik considered Daugherty's various schemes, he began to wonder. What if a team lined up in nothing but unbalanced wide-receiver sets, making them constitute the entirety of the offensive attack? And what if the receiver—in Blaik's words the "far flanker"—was positioned far wider than was normal?

Unbalancing his offensive line, Blaik knew, would not only give his offense overwhelming force on one side, but it would also compel the defense to make a choice—whether to remain in its normal alignment, conceding the advantage to Army's running game on the strong side, or to shift players over Army's extra blockers, leaving itself exposed to a play that went the other way. Splitting the end extremely wide on the strong side would break up the defensive front: It would draw coverage either from the cornerback on that side or from the safety on that side, who would have to be replaced in the deep secondary by the other cornerback. It would not be possible, in other words, to both cover the far flanker and maintain the integrity of the defensive secondary unless a player was removed from the defensive front. "And this man," Blaik wrote years later, "could not be spared, because we still had all our backs in close attacking deploy." Blaik couldn't remember another scheme like it in his twenty-five years as a head coach, but he knew instinctively that it would work. With an unbalanced offensive line and a far flanker, he felt he had discovered a way to spread out defenses, thus opening the field to his offense, whether Army wanted to run or pass.*

Blaik told nobody of his plan when he returned to West Point. Instead, when he met with his staff on New Year's Day, he simply gave his coaches a week to come up with their own solutions to Army's manpower problem. At the ensuing meeting, he listened quietly to their proposals. After the last one, he stood, walked to the front of the room, and diagrammed his new formation—unbalanced line, far flanker—on the chalkboard. "This is what we're going to run this year," he said.

His assistants exchanged questioning looks. None were impressed. "That's not very much, Colonel," said Tom Harp. "It's just an unbalanced line with a wide receiver."

"But he's way out there," said Blaik, tapping his piece of chalk on the board where he had placed the far flanker. This response was met with silence. Everybody had seen something like it before, and nobody thought it would make much difference.

Blaik ended the meeting soon after, ordering his staff to reconvene after lunch. His mind was made up, but he wanted to make his assistants understand. He was counting on them, after all, to help him build an attack around the formation. "Let's go up to Michie," he said, "and we'll see how it looks up there."

During the American Revolution, the Continental Army built West Point as a fortress to prevent British ships from sailing up the Hudson River and dividing the colonies. The academy sits on a rocky promontory along the Hudson's western shore, around which the

---

* The principle of spreading out defenses was nothing new. In 1952, shortly after his nineteenth and final season as the coach at TCU, Dutch Meyer—who tutored such passing marvels as Sammy Baugh and Heisman Trophy winner Davey O'Brien—published the landmark primer *Spread Formation Football*.

river bends sharply to the east before continuing the journey south to its terminus in New York Harbor. The terrain rises majestically from the water's edge to the west in a series of cliffs and plateaus. On the first plateau, nearly two hundred feet above the Hudson, is the hub of the academy, which includes the cadet barracks, the academic buildings, and the gymnasium, as well as the Plain, the vast parade ground where Army played football from 1890 until 1923. On the second, looming more than one hundred feet above the first, is the Cadet Chapel, stately and immense with its broad bell tower, separated from Michie Stadium to the west by the still waters of Lusk Reservoir. The landscape, seemingly all gray stone and cliff, is solemn and forbidding, never more so than in the dead of winter. It is with good reason that cadets refer to the cold months after the Christmas break as the "Gloom Period." Everything at the academy is shrouded in gray: the sky, the buildings, even the cadets themselves, clad in their uniforms and overcoats.

The afternoon Blaik took his staff up to Michie was just such a day. Snow was falling, and it was bitterly cold. As Harp trudged up the steep hill from the gymnasium to the stadium, doing his best not to slip on the icy ground, he mulled over the Colonel's plan. He still didn't think much of it, but like almost everybody else inside the Army program, he was in awe of the old man, who always seemed to be right when it came to football. Harp knew, too, that Blaik would have the final say. If Blaik had committed himself to the far-flanker concept, then Harp knew he would have to, as well.

But Harp didn't really begin to get excited about the formation until a line of scrimmage had been scratched out in the snow. Blaik had brought more than just his coaches along for the demonstration. He'd also drafted the staff of Army's practice squad—then known as the B Squad—led by head coach Barney Gill, a captain on temporary assignment to the academy's athletic department, and coaches from the plebe, or freshman, team. Blaik lined everybody up in what was essentially an unbalanced wing T formation. To the right of the center were just a guard and the weak-side end; to the left, a guard, both tackles, and the far flanker, who was split about fifteen yards wide. In the backfield, the left halfback lined up as a wingback, just behind and outside the left hip of the outermost tackle. Like the other members of the varsity staff, Harp had no idea the flanker would be set so wide. The typical split for a receiver in those days was not much more than seven or eight yards. Harp looked around at his fellow coaches, who were standing quietly in the falling snow. A few of them were grinning.

Now that Blaik had their attention, he explained that he didn't yet have any specific plans drawn up for how to put his idea into action. The one thing of which he was certain, he said, was that even though teams typically split a receiver wide only in passing situations, he felt it was crucial for Army to maintain a sound running game from its far-flanker formation. Nobody was objecting now. By the time the Army assistants followed Blaik off the snowy field and back down the hill, they had already begun to consider new possibilities. The staff would have just over eight months for planning and research before Army opened its 1958 campaign against South Carolina on September 27 at Michie Stadium. Spring practice would be the laboratory for their first experiments.

Chapter 2

THE PROMISE

IN THE SPRING AND SUMMER of 1951, Red Blaik had been rocked by the greatest calamity of his career—thirty-seven members of his varsity football team had been implicated in an academic cheating ring, among them his younger son, Bob, a rising first classman who had been penciled in as Army's starting quarterback for the fall. The ring was a clear violation of the cadet-enforced honor code, nearly as old and rigid as the academy itself, and regarded as the bedrock of its values. *A cadet will not lie, cheat, or steal, nor tolerate those who do.* After an investigation that lasted almost the entire summer, the academy dismissed eighty-three cadets for either participating in the cheating ring or failing to report it, including all thirty-seven of the football players.

Blaik was devastated. He had always promoted his team as the embodiment of the West Point ideal. The scandal not only stained his carefully cultivated professional reputation—it was not for nothing that he was known, sometimes derisively, as St. Blaik—but it also very nearly ended his career. More significantly, it shook the faith of the nation in one of its most trusted and beloved institutions. As Blaik later wrote in his memoirs, the entire affair "was a catastrophe."

The cheating scandal was hardly of any immediate concern to the Army coaches and players in 1958, none of whom, save for Blaik, had been at West Point seven years before. For the most part, their knowledge of the episode amounted only to what they had read in newspapers at the time. The incident is nevertheless essential to their story. Blaik, ever the stoic, certainly never spoke of it, but that did not mean that the painful memory of his catastrophe wasn't with him every hour of every day. And he burned to erase it. Indeed, his quest for redemption—both for himself as well as for the program he had built—was the mainspring for what was the third and final act of his professional life. Blaik had made his name as a young coach by molding Dartmouth into an Ivy League power in the 1930s, and he became a giant of the game by turning Army into a college football colossus for the better part of the next decade. But the greatest accomplishment of his long career was the resurrection of his program after it had been decimated by scandal.

The years following World War II are often recalled through a patina of nostalgia and are frequently hailed as a more wholesome era. But history is rarely so simple. By the spring of 1951 cheating in college athletics was in no way a new phenomenon, and a few incidents that immediately preceded the West Point expulsions had raised the bar of public outrage. In January, on the heels of two game-fixing scandals involving players from area college basketball teams, the Manhattan district attorney charged three players at the City College of New York with conspiring to rig the outcome of games. All three—center Ed Roman, guard Al Roth, and forward Ed Warner—had been key contributors the year before on the CCNY team that had won both the National Collegiate Athletic Association and the National Invitation tournaments, still the only team ever to pull off such a double. Four more of the Beavers' players were eventually arrested in the course of the investigation, as well as more than thirty players from six other schools, including the powerhouse programs at Kentucky and Bradley, the team CCNY had beaten in the finals of both the NIT and the NCAAs.

The root of the problem was gambling, an industry that had exploded around college basketball after the invention of the point spread in the mid-1940s. With spread betting, which depended on the accuracy of the bet rather than on the result of the contest, an enterprising gambler who wanted to fix a game no longer had to pay players to lose on purpose. Instead, the fixer merely had to convince players to "shave" points in order to keep the game's final result within the margin established by the point spread. For a few years, point shaving was college basketball's dirty little secret. But the CCNY scandal put it on front pages around the country. The Manhattan district attorney's investigation turned up evidence of eighty-six fixed contests, a number that most agreed represented merely the tip of the iceberg. The NCAA canceled Kentucky's entire 1952–53 season, and CCNY put its basketball program on indefinite suspension. Players who didn't serve jail time over their role in the scheme were cast out of organized basketball, and all were condemned in the press as "Judases" and "betrayers of America's youth." Nearly thirty years later, Ed Roman would lament, "The American people have a romanticized view of athletics. They want to identify with the entire fantasy that the world of sports has come to represent. Whenever you break a moral code that people are supposed to believe in, you are confronted with a stronger wrath than any burglar or common thief ever faces."

Nowhere had the public's view of athletics become more romanticized than at the United States Military Academy. At West Point, in the words of sports historian and critic Murray Sperber, Army football was sacred, and "its conquests under Blaik were woven in the country's recent military triumphs." Fullback Felix "Doc" Blanchard and halfback Glenn Davis, who had each won the Heisman Trophy while playing for Blaik's dominant wartime teams, were such crossover superstars that in 1947, during a break between graduation and the beginning of their active-duty commitments, they had played themselves in the Hollywood version of their lives, *The Spirit of West Point.** The Black Knights of the Hudson were not a typical college team for most Americans. Blaik had always emphasized to the press that, rather than just football players, his boys were cadets first and

---

* Davis, for one, was not impressed with the finished film, warning fans, "Save your dough, it isn't worth [the] 85 cents."

foremost, the army's, and the country's, future leaders. In a nation where respect for the military was high, where most people were close to someone who had served in World War II, this idea struck a deep emotional chord. Some of Blaik's former players were, even then, fighting and dying in the Korean War. The academy's Class of 1950 had been rushed to the front to meet the needs of an army that had been drastically reduced in the postwar years. On the eve of that year's Navy game, word reached Blaik and his team that the captain of the undefeated '49 squad, John Trent, a handsome end who had begun the year on Blaik's staff coaching the plebe team, had been killed in action only four days after arriving in Korea.*

The public and the press, then, were more than ready to believe Blaik when he told them that his boys were special players, on a special team, in a special place. That the downfall of his program was on an issue of honor instead of college basketball's large-scale criminal enterprise did not soften the blow for a dismayed country. If anything, it made the entire episode worse. "The profiteering of the Korean War, bribery in college basketball, the fur coats and deep-freezes of the Truman administration had shaken the nation, but they all paled beside the cheating at the Military Academy," wrote historian Stephen E. Ambrose. "Nothing ever illustrated quite so clearly how high was the pedestal on which the public had placed West Point as the reaction to the scandal."

When the story broke in early August 1951, the above-the-fold headline on the front page of *The New York Times* ran in 216-point type: WEST POINT OUSTS 90 CADETS FOR CHEATING IN CLASSROOM; FOOTBALL PLAYERS INVOLVED. The *Times'* venerable sports columnist Arthur Daley wrote, "It is a stark, sickening reality. Ninety West Point cadets, perhaps half of them athletes, face expulsion for violating the honor code. Caesar's wife, regarded as beyond reproach, is no better than the rest of them." Notre Dame football legend Moose Krause, an All-America tackle for Knute Rockne in 1932, as well as a hero of the Second World War, proba-

---

* Army fell to Navy in that game 14–2, the Black Knights' first loss in the series since 1943.

bly spoke for the majority of Americans when he said, "My heart sank that summer day when I heard about [the cheating scandal at West Point]. Although Army was our toughest rival for decades, I respected them so much . . . and their officer corps meant so much to me as an American. My gosh, their graduates had just led us to victory in the war. I hated the basketball fixes but the Army scandal was a lot worse."

The cheating that precipitated the expulsions involved a ring of cadets that had been formed to pass along the questions and answers to daily quizzes and midterm reviews. It first came to the attention of the academy's administration in early April of 1951, reported by a member of the swim team who had refused an offer to join. The scheme was simple. Relying on the honor code, professors gave the same daily writs (quizzes) to every class and administered them without a proctor.* It was an irresistible temptation. Members of the ring who took a quiz in an early period would pass along the questions— "passing the poop," in the slang of the ring members—to cadets who were to take the same writ in a later class. If time permitted, smarter members of the ring would work out the answers and pass them along. The practice, according to the findings of the academy's investigation, dated back to at least 1947. According to the first witness to appear before a three-officer board of inquiry on the morning of May 29, the ring had been "started by football players for football players."

It was late that same night that Blaik learned the details of the ring for himself. One of his players had called him at home early in the evening to say that several third classmen, or sophomores, needed to see him at nine fifteen. Blaik drove to the gym and climbed the stairs of its south tower to the projection room of the football office. There, where he had spent countless hours studying game film, divining the keys to Army's most glorious triumphs, he listened silently

* This writ schedule became standard procedure during the trying days of World War II, when the demand for officers was high, and Congress increased enrollment at the academy from 1,960 to about 2,500.

for nearly an hour as his players told him about the ring and the statements they had given to the board of inquiry earlier in the day. Some had incriminated themselves in their testimony. Some had lied. One player broke down sobbing to Blaik, "I'm going to be thrown out for passing the poop, and the other guys are too." What, they asked him, should they do?

Without hesitation Blaik said, "You men, leaders of the academy, need to straighten out this situation by going to the commandant's staff and telling them what you know. If you and your fellow players set the example, the corps will follow." After they left, Blaik sat by himself in the darkened room, thunderstruck. He did not think the boys would be expelled, but he also knew that the honor code was inflexible. "No foreboding could have been greater than my own," he later wrote.

Blaik was aware that not everyone at West Point held Army football in high esteem, and he knew that by ordering his players to the commandant's office, he was sending them into the lion's den. As the head of the academy's tactical department, the commandant was charged with training every member of the Corps of Cadets to be a military man. In the spring of 1951, this was the responsibility of Colonel Paul B. Harkins, a rigid career soldier who had been deputy chief of staff in General George S. Patton's 3rd Army during World War II. Unlike the creative and emotional Patton, Harkins had a reputation for sober adherence to rules and regulations, traits manifested in his nickname—the Ramrod. Harkins and some members of his staff, including Lieutenant Colonel Arthur S. Collins Jr., who was the head of the board of inquiry, took a dim view of the Army football program, which they felt was stocked with athletes who did not belong at West Point.

Harkins and his coterie openly sneered at Blaik's public persona. In their opinion, Blaik was a draft dodger who had gone to West Point as a young man to play two more years of football rather than fight for his country in the First World War, and he had assumed the rank of colonel during the second only because he had demanded status equal to Navy's coach, who usually held the rank of commander. Now his power far exceeded his position, and they felt he was allowing his players to openly flout academy directives at the same time they were being indulged with special privileges. Harkins had a point. Blaik's boys were favored with academic tutors throughout the school year and were excused from certain afternoon classes and a raft of minor regulations to which all cadets were supposed to adhere. Most notorious among their perks was a six-week cram course on academy grounds—the "monster school" was its derisive nickname—offered to a dozen or so incoming football players every spring to prepare for the West Point entrance examination. Some of these privileges had been granted to Blaik early in his tenure, when Army was desperate to build a winner after the team won just four games in the two seasons after President Roosevelt had stripped West Point of its open-recruiting exception in 1938.*

Upon gathering his thoughts in the darkened projection room, Blaik quickly walked next door to the quarters of Major General Frederick A. Irving, the superintendent of the academy. It was a clear evening, and the moon had not yet risen. Standing in the darkness of the superintendent's front yard, Blaik threw pebbles at Irving's bedroom window until the general, wrapped in his bathrobe, appeared at the door and invited Blaik inside. Sitting in the living room, the coach laid out the story he had just heard, then implored Irving to ensure that the matter be given a sympathetic hearing. Blaik told Irving that Harkins was "a black-and-white man, with no shades of gray," and pushed for the matter to be handed over to the academic board. Irving was sympathetic but gave Blaik no guarantees.

The next morning, Bob Blaik, along with his roommate, who was due to be captain of the football team in the fall, came to see his father. Red Blaik had always tried to maintain a professional distance from Bob as a football player—so much so that when the boy escaped his cadet responsibilities long enough to visit his parents at home, he was forced to turn to his mother to learn the old man's opinion of his play. But Merle Blaik, who had been the family's lone representative at Exeter Academy football games when Bob had

---

* In 1940, the year before Blaik was hired away from Dartmouth, Army went 1–7–1 under coach William Wood, USMA '25.

spent a year at the New Hampshire prep school, rarely had much information, simply because her husband's reports rarely amounted to much more than "He didn't do anything wrong." But when Bob and his roommate divulged to the Colonel that they, too, had violated the honor code, the elder Blaik's businesslike demeanor finally dropped. Bob was a good student and a talented musician, and he told his father that his sin was that he knew about the cheating but did not report it. For the second time in twenty-four hours, Blaik was staggered. "My God!" he said. "How could you? How could you?" When Bob testified before the board of inquiry the next day, he said, "This has been a terrific blow to my father. It has broken his heart."

It was a grim summer. Members of the First Class, due to graduate within the week, had just returned from a one-day training trip in Aberdeen, Maryland, when they were called to testify. All denied participating in the ring. Most denied any knowledge of it, though one first classman accused the entire football team of being involved. Another was more direct:

> *In the past few years there have been some people brought into the academy to play football. Some of these like —— and ——, have no sense of honor whatsoever. I have heard the same opinion expressed by other cadets. There is no question but that the football team lives something of the life apart from the Corps, for example, they never take Tactics, while all other cadets do. They feel that one individual, Colonel Blaik, is largely responsible for this state of affairs because of the type of personnel that has been brought into the academy to play football, such as ——, —— and ——.*

Though the members of the board of inquiry concluded that sixteen seniors had almost certainly cheated, they could not prove it conclusively in short order. The entire First Class was allowed to graduate on schedule on June 5.

The underclassmen left behind were not so lucky. Blaik's advice to his players to tell the truth blew the investigation wide open. Though he and his coaching staff were never implicated, several players told the board that some cheating had taken place not only at team tables in the mess hall but also in the film room of the football office, as well as in the locker room. Blaik, who was also West Point's athletic director, had always been portrayed as a man in total command of his program, but the statements given to the board by members of the ring contradicted that image. Some of the testimony, even from his own players, gave the impression that his team had begun to run amok.

CADET 1: *"Passing the Poop" was a big thing . . . Everyone in the Corps knows who Blaik's Boys are and anyone who tampers with them is in trouble. This is the impression one gets from the first day of Beast Barracks [summer plebe training]. You even hear remarks like that in the hotel before entrance. It is said that Colonel Blaik is so influential that no one had better cross him.*

CADET 2: *I was surprised [to learn of the ring's existence], but it didn't come out of a clear blue sky as I heard a lot of joking about it while on football tables. The same thing has gone on at baseball and basketball tables but the men at those tables were generally members of the football squad.*

CADET 3: *A while back at spring football practice I told ——— to quit making 5.8's and 5.9's on his writs as everybody knew he couldn't do that. We almost got in a fight about it . . . I couldn't turn all these people in. They were my best friends and when you play ball together you just get very close.*

CADET 4: *I can't understand why the academic departments didn't figure out what was going on. I know many cadets who couldn't do any problems. When they made good grades on writs I figured that the instructors knew about it and just let football players get away with it.*

Blaik saw the problem as a breakdown in the system, with cadets who were already under tremendous pressure and living in close quarters confronted with a policy that mandated they all take the same tests. *What did you expect?* He also felt that leniency should be given to those who had told the truth, especially when some who denied knowledge of the ring—in particular members of the just-graduated First Class—were certainly lying. Despite his requests to testify, the board never called on Blaik, who likewise was refused a chance to present his case before the academic board. On June 8, the board of inquiry submitted its findings to the superintendent, with admissions of guilt from, or evidence of the same against, ninety-four cadets. The recommendation in most cases: dismissal from the academy. Harkins attached his own memorandum to the report, which read in part, "I think when the air clears, the whole thing will have a very salutary effect on West Point and the country. It will bring some of the athletic teams back closer to the Corps of Cadets. It will prove to all of us that, though we want to have winning teams and play to win, the teams must be made up of cadets who are members of the Corps and respect and live by the ideals and spirit of West Point. There can be no other way."

Before taking official action, the secretary of the army appointed a review board, consisting of Learned Hand, a recently retired federal appeals court judge from New York City, and two retired generals. This panel stayed at West Point for two days in late July, reviewing the board's findings and hearing testimony from cadets. Blaik at last got his chance to give his side of the story and was heartened when he finished his testimony. At least one member of the Hand board sympathized with Blaik's argument against the writ system, as well as with his feeling that it was unfair that not all who had cheated were receiving punishment.

But Blaik's testimony was grounded in his belief in what he had been told by his players—that most of them knew about the ring but did not take part themselves, and that the cheating was widespread throughout the corps. The evidence in front of Judge Hand told a different story. At least eighty-two of the implicated cadets had admitted to cheating before the board of inquiry, instead of only having knowledge that cheating was going on. And their offenses went further than just passing on quiz questions to other members of the ring. In most cases, "passing the poop" meant getting specific answers to questions. And the idea that cheating was rampant throughout the Corps of Cadets turned out to be an exaggeration spread by ring members, first as a means of discouraging attempts to expose the cheating, and later to diminish their own culpability.* What the testimony also made clear was that the insularity of the football program, and the perception of a protective aura around it, had encouraged the growth of the ring. In his report, Hand acknowledged that by affirming the findings of the board of inquiry he would "in effect [wipe] out the entire varsity football squad," ruining West Point's chances of fielding a top team "for at least 10 or 15 years." But he decided that any punishment besides dismissal would scuttle the academy's honor code. The formidable jurist had little choice but to uphold the board of inquiry's findings.†

Blaik was stunned. He had been sure that his testimony to the Hand board had hit home. Doug Kenna, who had earned All-America honors as the quarterback of Army's 1944 national championship team, was Blaik's defensive backfield coach in 1951. He remembers that Blaik, then preparing for his annual preseason retreat with the rest of his coaching staff to the nearby fishing camp at Bull Pond, went three straight nights without sleeping while he worried about all that had just happened and all that was still to come—and fuming that his enemies at West Point had won the day. He was convinced his only option was to resign in protest. On August 4, the morning after the news went public, he drove with Merle to New York to meet with MacArthur at the general's suite in the Waldorf Towers. Ten miles north of the George Washington Bridge, a tire on Blaik's car blew out. Already running behind, he left Merle on the

---

* From the findings of the board: "The best evidence that this practice is not prevalent in the Corps is the great care that these violators of the Honor System took to conceal their actions from those not involved . . . The men cheating took great pains to inform anyone who discovered it about the great number involved so that a report would not be made to the Honor Committee."

† The academy endured another, more extensive, cheating scandal in 1976, before revising the honor code to provide more leeway when judging matters of honor—expulsion for violating the code is no longer mandatory.

side of the road with the car and hitchhiked into the city. He arrived at MacArthur's door thirty minutes late.

It was not the first time that year that he had come to the Waldorf to visit his old friend. In April, President Truman, who had openly clashed with MacArthur for months over how forcefully to confront the Chinese in Korea, had fired the general from his position as commander of United Nations forces. MacArthur returned to the United States soon after—for the first time since 1937—and, despite the open insubordination he had shown to the commander in chief, was welcomed in New York on April 21 with a ticker-tape parade. Blaik called on him shortly thereafter. Many Americans, including Blaik, were then beseeching the seventy-one-year-old MacArthur to seek the Republican nomination for president in 1952. "The best hope for the future," Blaik wrote to him, "lies in fielding a new team in Washington."

But now Blaik was back for reasons of his own. After ushering the coach in the door, MacArthur's first words were, "They have set the academy back twenty years. Yes, at least that." He put an arm around Blaik's shoulders and led him into the living room. "Now," he said, "tell me the whole story." Over several emotional hours, Blaik briefed the old soldier on all he knew, complete with his take on what had gone wrong. When he was finished, he told MacArthur of his intention to step down. MacArthur stopped him. "Earl, you must stay on," he said. "Don't leave under fire."

Four days later, Blaik met the press for the first time since news of the scandal had broken. He chose as the venue his favorite meeting place in all of New York City, Mamma Leone's, a bustling Italian restaurant on West Forty-eighth Street in Manhattan. The sprawling establishment was owned and operated by Gene Leone, whose son-in-law was a major stationed at West Point, and who made such an effort to ingratiate himself with the academy crowd that he had been made an honorary member of the Class of 1915.*

---

* This was not an insignificant honor. Known as "the class the stars fell on," USMA '15 is the greatest class in West Point's history. Of the 164 graduates, fifty-nine rose to the rank of brigadier general or higher, two to the rank of full general, and two, including

Restaurant staff who found uniformed cadets and officers standing in the long lines that were common at the popular spot quickly ushered them to the front and seated them at the best tables. The same treatment was also accorded the Army coaches and their wives. Blaik hated to meet with reporters, and rather than hold an open press conference, he opted for a private luncheon in a friendly setting with the forty New York–area writers to whom he was closest, including his old friend Stanley Woodward, Red Smith of the *New York Herald Tribune*, Jimmy Cannon of the *New York Post*, Joe Williams of the *New York World-Telegram*, and Dan Parker of the *Daily Mirror*. Earlier that morning, Joe Cahill, the academy's sports public relations head, had called Blaik at his hotel to warn him about "a mob scene in front of Leone's." Outside of the restaurant, Blaik had to fight his way through photographers, newsreel cameramen, and a crowd of onlookers that gave the luncheon the feeling of "a Hollywood premiere," in the words of one reporter. As he elbowed past them on his way to the front door, Blaik groused, "Jesus Katy."

He waited until lunch was over before rising to tell his story. Blaik may not have relished talking to the press, but that fact did nothing to diminish his ability to command a room. He gave no excuses for the cadets who had cheated, and he admitted that a measure of responsibility for the scandal fell on him alone. Blaik then stunned the crowd by telling them that his own son was among the cadets dismissed from the academy, before extolling the virtues of, as he called them, "the ninety scapegoats." He went on to say, "I believe in the youngsters with whom I've been dealing. I know their families. I know them. I know they are men of character . . . My entire endeavor from now on shall be to see that these boys leave West Point with the same reputations they had when they came in." When Blaik announced at the end of his speech, as the lunch stretched

Omar N. Bradley, to the rank of General of the Army and the office of Chief of Staff of the Army. One, Dwight D. Eisenhower, became president of the United States. Ike, in particular, was a big fan of Leone's—so much so that in 1967 the former president wrote the foreword to the newly published *Leone's Italian Cookbook*.

into its third hour, that he would remain at West Point, the assembled newsmen, shedding all pretense of objectivity, stood and cheered.

The press conference at Leone's marked the beginning of Red Blaik's public defense of the cadets who had been dismissed in the wake of the scandal. It was a cause he would pursue with great zeal, and with an increasing amount of bitterness, throughout the rest of his long life. His arguments were not without merit. Though the official report of the board of inquiry made much out of the role of Blaik's team in the scandal, the changes the academy actually made to the football program were minimal and mostly cosmetic. Indeed, in 1952 the academy renewed Blaik's contract as both coach and athletic director. And save for some adjustments to the daily schedule for players, the major refinement was the removal of the "monster school" from West Point to the nearby town of Cornwall. According to the Bartlett Board, a board of officers convened at the end of the summer of 1951 to address the underlying causes of the scandal, a similar program at the Naval Academy far surpassed the size and scope of Blaik's preparatory course. The report of the board went on to note: "There is rather conclusive evidence to indicate that 30 to 50 prospective Navy athletes each year are given a full year in prep school at the expense of a so-called alumni organization. The modest efforts [at West Point] yielded 5 admissions out of 22 boys in the school last year." To Blaik, the underwhelming nature of the changes to his program were tantamount to an admission that it had not, in fact, been at the root of the entire episode, that his boys bore only as much responsibility for the scandal as everyone else at the academy.

The dismissed cadets received, to Blaik's dismay, administrative, rather than honorable, discharges from the service. Many of the disgraced players went on to other schools to continue their football careers. Several went to Notre Dame at the behest of Joseph P. Kennedy, the patriarch of the Massachusetts political dynasty. Bob Blaik enrolled at Colorado College. On the evening of September 3, shortly before he departed for Colorado Springs, Bob asked his father, "Dad, do you believe it would have been better to have lied?" In a letter to

MacArthur the next morning, Earl Blaik recounted the conversation but never divulged his answer to Bob's wrenching question. The Colonel still loved West Point, but he never got over what he saw as the injustice done to him and his boys by the academy's administration. Even as the stain left by the scandal began to fade and attitudes toward the dismissed cadets started to soften, he knew the official record would always remain. Blaik felt his team had been used as a whipping boy by a hostile tactical department, which had, out of antipathy to him, ensured that Army football would always carry the stigma of the scapegoat and would be forever remembered as the cause of West Point's deepest humiliation.

The 1951 football season was a disaster. Rather than a contender for the national title, Blaik fielded a team of, as he called them, "silhouettes." There was some talent in the newly promoted Third Class, who had been plebes the year before (no members of the Class of 1954 had been among the eighty-three cadets dismissed from the academy over the summer), but little experience, and Blaik had to round out the rest of his roster with marginal players from the B Squad and a raft of enthusiastic volunteers from among the Corps of Cadets. This last group, in the words of one assistant, consisted of "anyone who would agree to go out and get killed on Saturday afternoons." The Black Knights finished the season with just two wins against seven defeats, the worst record of Blaik's career. In the finale, Navy showed little mercy, opening in a single-wing offense and promptly driving for a score. The single wing had once predominated in college football, but nobody at West Point had seen it in nearly a decade. The Midshipmen drubbed a thoroughly befuddled Army team 42–7 in what was, at the time, the Cadets' most lopsided defeat since the series began in 1890.

The Black Knights were more competitive in 1952, going 4–4–1 but losing again to Navy. More troubling to Blaik, however, was his sense that a rift still existed between his football program and the Corps of Cadets. As the 1953 season approached, he made the first move toward reconciliation, meeting on the evening of September 2 with forty-five cadet captains—first classmen who had been plebes in the spring of 1951—to speak, as he wrote in a letter afterward to

MacArthur, "about Corps athletics and the regaining of a soul for the academy." On the practice field, he set about convincing his team, which had lost eleven games in the previous two seasons, that it could, and should, be a winner. Little was expected from Army that fall, but the Black Knights had jelled quickly and begun the season with two wins in their first three games. Up next was a meeting with seventh-ranked Duke at the Polo Grounds on October 17, a game Blaik seized upon as a chance to administer a dose of "psychological medicine." As he explained years later, "How else could I get this Army team truly thinking the way Army teams had thought before the expulsions?"

On a humid Indian-summer day, Blaik's fired-up band of overachievers played themselves right into West Point legend. With the entire corps on hand, and in full cry, the Black Knights upset the favored Blue Devils with the aid of a dramatic goal-line stand late in the fourth quarter. As time ticked away with Army clinging to a 14–13 lead, cadets spilled out of the stands and crowded the sidelines. The game ended when quarterback Pete Vann, playing from his safety position on defense, broke up a last-second Duke pass in the end zone. Red Smith described the scene: "Suddenly the stained white jerseys of the West Point team disappeared, swamped under wave upon wave of blue-gray soldier suits. West Point Cadets never break ranks. This time they practically broke their heroes to pieces." In the locker room, as his boys leather-lunged their way through choruses of "On, Brave Old Army Team," Blaik and his coaches, including Vince Lombardi, wept tears of joy. The victory could not erase the cheating scandal from the history books, nor could it put an end to the bitterness the incident engendered over the football team's role in the affair—bitterness that lives on more than sixty years later—but it completed the reconciliation Blaik sought between his present team and the Corps of Cadets. With their own sweat, his boys had washed themselves clean. Whatever remnants of the scandal that still clung to them when the game began were left on the locker room floor after Lombardi, gleefully wielding a pair of scissors, went from one player to another and cut the soaking T-shirts from their exhausted bodies.

Blaik had not only returned his team to the corps, he had re-stored it to what he saw as its rightful place among the nation's elite programs. A little more than a month later, the Black Knights beat Navy for the first time since 1949. They finished the season 7–1–1, ranked fourteenth by the Associated Press, and won the Lambert Trophy as the top college football team in the East. The Touchdown Club of Washington, D.C., named Blaik the national coach of the year. Though the heights for his team were high indeed, they were far from what the coach—the man who had instilled in Lombardi the notion that winning isn't everything, it's the only thing—had once known. Blaik talked often with MacArthur about his desire to bring Army football all the way back to its former glory. To both men this meant only one thing: going undefeated.

Chapter 3
THE SOLDIER'S SON

FOR RED BLAIK, spring practice was not so much about football as it was about testing the limits of his players' physical endurance. The offensive and defensive systems he employed at Army had never been complex. Rather than cram his playbook full of multiple formations and schemes, Blaik chose instead to rely on a small number of plays that he could teach his teams to run with violent precision. He had tailored his simple but exacting approach specifically for the disciplined, detail-oriented cadets of West Point, whose lives were already overloaded with academic and military responsibilities and needed no additional complications. At practice in the afternoons, while the corps marched on the Plain in preparation for the academy's weekly ceremonial parades, Blaik put his boys through his own version of close-order drill. The Cadets might run an end sweep or a draw play more than twenty times before he was satisfied. And the attention of Blaik's coaching staff to the finer points of each maneuver was so thorough that Tom Harp used to cut footprints from sheets of cardboard and place them on the turf, the better to show his backs the exact steps he expected them to take—like a full-contact Arthur Murray dance course. Everything was done at top speed. Practices were ninety minutes of full pads and full go, with players running from drill to drill at precisely timed intervals. One of Blaik's most oft-repeated mantras was *You have to pay the price*. And every year, as March mellowed into April, he sought out the eleven players who were most willing, and most able, to live up to his ethic. In the spring, an Army football player went out every day to prove to the coaching staff that he was willing to hit somebody, and to be hit by somebody else.

Few players were more ready on both counts than senior fullback Harry Walters. At five foot ten, he was one of the shortest men on the roster, but no one competed with a bigger chip on his shoulder. Blaik had recruited Walters out of Cincinnati's Mariemont High, one of the smaller public high schools in Ohio, and from his first days as a plebe Walters had played the game as if he had something to prove. He loved the contact of football, the collisions and the hitting, and few Army players took Blaik's admonition to "pay the price" more seriously. As a fourth classman in 1955, Walters suffered a concussion in a game against Syracuse. In 1956, his two front teeth were knocked out during a practice. During another training session that same year, he broke his back, an injury that went undiagnosed, and that caused him pain, for nearly twenty years. He endured so many bloody noses in his career that after his junior season the Army coaches ordered him to get his nose cauterized. He was a fullback on a power running team and he got hit on almost every play, but he always made it a point to bounce back to his feet and dash back to the huddle after getting knocked to the ground—a practice for which the Corps of Cadets cheered him lustily on autumn Saturdays.

Nobody was more aware of Walters's intensity than Red Blaik. One of his greatest strengths as a coach was his knack for finding ways to motivate his players. Like MacArthur, he had a gift for inspiring oratory—his comparisons of football to combat were legion and sincere—and he was more than capable of delivering a locker-room stem-winder. But Blaik also had a knack for pushing his players' buttons. And he needled Walters frequently because he knew that the best way to get his fiery fullback in gear was to make him angry.

This led to a surprising outburst in the opening week of spring practice in March 1958. During a goal-line drill for the first-team offense, B Squad defensive end Russ Waters had struck Walters squarely on the right hip with a knee as the fullback attempted to hit him with a roll block. Waters was unhurt, but Walters crumpled to the ground in agony, momentarily stunned with a hip pointer. The play had come up short of the goal line, and Blaik, fuming over poor execution, lost patience with the delay. He had been watching from a position just behind the Cadets' backfield, and he barked at Walters, who was lying motionless on the turf, "Jesus Katy, Walters! Get up and get back in the huddle!"

Blaik did not know Walters was hurt. His outburst was not intended to be cruel. He was merely trying to goad his gung-ho fullback. But he had misjudged the moment. Seething, Walters struggled to his feet and limped back to the huddle, the crooked grin he usually wore on his face now a menacing snarl. "Give me the fucking ball!" he hissed. Quarterback Joe Caldwell deferentially called for a fullback dive. Walters, a runner with a tremendous starting burst—"Nobody could beat me at forty yards," he says today—took the handoff and bored into the heart of the line, knocking over two defenders on his way into the end zone. Still on his feet, he laid a final hit on a defensive back for good measure. Then he turned to Blaik, who was still standing about five yards behind the line of scrimmage, and rifled the football in the coach's direction before limping off toward a stadium tunnel, on his way to the locker room to see trainer Ed Pillings.

Blaik, like everyone else, stood silently rooted to the turf for a few seconds in stunned amazement. But he quickly realized his mistake, and without a word he marched after Walters, jogging to catch up to him underneath the grandstand. Blaik put a hand on Walters's shoulder pads, waited for him to turn around, and said, "Mr. Walters, I lost my temper. I'm sorry." The unprecedented episode had prompted an even more unprecedented response—a personal apology from Red Blaik.

The whole affair was a rather stunning welcome to Army football for Russ Waters. The easygoing end had gone out for the team in the spring of 1958 almost as a lark. A skinny, towheaded third classman from the small farming town of Sylvania, Georgia, he stood six foot two but weighed just 170 pounds. Waters was a stand-out sprinter on the Army track team and was perhaps the fastest cadet at the academy, capable of running the 100-yard dash in under ten seconds. But he hadn't played football in more than two years, since the fall of 1955 when he had been on the freshman team at Georgia Tech. An end for the Yellow Jackets, Waters had given up the game because he felt his lanky frame put him at a disadvantage against players who outweighed him by as much as forty pounds. His older brother George had graduated from West Point in 1953, and Russ, after a second year at Tech, had decided to give the academy a try.*

Waters had been happy on the track team and had never once regretted his decision to quit football. He'd never even considered playing for Red Blaik until November 1957, when Chuck Gottfried, Blaik's ends coach, invited him to try out. Gottfried moonlighted with the track team as an instructor for Army's discus and hammer throwers, and he had approached Waters after an indoor track workout, saying, "Russ! I've been watching you run. Why don't you come out for spring football?" The offer had been made in earnest—with just twenty-five slots open to football recruits each year, it was not unusual for Blaik and his staff to poach talent from the academy's other athletic teams.

Waters liked Gottfried. Most people at West Point did. The coach, who kept his brush-cut brown hair cropped as close as any cadet, was a popular character in the athletic department. Hard-nosed and passionate, he still resembled the All–Big Ten lineman he had been at Illinois more than a decade earlier, and his open face and quick smile softened what was an otherwise imposing figure. A native of East St. Louis, he spoke with a thick, urban timbre that transformed such words as *these, them,* and *those* into *dese, dem,* and *doze,* and his tendency to butcher the English language was a constant source of

---

* Russ's younger brother, Bob Waters, was a backup quarterback and defensive back for the San Francisco 49ers from 1960 to 1963.

delight to colleagues and cadets alike; at his wit's end during a debate over game strategy, he had once told Tom Harp that he felt "sty-mated."

Waters told Gottfried that the offer was intriguing but explained that he had not played in nearly three years. Gottfried said that wouldn't be a problem, and Waters returned to the barracks to weigh his options. West Point wasn't a big school, and he was close friends with a handful of football players, including his classmate Otto Everbach, a third-string end for the Cadets. With his buddies in mind, and the vague notion that it might be fun, Waters agreed to try out for the team in the spring.

But things had gotten grimly serious on the first day. Waters had been issued an orange practice jersey, which designated him as a member of the B Squad—members of the varsity wore black. "Cannon fodder," he thought to himself. He became even more concerned after Gottfried began working with him before and after practice each day to go over the finer points of playing defensive end, which would require the sort of physical contact Waters disliked. He might have quit but for the fact that Gottfried, who was full of bluster on the practice field and liked to emphasize his instructions by grabbing the face bar of a player's helmet, proved himself a patient and understanding tutor.

Gottfried, however, was not investing so much time and effort in a skinny B Squad player out of mere kindness: Waters, after all, would also play on offense. Blaik wanted his far flanker to stretch defenses both before and after the snap of the ball, but he did not have many players who had enough speed to do both. Waters, the fastest cadet at West Point, would provide valuable depth at the new position. The issue of who would be the starter had already been decided. Blaik knew exactly the man he wanted for the job.

William Stanley Carpenter Jr. grew up dreaming about playing football at West Point. He was raised on Philadelphia's Southwest Side, only a few miles from Municipal Stadium, the stately horseshoe where Army and Navy had played nearly every year since 1936.* As a boy, Carpenter had been enthralled with the pageantry that surrounded the rivalry, as well as with the Cadets' legendary backfield tandem of Doc Blanchard and Glenn Davis, Mr. Inside and Mr. Outside. When the Black Knights of the Hudson were the most powerful force in college football, Bill Carpenter had been one of their most devoted acolytes. And when Army made its yearly visit to Philadelphia to play Penn at nearby Franklin Field, a young Carpenter used to delight in hoodwinking sympathetic ticket vendors into letting him past the stadium gates. All he had to do was wait until the game had begun, then conjure a few tears and sob that his parents had let him go to the restroom by himself and *somehow* he had wound up outside the stadium. It never failed.

But Carpenter's fascination with West Point and the military went deeper than just the pomp and dominance of Army football. In 1944, when he was seven years old, his father, William Sr., had been drafted into the army. Though he still bore a remarkable resemblance to the tall, strapping single-wing halfback he had been at Camden High two decades before, William was actually thirty-seven years old at the time. He and his wife, Helen, had survived the Depression by moving in with his parents on their small farm outside of Woodbury, New Jersey. There the family got by on food they grew themselves, as well as money earned selling whatever produce they did not eat. By the time Bill, the couple's only child, was born in 1937, William had found work as a car salesman, and he also occasionally earned extra money playing semipro football. He doted on his newborn son and refused to let his wife tend to the boy when he would cry after dark. "You have him all day," William told her. "He's mine at night."

William eventually found a steady job at the Baldwin Locomotive Works, a sprawling steam engine plant in the nearby suburb of

---

* Because of gasoline rationing during World War II, Army and Navy had skipped Municipal Stadium in favor of smaller venues in 1942 and '43, trading home dates in order to cut down on the size of the crowds.

Eddystone, Pennsylvania, just across the Delaware River from Woodbury. To shorten his commute, he moved his family off the farm and into a small two-bedroom row house on Chester Avenue in the working-class Philadelphia neighborhood of Kingsessing. William had not been drafted during the early years of World War II. Baldwin Locomotive was one of the primary manufacturers of the Sherman tank, and both his age and his employment in an industry crucial to the war effort had kept him with his family. But by 1944 the army needed all the infantrymen it could get. He completed basic training at Fort Stewart, Georgia, in December and promptly shipped out for Europe. In January 1945, William joined the 99th Infantry Division in Belgium, where he was assigned to the 393rd Infantry Regiment as an ammunition carrier. The 393rd had just seen some of the most intense combat of the entire war, having been in the path of the German advance in the snow-covered Ardennes forest on the northern shoulder of the Battle of the Bulge. William arrived just as the regiment was beginning its counterattack.

He was the oldest man in his unit, known to one and all as Pops, and he wrote regularly to his wife and son, even as his division relentlessly pushed its way to the East. The 393rd spent twenty-four days on the offensive in March and was one of the first Allied units to cross the Rhine River into the heart of Germany, doing so at the Ludendorff Bridge in the town of Remagen. William's messages to his boy were always short and encouraging. The notes to Helen were neither specific—soldiers' letters were subjected to heavy censorship—nor, with his unit constantly on the move, were most of them very long. Occasionally, however, they contained telling details: "Had a hot meal for the first time in two weeks" or "Took a shower this month."

William never saw the end of the 99th's advance through Germany. On April 11—one day before the death of President Roosevelt and twenty-seven days before Germany's surrender—while his company was engaged in heavy fighting near the town of Hilchenbach, he was killed by a round from a German 88 mm gun. The news arrived at the Carpenter home on Chester Avenue by Western Union telegram. Bill was suddenly the man of the family. "I was worried about him," Helen said years later. "I knew he was grieving inwardly. He wasn't eating like he should. He wasn't playing like he should. He wasn't himself."

Helen found salvation—for herself and for her son—close to home. Clifford Dunn, who was soon to become the comptroller at the Philadelphia Navy Yard, lived just a few blocks from the Carpenter home. A burly man with a shock of thick, dark hair, he was forty when he and Helen married in 1947. The couple soon moved from Kingsessing to the town of Springfield, in the city's western suburbs. In spite of his imposing size, Dunn was a supremely gentle soul, and he soon developed a close bond with Bill, with whom he shared a love of the outdoors. Dunn was an avid horseman, and since he could not afford a mount of his own, he used to volunteer to take care of the horses at the nearby Rose Tree Hunt Club on the weekends. On most Saturday mornings, he and Bill would ride cross-country together over the hunt's sprawling grounds.

In 1954, by the time Bill was a senior at Springfield High, he stood six-two, weighed 190 pounds, and starred for both the track team, as a sprinter and low hurdler, and for the football team, as a halfback. In the fall, he had scored sixteen touchdowns. In the spring, he had led Springfield to its first-ever Delaware County track and field championship, winning the 120-yard low hurdles and placing second in the 100-yard dash. He also won the long jump, leaping twenty-one feet nine inches on his first and only attempt. But he did not stay to collect his medals. Instead, he left to visit West Point, which had been recruiting him to play football. A raft of big-time colleges, including Duke, Penn State, and Syracuse, were also pursuing him, but there was only one place he wanted to go.

There is nothing unusual about a son following in the path of his father. It happens all the time, whether the old man was a pharmacist or a farmer. But in Carpenter's case the pull toward the military was almost overwhelming. In 1993, on the occasion of his retirement from the Army after a thirty-two-year career as an infantry officer, he explained to William Nack of *Sports Illustrated* what he loved most about soldiers: "I like what they stand for," Carpenter said. "I like what they do. I like to listen to them talk and laugh. I like to listen to their tales. I like to be around them. I just like them." It was an eloquent explanation of his life's animating force, and at its heart was a lone infantryman with whom Carpenter could never talk or laugh, and whose tales he had never heard. If William S. Carpenter Jr. first thought of attending West Point because of Blanchard and Davis, there can be little doubt that he ultimately chose to play for Red Blaik because of William S. Carpenter Sr.

Bill's only other campus visit had been to Duke, where he had been escorted for the weekend by a young quarterback named Sonny Jurgensen. But Carpenter's mind had been made up from the moment he had caught sight of West Point's immense granite buildings. So prized was Carpenter as a recruit that he was treated to a rare lunch at the Blaik household. During the meal, Blaik asked him if he would be interested in playing for Army. Carpenter was in awe of Blaik, but he did not mince words. "Colonel, I don't think I can pass the entrance exam," he said. Blaik told Carpenter that if he wanted, he could study for the test at the football team's six-week prep school in Cornwall—the once notorious "monster school" that had caused so much controversy in 1951. Carpenter protested that he didn't think the prep course would do him much good, confessing, "I haven't had any math, Colonel."

It was not an exaggeration. At Springfield High, Carpenter had abruptly stopped taking courses in the subject after a dispute with one of his instructors. He had thus graduated without any preparation for a subject as demanding as calculus, which was the primary focus of West Point's notoriously rigorous plebe math course. But Blaik had a solution. Rather than have Carpenter enter West Point in 1955, he would send him for a year of coursework at the Manlius School, a military preparatory academy outside Syracuse, New York.* Blaik typically had several prospects attending the school at any given time courtesy of the Delafield Fund, an alumni booster organization that paid for tuition, room, and board—all Carpenter had to come up with for his year at the school was the money to pay for

---

* Carpenter describes Manlius thusly: "a school for dumb jocks and rich under-achievers."

books and uniforms. In his year at Manlius, he filled out to a solid 200 pounds. And running on synthetic tracks rather than the cinders of his high school days, he lowered his time in the 100-yard dash to 9.9 seconds. Carpenter arrived at West Point for Beast Barracks in the summer of 1956 prepared for the academy in both body and mind.

The plebe coach at West Point in 1956 was none other than Captain Felix "Doc" Blanchard, the legendary fullback from Blaik's storybook teams of the previous decade. Blanchard, an air force pilot, was also Blaik's top recruiter, a glamorous, godlike pitchman who was often able to lock up a commitment from an awestruck young player simply by walking into his living room. In order to meet his monthly seat-time requirements for the air force, Blanchard used to fly himself on his own recruiting trips, taking off from nearby Stewart Air Force Base in a Lockheed T-33, a two-seat jet trainer. His practice uniform never varied: a loose-fitting long-sleeve rubber shirt over a pair of Army Athletic Association gym shorts, from which extended the most muscular set of legs Carpenter, or any of the other Army players, had ever seen. Blanchard was not a tall man, but he was nearly as solid as he had been during his playing days. And though his manner was soft-spoken and friendly, his coaching style had all the subtlety of a falling anvil. His job was not merely to show the plebes how to play football but to show them how Blaik expected them to play *Army* football—and this Blanchard did with hard-hitting precision, never hesitating to insert himself into the middle of a drill in order to demonstrate its proper execution. No pads, full speed. In the words of one former player, "He'd put you on your ass in a heartbeat."

Carpenter had played only one game for Blanchard as a plebe before undergoing surgery on his right knee, which had caused him nagging pain ever since it had gotten twisted during a high school game. To protect the joint, he had always wrapped it heavily with athletic tape before playing football. But he reinjured it at West Point one morning as he was sprinting down a flight of stairs in the gymnasium, hurrying to change out of his gym clothes in order to make his next class on time. Carpenter took a bad step and the knee gave out, sending him sprawling to the floor. He hobbled to class on time, but his instructor sent him straight to the hospital. The next day, he was in surgery to repair the medial meniscus, the cartilage on the inner half of the knee between the femur and the tibia. This was in the days before arthroscopic surgery, and doctors had to open up Carpenter's joint in order to clean out the damaged cartilage.

A more severe injury had waylaid Carpenter on the eve of his sophomore season. In August 1957, he had been hurt in a jeep accident while returning to West Point for two-a-day practices from nearby Camp Buckner, the site of the Third Class summer training encampment. Eschewing a bus ride back to the academy with the rest of the squad, Carpenter had chosen instead to catch a lift with three teammates. In the jeep with him were two other ends: Otto Everbach, his classmate, and Dick Warner, a first classman, as well as a B Squad halfback named Fred Kaiser. Hitched to the back of the jeep was a small olive-drab U.S. Army trailer, filled to the brim with foot lockers. Kaiser and Everbach rode in back. Carpenter was sitting shotgun next to Warner, who, in the words of Everbach, "was the kind of driver who liked to look at you when he was talking." Nobody was wearing a seat belt, and rather than taking State Route 293, the main road back to post, Warner had opted instead for a shortcut, turning down one of the meandering dirt roads that crisscross the undeveloped interior of the West Point reservation. For the first few miles of the short drive, the four cadets had buzzed uneventfully past rifle ranges and training grounds before the road turned sharply to the left. As the jeep, which had no doors and a canvas top, rounded the corner, they found themselves directly in the path of an approaching U.S. Army truck, bearing down on them from no more than twenty yards away. Warner swerved sharply to the right to make room, but his right front wheel slipped off the dirt road and into a drainage ditch. To get out of the ditch, he jerked the wheel back to the left, a maneuver that caused the trailer behind the jeep to jump and whip hard to the right. Warner jerked the wheel back to the right to try to get the careening trailer under control, but the move only made its swing more violent. After a final correction by Warner, the trailer flipped over to the right and tipped the jeep with it. Carpenter, his world turning upside down, instinctively stuck out his right foot in a vain attempt to keep the jeep upright. It rolled over his foot and ankle and came to rest on its canvas roof. Carpenter's ankle was gushing blood, cut nearly to the bone. His season was effectively over.

Blaik had been eager to get Carpenter into the lineup that fall but because of the injury had to wait until the third game of the season to even get him into a uniform—when Army traveled to Philadelphia on October 12 to play Notre Dame at Municipal Stadium. Carpenter never saw the field during the Fighting Irish's 23–21 comeback victory, but he suffered a setback nonetheless. While he was kneeling along the sideline, a teammate warming up behind him stepped on his ankle, reopening the wound. Carpenter did not dress again until the Virginia game two weeks later, when he made it onto the field for a few meaningless plays during an unexpectedly tough 20–12 victory. He saw limited action in every game thereafter, primarily as a backup to Dick Warner, but he did not register an offensive statistic.

A healthy Carpenter was just one reason for Blaik to be optimistic in 1958. Though the Cadets brought back only three players who had started against Navy, each one was a standout. Guard Bob Novogratz, a long-armed former wrestler, was a terror as an inside linebacker for Blaik's defense. And with the halfback tandem of Bob Anderson and Pete Dawkins, Army would again have the best backfield in the country. Anderson, a brawny yet graceful runner out of Cocoa Beach, Florida, had been an All-America as a third classman in 1957, when he had averaged over six yards a carry and scored fourteen touchdowns. Dawkins, a blond-haired, blue-eyed rising first classman who had come to West Point in 1955 as a quarterback, was both a dangerous runner and a naturally gifted receiver. Of the eight scoring passes the Black Knights' rush-oriented offense had completed the year before, Dawkins had caught three, averaging a whopping twenty-one yards per reception. He and Anderson had combined to score twenty-five of Army's thirty-seven touchdowns in 1957, prompting the press to dub the pair the "Touchdown Twins," just as it had done with Doc Blanchard and Glenn Davis a decade earlier. Blaik was certain that if he was successful in implementing a more open game with his far-flanker scheme, there would be many more touchdowns to come.

The introduction of the far-flanker attack turned out to be so unremarkable an event that most of the Army players have no recollection of the first time they saw it drawn up on the chalkboard. Whereas Blaik's assistant coaches had all eventually grasped the singularity of the scheme, to the players it had never seemed anything but straightforward. They were thoroughly used to following orders, and once they had been instructed on how they were to line up and where they were supposed to go, they did exactly as they had been told and waited for the next set of orders. Indeed, to most of the players, little seemed to have changed. Blaik was primarily concerned with finding new starters that spring, and the Cadets simply ran their regular offense out of the far-flanker formation rather than work on new plays. The biggest adjustments Blaik and his coaches made were along the unbalanced offensive line. The far flanker always lined up to the wide side of the field: If the ball was spotted to the left of the field's vertical center line, Carpenter would split right; if the ball was spotted to the right, he would split left. In order to simplify blocking schemes, Blaik decided that the Army linemen would likewise flip sides to match the far flanker. Thus the guard and end on the weak side of the Cadets' line were always the same players, as were the linemen to Carpenter's side of the field. This meant that the seven men on the line of scrimmage had the same assignments on every play, whether Army was running from unbalanced right or unbalanced left, sets that Blaik eventually dubbed Bazooka and Bataan. And to minimize the number of adjustments the linemen had to make against different defensive fronts, new offensive line coach Bill Gunlock, who had been hired away from Bowling Green on February 17, installed a rudimentary system of zone blocking. Rather than blocking a specific defensive lineman or

OFFENSIVE FORMATIONS

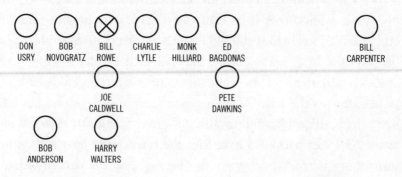

BAZOOKA

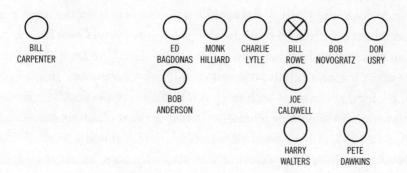

linebacker, an Army lineman would block a particular area, hitting whichever defender came into it.

The defensive coaching staff also bought into the spirit of simplification. Blaik had given line coach Frank Lauterbur and secondary coach Dale Hall only one instruction: Abandon the Oklahoma Defense. Against opponents with superior size and depth, sticking with the Oklahoma seemed as self-defeating as continuing to run the offense from the T formation, since the key to the scheme was for defenders to hit and control the offensive blocker in front of them. The Oklahoma Defense, in other words, was "impact football." Blaik instead wanted an aggressive defense that attacked the ball with speed rather than trying to control the line of scrimmage. "Let's give the boys some freedom," he told his coaches. Hall and Lauterbur came up with a defense they called the Offset 5-4, with defensive linemen and outside linebackers positioning themselves opposite the gaps in the offensive line. Additionally, the Cadets' defensive linemen would angle to either the left or right, depending on the defensive calls—"Chuckles" to the left; "Monster" to the right—of linebacker Charlie Lytle. Hall and Lauterbur also designated fullback Harry Walters as the Monster back and gave him the freedom to attack the line of scrimmage wherever he wanted. The aggressive scheme, which included an unusually high number of linebacker and safety blitzes, was designed to quickly break into the offensive backfield, disrupting plays before they had time to develop.

The only real hitch to any of the changes was the far flanker itself. Positioned about fifteen yards wide for every snap, Carpenter had to sprint back and forth to the huddle on every play, a requirement that became more arduous in Army's high-tempo offense when his receiving routes took him far downfield. "I was tired," he says. "I told the coaches I wasn't sure how long I could keep doing this." In the context of today's game—with its multiple wideouts, no-huddle offenses, and wide-open passing games—Carpenter's complaint seems absurd. But in 1958, college football was essentially iron-man football. The NCAA's substitution rule did not allow a player to return to the game in the same quarter in which he was taken out for a substitute (except for the last four minutes of the second and fourth quarters), which meant that it would not be easy to get Carpenter extra rest. Under the previous unlimited substitution rule—drafted in 1941 to compensate for the dearth of skilled players available during World War II—college football had come to be dominated by the platoon system, which allowed coaches to develop specialized units of offensive and defensive players. Blaik loved platooning, which he saw as mimicking the dynamics of a military outfit, and he exploited it to his advantage with his talent-rich wartime teams. But not everyone in college football was of the same mind. The athletic director at Tennessee, General Robert Neyland, a 1916 graduate of West Point, decried the platoon system as "chickenshit football."* In January 1953, the NCAA, citing its desire to reduce the financial burden on small schools that could not afford the oversized rosters demanded by the platoon system, changed its rules to bring back iron-man football.

It was for this reason that so many Army starters had averaged well over fifty minutes per game in 1957—a situation Blaik expected to be repeated in 1958. As spring practice came to a close in April, the coach was optimistic about the potential of his far-flanker attack, but he was uncertain about how to make it work within the limits of iron-man football. He felt that if he could figure out how to help Carpenter conserve energy, the only other question he had left to answer was the identity of his starting quarterback. The Black Knights did not have even one experienced passer on their roster, but somebody was still going to have to be able to throw Carpenter the ball.

---

* Neyland had been a star lineman at Army before going on to become one of college football's greatest coaches, winning four national titles with the Volunteers—the last in 1951.

Chapter 4

OLD ENEMIES

EVER SINCE HIS SON Bob had been expelled from West Point in 1951, Red Blaik had struggled to find a reliable starting quarterback. He had always built his West Point teams around the running game—Army had averaged just 7.7 throws per game in 1957 and 5.6 in 1956—but in order to keep opposing defenses honest, he needed someone who was capable of completing the few passes he was required to throw. The Cadets' best quarterback of the postscandal era had been Pete Vann, the strong-armed gunner who had led Army to its famous victory over Duke in 1953. But the pickings had been slim ever since. In 1955, Blaik had been so desperate that he had shifted All-America end Don Holleder under center. The left-handed senior was far from a reliable passer, but he was the Cadets' best all-around player, as well as an exceptional leader. The choice had nevertheless looked like a disaster in the early going, as Army lost two of its first four games. Holleder completed one of eight passes in a 26–2 drubbing at Michigan and was little better in a 13–0 loss to Syracuse at Michie Stadium.* The newspapers began referring to the quarterback as "Red Blaik's Folly."

"A coach has never known trouble," wrote Blaik years later, "unless

---

* Syracuse was led that day by a junior running back named Jim Brown.

he has the senseless temerity to change an All-American end into a 'T' quarterback in one season."

Holleder's legion of vociferous doubters even included the superintendent, Lieutenant General Blackshear M. "Babe" Bryan, who had been a teammate of Blaik's in 1919, as well as a fellow Army assistant a decade later. But Blaik stuck with Holleder in spite of the growing public outcry. More importantly, the team rallied behind him. Heading into the Navy game, the square-jawed, blue-eyed Holleder had willed Army to a 5–3 record despite completing less than 34 percent of his passes. The Black Knights were heavy underdogs to the eleventh-ranked Midshipmen, who were led by All-America end Ronnie Beagle and unflappable quarterback George Welsh, the nation's leader in passing and total offense. The night before the game, Blaik gathered his players for, as he called it, "a bedtime story." Speaking deliberately, he said, "I have grown weary of walking across the field to offer congratulations this year to [coaches] Bennie Oosterbaan of Michigan, Ben Schwartzwalder of Syracuse, and Jordan Oliver of Yale. Now I'm not as young as I used to be, and that walk tomorrow, before one hundred thousand people, to congratulate [Navy coach] Eddie Erdelatz, would be the longest walk I've ever taken in my coaching life."

This pronouncement was met with silence, until a single voice spoke up from the huddle of players: "Colonel," said Holleder, "you're not going to have to take that walk."

The first half of the 1955 Navy game was a nightmare for the Cadets. Holleder's only pass had been intercepted, while Navy gained over 200 yards and built a 6–0 lead. But with determined running by halfback Pat Uebel, who rushed for 125 yards, and dominant line play, Army fought its way back over the final thirty minutes. The Cadets ran for 283 yards, gained none through the air, and won 14–6. Holleder had led Army to a famous victory, if not a handsome one, and "Blaik's Folly" became one of the coach's greatest triumphs.

Holleder was still something of a national celebrity a little more than a month later, in January 1956, when he flew with Doc Blanchard to Miami to visit a prospective Army recruit, a young quarterback named Joe Caldwell. A diligent and intensely smart student, Caldwell had been planning to play football at Florida, his father's alma mater, where he intended to major in engineering. Blanchard and Holleder did not discuss much football with the boy—they instead spoke more about the bachelor of science degree in engineering that every cadet earned upon graduation—and they did not stay long, just enough time to eat a quiet dinner with the family. Before leaving, they invited Caldwell up to West Point for a visit. He had not been considering Army. But the two men—two of the most famous players Red Blaik had ever produced—had made an impression, and he agreed to make the trip. A few weeks later, Caldwell flew by himself to New York to visit Blaik and see the academy. When he returned, he surprised his friends and family by telling them that instead of Florida, he was going to play football at West Point.

Joe Caldwell was nearly as tall as both Bob Anderson and Pete Dawkins—and he had almost three inches on Harry Walters—but his rail-thin frame made the junior quarterback the least imposing member of the Army backfield. Caldwell weighed just 158 pounds when he checked in for spring ball in 1958, still nearly as gangly as he had been when he arrived at West Point two years before. With his freckled face and gap-toothed grin, he bore more than a passing resemblance to Alfred E. Neuman, the mascot of *MAD* magazine. With no discernable waistline, Caldwell's lanky upper body ran more or less straight down into a pair of skinny legs. Had he not been blessed with an accurate right arm, it's hard to imagine that he would have ever made it onto the field at West Point. As it was, Blaik felt Caldwell was one of the best passing prospects Army had recruited in many years, a fact that did not stop the coach from referring to his rawboned quarterback in the press as "the urchin."

Caldwell was from southwest Miami, the youngest son of John, a mechanical engineer, and Ethel, a Sunday school teacher. From his father, Joe inherited his love for football. On autumn Saturdays, John would wheel three televisions into the family living room so that he and his two boys could watch as many games as possible, overdosing on college football straight through Ethel's ritual fried chicken dinner. From his mother, Joe inherited a passionate religious faith. He was a quiet and profoundly decent teenager, a straight-A student at sprawling Miami High. When he was seventeen, Caldwell purchased a brand-new 1956 Chevrolet Bel Air with money he had saved from the paper routes he had been working since the day he turned twelve years old. His brother, John, older by eighteen months, also worked as a paperboy, and the two competed to see who could throw more newspapers onto the front porches along their respective routes. By his senior year of high school, Joe was throwing anywhere from 250 to 300 papers every morning.

As a senior in 1955 he had been at the helm of one of the top prep football programs in the country. The Stingarees regularly dressed one hundred players for home games—enrollment at Miami High was nearly four thousand that year—and were so good that most other Florida schools refused to play them. As a result, they often traveled to find opponents, flying several hours to play schools from as far away as Birmingham, Alabama, and Chattanooga, Tennessee. They also traveled by plane to play the road leg of their yearly home-and-home series with Jacksonville High, which was 350 miles to the north. Caldwell was not a rifle-armed passer, but he was highly intelligent, and his quick release and knack for finding open receivers made him devastatingly effective. Miami went undefeated that season and was widely acclaimed as state champion by Florida's sporting press.*

Blaik was not worried about Caldwell's arm. He was concerned that the skinny junior wouldn't be able to remain healthy through an entire season. With the NCAA's strict substitution rules, Caldwell would have to play a significant amount of defense—though Blaik had a pair of bigger, stronger quarterbacks in third classmen Glen Adams and Frank Gibson who were capable of spelling him at safety. And on offense, Caldwell would have to be able to stand in the pocket and take a hit. His stint with the varsity in 1957 had given the

---

* The Florida High School Athletic Association did not hold its first championship football tournament until 1963.

coach no confidence on this point. Caldwell had lasted just two min-utes in the opening-day win over Nebraska, missing on all three of his passes before breaking his jaw as he attempted to throw a block.

Many of his teammates saw a quiet strength in Caldwell—a modest and intellectually sharp cadet whose only serious pursuit outside of academics and football was as a Sunday school teacher at the Cadet Chapel—but Blaik saw a player on whom he had not yet been able to get a good read. The coach, despite his reserved and dignified manner, was at heart a deeply emotional and sentimental man. His players may have felt that he kept them at a distance, but Blaik saw himself as their confidant and mentor. In 1955, Holleder and Blaik had become almost codependent, with the quarterback sometimes emotionally confiding his insecurities to his coach, who would respond by putting his arms around Holleder's shoulders and quietly reassuring him. Blaik did not have that sort of relationship with Caldwell, and it frustrated him. He groused to MacArthur on the eve of the 1958 season, "[Caldwell] seems to be that type of ca-det who agrees and thoroughly understands, and gives you a 'yes sir' 'no sir' answer with disarming enthusiasm, but then never get[s] untracked in action."

In order for Blaik's new offense to work, Army was going to have to be able to make opponents pay if they simply ignored the far flanker or covered him with only one defender. To do this, Blaik planned to throw the ball more, which meant that, despite his reser-vations, he had little choice but to stick with Caldwell. He was the best passer on the team. There was no one else. With Adams and Gibson set to play significant roles on defense, Blaik rated second classman Bob Rudesill—a baseball player who had struggled with injuries of his own—as Caldwell's offensive backup. But as the coach told MacArthur, Rudesill was "no passer." Red Blaik's fate would be bound to the urchin.

For all the optimism Blaik felt coming out of spring practice in 1958, there was one issue on which he had been supremely disappointed. For months, he had been trying to address his team's chronic lack of depth, a problem that dated back to the 1951 cheating scandal, when the academy's administration had begun to curb the number of football recruits included in each new class. The allotment for Blaik's program had been whittled down over the years to about two dozen, a number that the coach wanted bumped up to thirty-five. In December 1957, Blaik submitted a request for that amount to the athletic board. In his role as director of athletics, of course, Blaik also sat at the head of the board, but in spite of his position of authority, his fellow board members voted to knock the number down slightly, to thirty-three, reasoning that the new superintendent would not accept his request without some modification. The superintendent was now Lieutenant General Garrison H. Davidson, and he had exercised tight control over Army's recruiting efforts in all sports, particularly football, since taking over for Babe Bryan in July 1956. The board passed its request to Davidson in January 1958, and one month later, on the eve of spring practice, he had knocked the allotment for football recruits down to twenty-five, a decision that prompted Blaik to lament in a letter to MacArthur, "Never in all the time I have been at West Point has the approach to success been so needlessly difficult." Blaik also made a point of insisting, "There is nothing personal in my attitude."

But that was not true. Garrison Holt Davidson, known as Gar to family and friends, was no stranger to Army football, or to Red Blaik. In 1924 and 1926, Davidson had been a five-foot-ten, 168-pound end for the Cadets. Colonel Lawrence McCeney "Biff" Jones, the Army football coach, had thought so much of his leadership abilities and football acumen that, after Davidson's graduation in 1927, he had hired the square-jawed second lieutenant as the ends coach for the plebe team. Davidson joined the staff in the fall, at precisely the same time as Earl Blaik. The two men clashed almost immediately.

As a head coach, Blaik modeled his style on the deliberate approach of the reserved, fastidiously organized Jones. But in his first job as a full-time assistant—Jones had been forced to pay a personal visit to Blaik's father in order to convince him to grant his son a temporary release from his business obligations in Dayton—Blaik, who was in charge of the Army passing game, saw it as his duty to be a disciplinarian, the noncommissioned officer to Jones's commander. To his players Blaik was a hard-driving, unforgiving martinet, and he was so universally loathed by the Cadets that they bestowed upon him the unaffectionate nickname "the Whip." Things got so bad that the varsity backs and ends, many of whom had played with Davidson just the year before, went to their old teammate and asked him to speak to Jones about what they saw as abusive treatment. They told Davidson that if Blaik did not let up, they were all going to quit.

At the time, the members of the Army coaching staff lived together in West Point's Bachelor Officer Quarters (BOQ), where they ate dinner together at a long table in the dining room every night. The staff was extremely close, and the environment for the most part was collegial. But Davidson had seen enough of Blaik's antics that fall to know that the players' complaints were true. He went to Jones about the matter, an act of betrayal for which Blaik never forgave him.

Davidson was a man of initiative who had strong convictions about right and wrong, and he was morally certain that he had, at the risk of personal scorn from his friends and colleagues, done the right thing. The son of a career soldier, he had been raised in the Bronx by his father's parents, Genaro and Martha Davidson. Genaro had for years been the property man for Edwin Booth, America's most famous Shakespearean actor, and he and Martha were both fond of quoting the Bard to each other and to their grandsons.* One of their most oft-repeated lines was from Act I of *Hamlet*: "To thine own self be true." It was a lesson that young Gar took to heart. An Eagle Scout before he became a cadet, Davidson was such a straight arrow at West Point that rather than violate the prohibition law, he used to travel to Canada—vacationing at the summer home of a classmate on Ottawa's Lake McGregor with football teammates Red Reeder, Moe Daley, and Harry "Fats" Ellinger—in order to have a drink. Davidson was an outstanding student and one of the top leaders in his class. He served on one of the academy's first honor committees and, as a first classman, had been appointed

---

* Booth was the brother of presidential assassin John Wilkes Booth.

the cadet commander of Beast Barracks, a position that carried with it the informal title "King of the Beasts."

The normal progression for Davidson from such a prominent assignment would have been for him to be named First Captain, the highest-ranking position in the Corps of Cadets. But that promotion never came. With rumors swirling around Washington, D.C., about another possible congressional investigation of hazing, the new commandant of cadets, Colonel Campbell Hodges, ordered Davidson's Beast Barracks detail of first classmen to refrain from yelling at plebes; new cadets were instead to be corrected and reprimanded in hushed tones by their company tactical officers. In a meeting with Davidson, senior representatives of the Beast detail voiced their objection to the order, saying it undermined the cadre's authority, and urged him to carry the protest to the commandant. Davidson agreed with their argument, and he confronted Hodges in a private meeting. The commandant dismissed Davidson's reasoning and took offense at what he saw as open insubordination. Davidson never rose to be First Captain of the Corps of Cadets. But he also never regretted his decision, believing solemnly in an earnest plea from the Cadet Prayer: "Make us to choose the harder right instead of the easier wrong, and never to be content with a half truth when the whole can be won." Gar Davidson had not backed down to the commandant, and he was not about to back down to Red Blaik.

Going forward, the two men kept their distance from each other, maintaining a peaceful, if uneasy, coexistence on the Army coaching staff for five years. Biff Jones gave way to Major Ralph Sasse as head coach in 1930, and both Blaik and Davidson stayed on as assistants. Blaik loved working for the dashing Sasse—the first American combat officer to set foot on French soil in World War I—who gave his assistants tremendous freedom. Sasse turned over almost total control of the Cadets' attack to Blaik and offensive line coach Harry Ellinger, Davidson's former teammate. Other members of the staff referred to the head coach and his two lieutenants as "the Big Three," and Blaik later compared his role to that of a "chief of staff." He was becoming more and more convinced that, as he put it, "building houses was less rewarding than building men," and the prospects for his permanent return to the family business in Dayton continued to diminish.

Sasse's club had gone 9–1–1 in 1930, losing only to one of Knute Rockne's greatest Notre Dame teams. But in a 6–6 tie with Yale in the fifth game of the following season, tragedy struck. A slender Army end, a game reserve named Richard Brinsley Sheridan Jr., who weighed all of 149 pounds, was injured while covering a kickoff early in the fourth quarter. The first man down the field, Sheridan had met Yale's kick returner, Bob Lassiter, head-on. Lassiter was a high-stepping runner, and one of his knees caught Sheridan in the back of the head, fracturing his fourth and fifth cervical vertebrae. Sheridan was taken from the field on a stretcher and rushed to the hospital. A distraught Sasse remained on the sideline through the final gun but rushed to Sheridan's bedside immediately afterward, keeping vigil there throughout the next two days, before the young man passed away on October 26. Sasse finished the season, even using the memory of Sheridan to inspire Army to a 12–0 upset of Notre Dame on November 28. But he could not shake the lingering anguish. After the season, he asked to be relieved of his duties and returned to a post with the cavalry. He stayed on in 1932 at the request of the athletic board, but he again petitioned for a transfer at the end of the season. This time, there were no objections.

That October, the academy announced that Gar Davidson, who was still a second lieutenant, would succeed Sasse at the end of the 1932 season. Just twenty-eight at the time, Davidson was the youngest football coach in West Point history. The preference at the academy was that the head coach be an active-duty army officer, as well as a graduate, so Davidson's promotion to the top job was not entirely unexpected. But it was nevertheless a wounding blow to Blaik, who felt that he, Sasse's "chief of staff," was ready to take over. Sasse, after all, had gone before the athletic board and endorsed Blaik as his choice for the job. Soon after Davidson's promotion, in November 1932, Blaik wrote to MacArthur that his rival was "youthful and lacks worldly experience," and that he had "neither the drive nor the personality of Sasse nor the football brain of a Jones." Blaik, having already spurned coaching offers from Princeton and Ohio State, was stuck at West Point under his nemesis. He lasted just one season working for Davidson, growing in his conviction that the 1933 season would be his last on the banks of the Hudson. "For one thing," he later wrote, "the rapport Harry [Ellinger] and I had enjoyed with Sasse was missing." In January 1934, Blaik signed a three-year contract to take over as the head coach at Dartmouth. He promptly hired Fats Ellinger as an assistant.

Gar Davidson was getting married in Omaha, Nebraska, when he learned of Blaik's departure. Nobody from West Point had called to tell Davidson anything—he'd had to read about it the next day in the *Omaha World-Herald*.

Davidson enjoyed a successful five-year run as the coach at West Point. He won thirty-five of forty-seven games and, more importantly, beat Navy three times before finally departing for Hawaii to take a troop command in 1938. During his tenure on the sideline, he had been required to send weekly updates on the team to General MacArthur, first to Washington, D.C., when the general was army chief of staff, and later to Manila, after he took over as field marshal of the Philippine army.

While Davidson had earned a measure of acclaim as a football coach, it paled in comparison to that which came his way as a soldier. In 1942, Patton personally selected Davidson as the deputy engineer for the Western Task Force in the Allied invasion of North Africa. Davidson stayed with Patton when the latter took over the 7th Army for the invasion of Sicily a year later. It was in a battlefield ceremony there in the summer of 1943 that Patton had used his own general stars to promote Davidson to the rank of brigadier general. He stayed with the 7th Army through the invasion of southern France in August 1944 and the subsequent push into Germany.*

---

* Davidson had chosen the landing point for the French invasion, on the coast east of the city of Toulon, where there was no high ground for the Germans to command as they had in Sicily and at Normandy.

Davidson was only home for a few years after the war before he was called back to combat duty in Korea. There he oversaw the fortification of the defensive positions around the port city of Pusan, where United Nations forces were in a desperate fight to avoid being driven off the peninsula altogether. He chafed under MacArthur's command in Korea—the general had flown the Pusan perimeter during its construction and ordered changes that Davidson felt weakened the overall position. Nevertheless, he and MacArthur, and Red Blaik, too, were of the same mind about football as a training tool for soldiers. Davidson had seen enough evidence in two wars to convince him of that.

Blaik and Davidson both saw the academy's response to the cheating scandal as absurd. But where the coach saw the lack of reforms as both an indictment of the administration and a tacit vindication of his program, the superintendent saw inexplicable neglect. He set about following through on the Bartlett Board's recommendation that the duties of head football coach and athletic director be split. Davidson also reined in Blaik's recruiting program for football players by insisting on equality for all sports. In Blaik's words, "This meant the downgrading of football and the elevation of squash, soccer and other sports to a parity with the primary sport." To Blaik, the football program was worthless unless its overall goal was victory; to Davidson—who in his later years admitted that he would have preferred Army to play only an Ivy League schedule—the game was a means to an end, a supremely physical way to train leaders of character. It is a conflict as old as college football: What is the role of the game in the life of a school? Davidson, a man of high honor, had been appalled by the 1951 cheating scandal and blamed it on the academy's overemphasis on football. One of his goals when he arrived at West Point in 1956 was to get football, and Red Blaik, under control.

Barney Gill, Army's B Squad coach, knew nothing of the enmity between Blaik and Davidson until one chilly spring day in 1958. During a practice at Michie Stadium, Gill happened to look up into the stands, where he saw Davidson, bundled in his overcoat, sitting alone. Gill, an army captain, took it upon himself to walk up into the seats, say hello to the general, and ask if he could answer any questions. Davidson politely demurred, and Gill returned to the field, thinking nothing more of the encounter. Blaik said nothing at practice, but later, in the locker room, the coach confronted Gill and subjected him to a withering cross-examination. The conversation began innocuously, with Blaik asking, "What did the boss have to say?" Gill replied that Davidson had just been watching the team practice. But when Blaik bore in for the details of Gill's conversation, his tone changed. "He kind of raised his voice and I thought, 'Oh, *shit*,' " says Gill. "He crawled all over my ass for going up there. I thought he was going to run me out of the program."

The message was clear. When it came to Davidson, the assistant coaches were not to speak to the superintendent unless he first spoke to them. And the only information that would be divulged to the general was the information that Blaik wanted him to know. What had begun as a personal rivalry between Blaik and Davidson had escalated into a struggle over the future of Army football.

In the last week of July, Blaik and his staff made their annual summer sojourn to Bull Pond. The military academy covers roughly sixteen thousand rolling, wooded acres that extend west and south from the riverside promontory that was the site of the first fortress at West Point, and the reservation contains more than a dozen ponds and lakes, a number of which have a maximum depth of less than ten feet. Bull Pond, at seventy-nine feet, is one of the deeper waterholes in the area, though Blaik claimed that the added depth did nothing to improve the poor quality of the fishing. Nestled in the highlands of the Central Valley atop a thousand-foot rise, Bull Pond is relatively remote, and in 1958 there were just four cabins, including a boathouse and a caretaker's quarters, on its twenty-five acres. Officially, the encampment was intended as a vacation spot for the superintendent, but it was traditionally also made available to other senior officers on post. At the end of July and the beginning of August, Blaik and his staff had the run of the place.

The only people permitted to accompany the coaches on this trip were men who were close to the football program, including the graduate manager of athletics, Colonel Fran Roberts, and a collection of Blaik's cronies from both outside and inside the academy: Stanley Woodward; *Look* magazine's Tim Cohane; Willard Mullin, the sports cartoonist for the *New York World-Telegram*; and Colonel Russell "Red" Reeder, an Army assistant coach under Davidson and a veteran of D-Day. The current assistants mostly bunked together in Cabin Number Two, referred to by campers as "the Mother Lodge," while Blaik and the rest holed up together in the Superintendent's Cottage, which contained the camp's only kitchen.

One mirthful evening nearly a decade before, the scholarly, pipe-smoking Cohane had introduced campers to his Bull Pond All-America Team, a spoof on the College All-Star teams he selected for *Look* every year. As David Maraniss wrote in his authoritative biography of Vince Lombardi, *When Pride Still Mattered*, "The sensibility of the Bull Pond All-America Team reflected Cohane's perspective on major college football, which was shared by [his fellow campers]: he revered it, despite its flaws, which he preferred to deal with through jokes rather than hand-wringing editorials and official investigations." His roster included Excalibur Slime, the "maniacally aggressive end" from King Arthur's Knight School; Increase Yardage, Harvard's "famed fullback and cum laude student in underwater fingerpainting"; and Chuckles Axmurder, the "murderous end" from Bedlam Hall. It was during the 1958 trip to Bull Pond that Blaik had, on the recommendation of Dale Hall and Frank Lauterbur, created the Chuckles Axmurder Award, to be given to the outstanding defensive player of each game. Willard Mullin even dashed off a rendering of the fictional All-American for the certificate—a dazed football player whose helmet had been split open with an ax.

Besides a mid-retreat meal catered by Gene Leone, the Bull Pond campers subsisted on breakfasts and dinners prepared by a kitchen staff that visited from West Point every day. They otherwise spent their time fishing, golfing, swimming, or just relaxing. Each night on the screened-in porch of the Mother Lodge, they watched Hollywood movies that were provided by the U.S. Army Signal Corps and

Army highlight reels from Blaik's vast film archives. If the movie was of no interest, there was always the backroom bar in the same cabin, where Red Reeder gleefully dispensed, in the words of Blaik, "sarsaparilla, root beer, and other more deadly washes." It was during one of these casual evenings that Blaik had first drawn up his far-flanker formation for his visitors. Stanley Woodward took one look at the diagram and said, "You ought to call him the Lonely End."

On August 15, Blaik attended the Chicago Charities College All-Star Game, the annual clash between the reigning NFL champion (in this case, the Detroit Lions) and a select team of graduated collegiate seniors. He was less concerned with the game—which was won by the All-Stars 35–19, in front of seventy thousand fans at Soldier Field—than he was with visiting old friends. In particular, he was anxious to see Andy Gustafson, the head coach at Miami, where Bob Blaik was currently working as an assistant. The affable Gustafson had been one of Red Blaik's first hires at Dartmouth, and the two had stayed together until 1947, when Gustafson left West Point to take over as the head coach at Miami. No other assistant had spent more time working for Blaik, and the two men had remained close; Blaik still sought out Gustafson for counsel on football matters. Indeed, it had been Gustafson who had turned Blaik on to Joe Caldwell after Gustafson had been unable to convince the boy to play for the Hurricanes. When Gustafson got a look at Blaik's far-flanker scheme, he was taken aback by the amount of running the formation would require from Carpenter. "Earl," he warned, echoing Blaik's concerns at the end of spring practice, "you will run him into the ground."

On a plane ride from Chicago to Oklahoma to visit his older son, Bill, Blaik considered the problem. With the limits on substitution and Army's lack of depth, Carpenter was going to have to play more than fifty minutes in most games. If he stayed out of the huddle, Blaik reasoned, it would help to conserve his energy. Relaying the plays to him would be easy enough—all that was needed was a system of signals similar to the ones used by baseball teams as a matter of routine. As he deliberated on this, Blaik realized an even greater benefit to stationing Carpenter wide throughout the game. "Most important," he said, "[the far flanker] would force the defense, or at least a vital part of it, to commit its intentions immediately. This would give the quarterback a chance, much earlier in the twenty-five seconds allotted for getting the ball in play, to assay the defensive alignment and call the proper play to negate it."

When Blaik returned to West Point, he quickly devised a system of signals for Carpenter. The far flanker's first look would be to the quarterback standing just outside the huddle. If the quarterback's feet were together, the play was a run, and Carpenter, according to his official orders in the Army playbook, was authorized to "do as you please." When Caldwell stood with one foot in front of the other, the play was a pass. Carpenter would then look to the halfback—either Dawkins on the right or Anderson on the left—for another signal that would tell him the pass route he was supposed to run. If the halfback touched his chinstrap, Carpenter would slant across the middle of the field. A hand to the eyes meant he was to run a post pattern. Tightening the belt was a come-back route. Touching the thigh guard was a hook. A hitch of the pants was a deep fly route. It was simple.

The Space Age had begun less than a year before, in October 1957, when the Soviet Union had launched *Sputnik I* into a ninety-six-minute orbit of Earth. At that moment, the country's military focus turned from the tank, warplane, and common foot soldier to the rockets and missiles capable of winning a war in the heavens. Given Blaik's intention of opening up the Army offense, it was appropriate that the Cadets began fall training on August 29, 1958, with a Nike Ajax missile at the north end of their practice field. The first day of the new season was traditionally a photo op that was open to the press, and the Army players wore their game uniforms and posed for file photos. Nobody was in greater demand with the reporters than halfback Pete Dawkins, who had already assumed command of the Corps of Cadets as First Captain—a promotion that made him the most accomplished cadet in the history of the academy. Both Robert E. Lee in 1829 and Douglas MacArthur in

1903 had been First Captains who ranked in the top 5 percent of their classes academically. Dawkins ranked in the top 5 percent of his class, but he was also president of the class and the captain of the football team. No other cadet in the history of West Point had ever achieved all four distinctions at once. Bill Carpenter, in his role as the far flanker, may have been the cornerstone of this Army team, but Pete Dawkins was its public face from Day One.

Blaik only hinted to reporters that he planned to throw the ball more, saying in general terms that a "more open game" would be necessary to spare his team the physical pounding it had been taking in recent years. He gave nothing away about the far flanker or the unbalanced line. But he did go into specifics when he discussed his reasons for the new approach. Without ever mentioning the superintendent by name, Blaik laid the blame for his current predicament at the feet of Gar Davidson. "Army doesn't have the depth of material to play our schedules," Blaik said. "We have been getting away with murder, but some day it is going to catch up with us. I have been trying to get them to do something about it, but we are limited to twenty-eight and you know what the attrition is at the academy with the heavy schedule of work and the academic requirements."*

The first chance to test Blaik's far-flanker scheme had come in the annual scrimmage against Syracuse on September 13. The day had begun auspiciously, with a visit from MacArthur. Neatly attired in a dark suit and Panama hat, he addressed the team in the locker room before the game. Under a table near the general, a reel-to-reel tape recorder was running. The only sound in the room besides MacArthur's voice was that of the player's cleats click-clacking on the concrete floor. As he was fond of doing, MacArthur spoke of football and war as endeavors that were inextricably linked. "Football," MacArthur began, "has become a symbol of America's greatest qualities: loyalty, courage, stamina and coordinated efficiency. Throughout my

---

* Between the time Davidson cut the number of recruits to twenty-five and the time new plebes arrived for Beast Barracks, three slots allotted to other sports had gone unused. The athletic board gave them to the football program, allowing Blaik to secure a total of twenty-eight recruits.

long career, through war and peace, it has been West Point football players that have gained my greatest reliance." He went on to cite John Trent, the 1949 Army captain who had been killed in Korea. Then he moved on to Trent's teammate, All-America quarterback Arnold Galiffa, who had been awarded the Bronze Star. Galiffa, MacArthur said, "lobbed grenades at the enemy as he lobbed passes at West Point."* He concluded by saying, "Remember when you go out on that field, you play not just for yourselves, not just for your teammates or for the corps, but for the ghosts of a million American fighting men who gave their lives for their country. Now go out there and win."†

MacArthur's speech fired the Cadets up, but its effect on their play was minimal. Caldwell, according to Blaik, played as if he were in a "haze" and did not perform as well under center as Glen Adams, his defensive replacement. Army fumbled the ball seven times, completed only three of eleven passes (with two interceptions), and committed ninety-five yards' worth of penalties. But Blaik did not see the overall effort as a negative. The sense that the team had not played well, he wrote to MacArthur on September 15, "is shared by the entire squad, and such personal appraisal augers well for our practice sessions."

The most important lesson that Blaik and his coaches took away from the scrimmage was that they needed to involve Carpenter even more in the attack. The far-flanker formation had confused Syracuse initially, but the Army offense had been unable to press the advantage. This was partly due to Caldwell's indecisive play, but it was also because the Syracuse defensive backs quickly figured out that, since the Cadets weren't regularly throwing the ball to Carpenter, they could get away with leaving just one man on him. The safety responsible for playing double coverage to the far flanker's side of the field instead held his ground in the middle, where he could more

---

* MacArthur wasn't the first to make this comparison. Press accounts from Korea had said that Galiffa had once thrown a grenade a record seventy-five yards in combat. Since official combat grenade-throwing statistics are not kept on file by the army or anyone else, we'll have to take their word for it.

† Says Pete Dawkins, "Remember, this was *scrimmage*."

easily provide run support and disrupt the pass routes run by Anderson, Dawkins, and Army's tight end, Don Usry. Carpenter, then, was of little use as a decoy unless Army was willing to throw him the ball whenever the opportunity presented itself. Forcing double coverage on the far flanker would create an unfillable gap in the defense that Anderson and Dawkins would then be able to exploit. It would mean even more passing than Blaik had intended, but there were plenty of reasons to think it would work. Carpenter was fast enough to beat almost any defensive back one-on-one, and he had also shown exceptional skill as a receiver. This he apparently owed almost completely to his own natural ability. "I can't remember anybody," says Carpenter, "ever talking to me about the technique of catching a football."

Blaik and his coaches retreated to their offices at the gymnasium. They had two weeks to tinker before the home opener against South Carolina, and as they were about to learn, the far-flanker formation lent itself to tinkering. Opening up the field would reveal innumerable new offensive possibilities. The commitment to increasing Carpenter's involvement in the passing game was not the first wrinkle Blaik and his coaches would add to the new attack, but it may have been the most important.

Chapter 5

THE LONELY END

ON THE MORNING of September 27, Red Blaik sat in his office, watching the rain outside beat against his window. Showers had been falling since before sunrise, forcing the cancellation of the season's first football review, a pregame ceremony in which the Corps of Cadets formed up by regiments on the Plain and paraded for thousands of spectators and a handful of the academy's top brass. This day's opponent was South Carolina, a tough, hard-nosed outfit that, like the Black Knights, was led by a pair of outstanding halfbacks. In 1957, King Dixon and Alex Hawkins had combined to score all four of the Gamecocks' touchdowns in a 27–21 upset of heavily favored Texas, and they were the centerpieces of a team that was expected to be one of the best in the Atlantic Coast Conference. The blond-haired Hawkins was a preseason All-America, a rugged and athletic runner who had a reputation for both delivering and absorbing a tremendous amount of punishment. He was a perfect fit in coach Warren Giese's grinding, ground-hugging offensive scheme. The bright and ambitious Giese was, at thirty-four, one of the younger head coaches in the country, and he had already coauthored an instructional book entitled *Coaching Football and the Split T Formation.*

South Carolina had been unranked in the preseason Associated Press college football poll while Army had been picked ninth, but the Gamecocks were nevertheless supremely confident entering the game. They returned twenty-three lettermen and seven starters from the year before and were coming off a season-opening shutout victory over a good Duke team on September 20 that had bumped them up to number eighteen in the AP poll. Classes had not yet begun in Columbia, but Giese and his staff had been drilling their players in two-a-day practices for more than a month, preparing them for the Cadets' power-rushing attack. South Carolina arrived in New York the morning before the game and set up camp just south of the academy at the Bear Mountain Inn, a rustic lodge constructed from the timber and fieldstone found naturally in the highlands that surround West Point. On a field adjacent to the hotel, the Gamecocks ran through what they felt was a flawless pregame practice. "Our kickoff guy was kicking the ball not only through the end zone but through the uprights," says Dixon. "We'd never seen anything like that before. It was just a beautiful, cold afternoon—windswept—and we had a great rehearsal."

For his part, Red Blaik was not so confident. As the rain continued to fall Saturday morning, he met with his assistants in the staff's conference room and asked them if they thought the weather would present a problem for the new far-flanker attack. What if Caldwell had trouble throwing the ball in the rain? How would both a slippery ball and a slippery field affect the receivers? Would it be more prudent, he asked, to wait for better weather to debut the far flanker—to bring Carpenter back to a tight-end position and return to the traditional T formation? Blaik conceded that the switch might present some problems at first to the players, who had been practicing the new offensive system for the better part of a month, but he did not feel that such a change would be impractical. Army's basic offense, especially the running game, was essentially unchanged from the year before, and, for the most part, the plays would remain the same.

Bill Gunlock was taken aback by Blaik's proposition. He had been at West Point since early February, when Blaik had hired him away from Bowling Green to be the Cadets' new offensive line coach, and at twenty-eight, he was the youngest man on the Army staff. A 1951 graduate of Miami, where he had played on the Redskins offensive line, Gunlock had only been able to join Blaik at West Point after he had backed out of a job he had already accepted from Minnesota coach Murray Warmath. Warmath, who had coached the Cadets' offensive line for Blaik from 1949 to 1951, had been waiting for approval of Gunlock's hiring from Minnesota's board of trustees when the Army job became available. The prospect of working with Blaik at West Point was thrilling to Gunlock. A job on the Cadets' staff was a plum assignment, and almost as important to him was the fact that Blaik was a fellow Miami alumnus. Gunlock had even been recruited to play for the Redskins by head coach Sid Gillman, a former Blaik assistant. But Gunlock nevertheless told Blaik that he didn't feel it would be appropriate to take the job at West Point after he had already accepted one at Minnesota. Blaik pressed the issue, encouraging Gunlock to come to West Point for an interview and telling him, "You owe it to yourself to come out here."

"He kept on talking," says Gunlock. "And it seemed like he was practically offering me the job on the telephone. So I said, 'OK, I'll come for a visit.'"

But before he left for New York, Gunlock called Murray Warmath. As well as anyone, Warmath understood Gunlock's interest in the West Point job. Warmath had, after all, gone straight from a position on Blaik's staff to a head coaching job at Mississippi State, staying in Starkville for two years before moving on to Minnesota. Warmath understood, but he wasn't happy. "God damn it," he said to Gunlock, "if you go out there, you're going to accept the job!" Gunlock took the statement as a tacit release from his commitment.

Gunlock had never before seen indecision from the Army coach. Blaik ran his office with purposeful efficiency, and when he made up his mind to follow the advice of an assistant, he allowed that coach a tremendous amount of autonomy. In just a few months at West Point, Gunlock had already made significant contributions to the Army playbook, and Blaik had adopted his zone-blocking scheme with minimal changes. So Gunlock spoke up with confidence when he told Blaik that he thought it would be best to stick with the far flanker, a sentiment echoed by Tom Harp, the offensive backfield coach, who said, "Colonel, if we only run this offense when the weather's good, then it's not a very good offense." Blaik stood silently at the head of the table for a few moments, then nodded his head in agreement. The far-flanker attack would make its debut in the rain and the mud at Michie Stadium.

Like everything else at West Point, football Saturdays followed an unvarying routine. The academy's weekend did not formally begin until Saturday afternoon, and so when Army played at home, Blaik's players slept in their barracks rooms, rose at a quarter to six, and went to breakfast at the mess hall with the rest of the corps before attending the first class of the day. "We had to be one of the only teams in the country that went to class on game days," says Harry Walters. Excused from the morning's second academic period, the players would then make their way individually or in groups to the gymnasium, where they would meet Blaik at half past nine and walk with him out to Trophy Point, the leafy overlook that affords a spectacular view upriver to nearby Storm King Mountain and the city of Newburgh. In the nineteenth century, the prospect had been popular with the artists from the Hudson River School, and since 1837 the academy had been using it to display captured artillery pieces from American conflicts dating back to the Battle of Saratoga in 1777. It was on this hallowed ground that Blaik typically delivered his final pregame comments.

On this rainy Saturday, however, the coach addressed his boys inside the entrance to the gym, telling them little more than that South Carolina was a good team, and that it was important that they get the season off to a winning start. He then dismissed them to the mess hall, where they sat down to their traditional pregame meal: well-done steaks, baked potatoes, string beans, and dry toast. Blaik, for reasons of his own, did not allow butter for the toast, only honey, and the beverage options were strictly limited to hot tea or ice water. In eighteen years at West Point, the deeply conservative coach's menu had changed only one time. In 1957, trainer Ed Pillings had enraged Blaik by substituting lima beans for string beans before an early-season game, a mistake he never made again.

When the players finished eating, they returned to the gym to dress for the game. Members of the backfield got their ankles taped, a safety measure not accorded to offensive linemen, who wore high-top shoes. The team then assembled in the first-floor wrestling room, where they sat down on the floor mats to wait for Blaik. By this time, the assistants were downstairs, too, standing along the padded wall by the entrance. The room was down a hallway from the freight elevator that ran to the coaches' offices three floors above. With the rest of the Corps of Cadets back in the barracks, the players and coaches were the only ones in the building, and they could clearly hear Blaik enter the elevator, lifting and closing first the gate and then the door. They could hear the whine of the motor as the elevator slowly made its way down to the ground level, where Blaik would once again lift the door and the gate. He would appear in the doorway exactly forty-five minutes before kickoff wearing his usual brown tweed suit and fedora. And then he would clap his hands once and say simply, "Let's go, men."

Bill Rowe, a lean, jug-eared three-year letterman, had been through this drill so many times that he used to count the seconds, all sixty of them, that it took Blaik to travel downstairs from his office—from the time he could hear the first rattle and crash of the elevator doors to the instant the coach stepped into the doorway of the wrestling room. Rowe hailed from Carlisle, Pennsylvania, a small burg nestled in the rich farmland of the Cumberland Valley. His father, Earl, was a dairy farmer, and his mother, Pauline, worked in a dress factory. The family, which included four brothers—in addition to Bill there were also LeRoy, Bob, and Ben—had built their own house out of timber salvaged from an abandoned barn and lived without indoor plumbing or a telephone. Before Blaik began recruiting Bill during his junior year of high school, the only things he knew about the academy were what he had heard from football teammates whose fathers were stationed at the nearby Army War College at Carlisle Barracks. To notify Rowe of his acceptance at the academy, Jim Schwenk, the graduate manager of athletics, had called Rowe's girlfriend, Mary Lou Beittel, who took the news to the Rowe household in person. Rowe had already received scholarship offers from other schools, but he stuck with West Point because Blaik had been the first to contact him, and also because he found the promise of three hot meals a day and a structured lifestyle appealing.

Rowe took naturally to life at the academy. Carlisle High School had provided him with a strong academic background, especially in math. Unlike several of his plebe teammates, he did not find academics to be a great burden. And his background in football was just as strong. Many of the drills that Doc Blanchard ran at practice were ones that Rowe had already seen in high school, and the former Heisman winner frequently used him to demonstrate proper execution and technique. Rowe had also played the same defense in high school that Blaik was then using at West Point—the 5-4 Oklahoma. "The majority of the people here, I was just ahead of them, football-wise," says Rowe, who was chosen by his teammates as captain of the plebe squad.

In the hours before the South Carolina game, Rowe, now a first classman, was as nervous as he had ever been for a game at West Point. His apprehension had little to do with the far-flanker attack. In the spring, Blaik had moved Rowe from guard to center, and he was anxious that he would miss a blocking assignment or, even worse, botch the center-quarterback exchange with Joe Caldwell. The tension added an extra edge to Rowe's typically spirited game-day demeanor. An intense presence on the field, he loved everything about football, especially the chances it afforded him to mete out punishment. He was renowned among his teammates as a ferocious hitter even in practice, and he had always been one of the more boisterous and vocal players on the roster. As Rowe and his teammates were filing out the doors of the gymnasium and onto the bus, he was thinking of ways to get everybody fired up, to release some of their built-up tension and have a little fun.

It wasn't a long drive up to Michie Stadium, just a slow and winding one. There was less than half a mile between the stadium and gymnasium, but much of it was straight uphill, and the bus had to make a steep climb past the Cadet Chapel and Lusk Reservoir, and past the thousands of game-day revelers who descended on West Point on football Saturdays. Blaik always sat in the front seat of the bus, and Rowe was just a few rows behind as the driver pulled out on to Mills Road to begin climbing the hill to Michie Stadium. Rowe looked out the window to his right, where the Hudson River was passing by underneath. The bus was quiet, and the mood was tense. Looking to his left, he caught the attention of several of his fellow first classmen, including reserve tight end Jack Morrison and fullback Harry Walters, and with a smile he called out in the manner of a revivalist preacher, "I see the river!"

His classmates answered, "I see the river!"

"I see the river!" Rowe yelled again, louder this time. The rest of the team, in on the joke by now, responded in unison. Then a voice called out, "What else do you see, Bill?"

"I see the chapel!"

"I see the chapel!"

"I see the stadium!"

"I see the stadium!"

"I see victory!"

"I see victory!"

By the time the bus stopped at Michie Stadium at thirty minutes after one, it was bedlam, with players hooting and hollering, and with Blaik sitting in the front seat smiling. The doors opened, and he led his players off the bus and into the locker room, where they paused only briefly before heading out onto the field to warm up. Kickoff was at two o'clock.

Joe Cahill, Army football's director of publicity, had wanted to send out invitations to the media for the unveiling of Blaik's far flanker against South Carolina. But the coach demurred. "Better not," he said. "Maybe the stuff won't work."

He needn't have worried. The Gamecocks were wholly unable to cope with any facet of the new offense. Army got off to a fast, if sloppy, start, though not before the referees made an adjustment of their own to Blaik's formation. As they explained to the coach before permitting his team to run its first play, rules required that Carpenter had to stand within the hash marks while his teammates huddled, after which time he was free to split as wide as he wanted.* With that detail out of the way, the Cadets took the opening kickoff and in just six plays drove sixty-one yards to the Gamecocks' 1-yard line, a march highlighted by a pair of gashing runs from Dawkins. On the first, running from the straight T in the Bataan formation, he took a handoff from Caldwell and angled left behind Bob Anderson and Harry Walters, who overwhelmed Carolina linebacker Lawton Rogers as Dawkins broke into the secondary. On the second, he took a pitch from Caldwell on a sweep around the left side. He had the option to throw the ball to Anderson, who had lined up as the wingback and was running a short out route toward the sideline, but there wasn't a defender within ten yards and he took off for the flag at the front corner of the end zone. Cornerback John Saunders saved a touchdown by pushing Dawkins out of bounds at the 1. The drive came up empty on the next play, however, when Caldwell's handoff to Walters hit the fullback on his right hip. The ball tumbled to the ground, and South Carolina recovered the fumble.

Caldwell was the only Army starter who did not look sharp to begin the game. He badly overthrew Anderson on his first pass, as the halfback was streaking all alone down the left sideline. He completed a screen to Carpenter on the next play, but his throw was above and behind his receiver. Caldwell's throws were consistently high throughout the first quarter, the classic sign of an overexcited quarterback—though his wildness did save him from a bad interception when Hawkins jumped in front of Carpenter on another screen but was unable to pull the ball down. The Cadets came up empty on their next three possessions, two of which ended when

---

* The rule, which applied to every player on the field, existed to prevent "hideout" plays, in which receivers would hide on the sidelines and step onto the field just before the snap of the ball. All players were required to return to the area between the hash marks after each down and before the next snap.

Caldwell threw too high or too long to Carpenter. This despite an opportunistic Army defense that blocked a punt and grabbed an interception to give the offense excellent starting field position for each drive.

It wasn't until the final minutes of the first quarter that Army finally put points on the board. Gamecocks halfback Buddy Bennett fumbled a direct snap and Bob Oswandel, the Cadets' backup nose tackle, fell on the ball at the South Carolina 12-yard-line. On first down, Caldwell pitched to Anderson on a sweep around the right side. But instead of trying to turn the corner, he pulled up and threw to Dawkins, who was dragged down at the 8-yard line. Dawkins ran for four yards on the next play, and then ran for four more to score the first touchdown of the game. With fifty-three seconds left in the opening quarter, Army finally led, 7–0.

The Gamecocks had planned to focus on stopping Anderson, but they had become so concerned with the passes to Carpenter that their defensive-line play utterly collapsed. Again and again, Dawkins was able to rip inside for long gains. Even more damaging was Carolina's inability to deal with the Cadets' halfback option play, which had so far worked best on pitches to Anderson, who would sweep to the right when Carpenter was split wide to that side. Dawkins, from his position as the wingback, would run a seven-yard out route, filling the space behind Carpenter, whose job was to take his defender deep down the field and out of the play. If the defensive back or linebacker in the flat covered Dawkins, Anderson had room to run. If the defender in the flat came forward to challenge the run, Anderson would simply lob the ball to Dawkins.

During an early second-quarter timeout, Army manager John Bryer was walking off the field with his arms full of water bottles when he noticed a set of Polaroid instant pictures on the ground at the feet of the Gamecocks' players, who were absorbed in a heated discussion. They had become so caught up in the mystery of how Carpenter knew what plays were being called that they had not realized that the Cadets were running their offense from an unbalanced line until their coaches in the press box had sent down pictures to show them what was going on. "We had been schooled and schooled and schooled to

HALFBACK OPTION (From Bazooka)

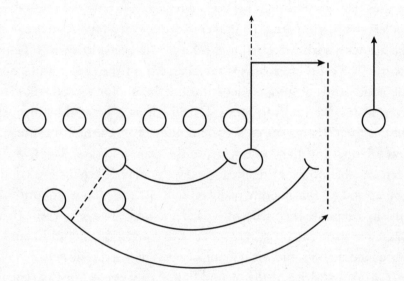

play a zone defense, and we knew exactly who we were supposed to key off of and so forth," says King Dixon, "but when they flanked out that lonesome end and he never went into the huddle, it really blew our minds. We were very structured in our defensive assignments out there and our coaching staff in those days did not do very much to give us leeway on the field. We just got frustrated."

Army drove seventy-six yards for a touchdown on its next possession, which ended with Harry Walters plunging over from a yard out to make the score 13–0. Blaik put in his reserves for the last series of the first half and watched them march sixty-three yards to another touchdown, this one scored by Steve Waldrop, the backup to Dawkins at right halfback. The Cadets led 19–0 and settled down to a quiet halftime, sucking on orange slices and quietly going over the first-half action with their coaches.

In the steamy South Carolina dressing room, players sat dazed and dripping at their lockers, silently changing into dry jerseys while

Giese huddled with his assistants; he had called them in with a few minutes left in the half in order to have extra time to come up with a counter to the wide-open Army offense. Giese implored the Game-cocks to stick together, promising that he and the coaching staff would devise a way to stop Army's far flanker. But King Dixon wasn't so sure. He was feeling a bit shell-shocked, not only because of the Cadets' whirlwind attack but also because every time Army scored, the academy's spirit squad fired off a howitzer loaded with a blank round. The echo of each shot reverberated off the valley walls, and the acrid stink of gunpowder hung in the air for several minutes. Even inside the dressing room, Dixon felt as if he could still smell the gunfire. "There were only two minutes left in the halftime break," says Dixon, "and the coach turns to the team and says, 'Guys, we've been together now for three years and we've never given up. Let's don't give up today.' But nobody really rallied." As the players stood to file out the door, another assistant coach shouted, "We've got 'em right where we want 'em, boys!" He spoke with conviction and spirit, but he persuaded no one, and his rallying cry met with grim silence.

On its first drive of the second half, Army needed just two plays to go fifty-six yards for another score—a halfback pass from Ander-son to Dawkins that covered thirty yards to the South Carolina 26, and a run up the middle out of a straight T formation, with Dawkins taking the handoff and angling left through a hole between Bob Novogratz, the weak-side guard, and end Don Usry. Dawkins broke untouched through the line, bounced the run to his right, against the flow of the play, and, running with a short, choppy stride, out-raced the Gamecocks' secondary to the corner of the end zone. After a missed extra point, the Cadets led 25–0.

King Dixon took the ensuing kickoff on the run at the South Carolina 9 and headed upfield, angling to his right toward the side-line. He slipped a flying tackle attempt by Walters at the 20 with a nifty twist and eluded a diving Usry at the 24 before pivoting back to his left, where he was hit low by Al Vanderbush, a sophomore guard who had broken into the starting lineup over first classman Charlie Lytle in the last week of practice. At the 23, Dixon went down under a swarm that included Bill Rowe, who hit Dixon hard and jarred the ball loose. Walters came up with the fumble recovery after a brief scramble. Army went right back to the halfback option on first down, with Anderson—who could have easily run for the touchdown—passing to a wide-open Dawkins for the Cadets' fifth touchdown of the afternoon, and the second in their last three plays. Tackle Monk Hilliard, pulling double duty as the placekicker, missed the conversion—his second miss out of three attempts—and Army led 31–0.

On the sideline after that touchdown, Blaik grabbed Anderson by the sleeve of his jersey and pulled the halfback close. Ever the conservative, he wanted Anderson to know that the first option on his team was *always* to run the ball. The coach admired Anderson's selfless attitude, but he also felt that the boy was, at times, "inclined to overdo it." Now Blaik looked him in the eye and said, "What's the matter, Anderson? Don't you want to be a hero anymore?"

On South Carolina's next possession, Dawkins leapt in front of a pass from Hawkins to Dixon and returned it thirty-three yards to the Cadets' 48. They needed seven plays to score from there, Army's third touchdown in the opening six minutes of the second half. Anderson, who completed five of six passes in the game, found Usry in the back of the end zone for a three-yard scoring strike.* Hilliard's kick was good this time.

Blaik, with his team leading 38–0, went to his bench as the third quarter came to an end. This time, his second-stringers let him down. The Gamecocks gained 50 of their 132 yards in the game on their next drive, which ended when quarterback Bobby Bunch snuck over the goal line for a touchdown from one yard out. Alex Hawkins then ran over from the 3 for the two-point conversion, cutting Army's lead to 38–8.† A chagrined Blaik sent his first team back in, and the Black Knights went seventy-two yards in eight plays for their final touchdown, the score coming on a ten-yard screen pass

---

* The box score for the game mistakenly credits Anderson with completing all five of his passes. For whatever reason, it failed to count an incomplete pass in the first quarter, when officials refused to call interference when Dawkins was hit from behind before the ball arrived.

† The 1958 season marked the debut of the two-point conversion in college football.

from Caldwell to Dawkins with just over three minutes left to play. It was the halfback's fourth touchdown of the afternoon and made the score 45–8.

Late in the third quarter, Blaik had inserted third-string end Russ Waters into the game for the first time, substituting him for Otto Everbach, the backup to Carpenter at far flanker. Despite the miserable conditions, Carpenter had caught four passes for ninety yards— including a thirty-one-yarder in the fourth quarter on a tipped pass that he gathered into his chest at the same time he was falling onto his back. Everbach played well in relief, but he had so far failed to distinguish himself. Waters, who had been bumped up from the B Squad to the varsity just a few weeks before the game, promptly made a notable defensive play, shedding two blocks to drop a sweeping Carolina halfback for a five-yard loss. Now, in the closing minutes of the fourth, he made a play that had Gottfried swelling with pride on the sideline. As Gamecocks quarterback Steve Satterfield dropped back to pass, Waters, as Gottfried had taught him, retreated into pass coverage. Army nose tackle Bob Oswandel hit Satterfield's arm as the quarterback released the ball, and Waters settled under the resulting floater for the Cadets' fourth and last interception of the day. Better still, and to the delight of Blaik, he returned it thirty-five yards. After the game, the coaches moved Waters ahead of Everbach as the primary backup at far flanker.

The Cadets' 45–8 victory could hardly have been more complete. They ran a whopping eighty plays for 529 yards. Dawkins, who ran nine times for 113 yards and caught four passes for 53 more, outgained the entire South Carolina offense by over 30 yards. Two of Anderson's five completions went for touchdowns. The Army defense had forced six turnovers, and the first-teamers had held the Gamecocks to less than 80 yards of total offense, never once letting them across midfield. The Cadets' dizzying opening-day victory was the biggest surprise of the new season—a surprise magnified by the mysterious and spectacular appearance of Red Blaik's far flanker. The Army coach was not renowned as an innovator, yet he had unveiled a highly prolific attack that was unique in college football. The Cadets weren't the only top-ten team to score a big victory that weekend.

Second-ranked Oklahoma had unveiled a flanker-spread scheme of its own in a 47–14 thumping of thirteenth-ranked West Virginia, but the Sooners' wide receivers had not been stationed nearly as wide as Carpenter, nor had they stayed at a complete remove from the huddle. Oklahoma had jumped to number one with its victory, but it was Army who caught the country's attention. Overnight, the Cadets became the sensation of college football.

Only 16,250 hardy souls had braved the rain to witness the debut of Blaik's far flanker. But the wretched weather and poor attendance did not dampen the enthusiasm of the members of the press who had been on hand that day at Michie Stadium. Writing in *The New York Times*, Allison Danzig compared Army to Blaik's great teams of the previous decade and described the far flanker thusly: "Operating from an unbalanced line in the wing T and straight T, with an end stationed 15 yards out as a flanker—the most revolutionary change Blaik has made in his attack since he installed the tight T in 1943—the Cadets went berserk from the opening kick-off." Stanley Woodward's "lonely end" moniker was splashed on front pages around the country, forever more to be honored with capital letters—the *Lonely End*. In a *Herald Tribune* column under the headline "Great Deceptions," Blaik's friend Red Smith played up the mystery of the scheme:

> He is a leper who plays off by himself, fifteen yards to right or left of center. If he approaches the huddle between scrimmages his schoolmates cry, "Unclean! Unclean!" and he retreats, getting the signals . . . by extra-sensory perception. Our war machine broke both the Japanese and German codes in World War II but this wasn't revealed until hostilities ended; Army's method of communication with the lonely end is, similarly, a military secret.

Speculating about what Army's upcoming opponents might think when they studied film of the South Carolina game, Smith wrote, "When they see a team coached by Red Blaik, the high priest of the overland game, throwing twenty-eight passes through the rain with a slippery ball, they simply won't believe it."

On Monday, Blaik dispatched B Squad coach Barney Gill to the weekly meeting at Toots Shor's with members of the New York sporting press. An easygoing good-timer, Gill was popular with Blaik's players—in large part because he cheerfully made his room at the BOQ available to those who were hosting dates for the weekend. Addressing the crowded room from a podium, Gill drew up Blaik's formation on a chalkboard and cheerfully refused all entreaties to divulge how Carpenter received the offensive signals.

Back at West Point, Blaik was still fretting over the quarterback position. He was not satisfied with Bob Rudesill as the primary backup to Caldwell, and he turned his attention to a young third classman named Tom Blanda. "We have been forced to go along with Rudesill, but he is no passer," Blaik wrote to MacArthur on September 29. "After the game I told the coaches regardless of his lack of background we must make every effort to bring Blanda along as the offensive substitute to Caldwell. He is tall and strong, a baseball pitcher, and like Caldwell is not fast." The son of a Slovak-born Pittsburgh coal miner, Blanda was a wiry eighteen-year-old—the younger brother of George Blanda, the kicker and backup quarterback for the Chicago Bears. The Army media guide, printed in advance of the season, noted that Blanda did "not figure prominently as a signal caller this fall," and Blaik doubted that the boy, who had played for a bad team at tiny Hempfield Area High School in Youngwood, Pennsylvania, was ready for big-time college football. But the coach liked Blanda's poise and felt that, outside of Caldwell, he was the best passer on the team. With the Cadets more dependent than ever on their passing game, there was little choice but to start getting Blanda ready to play.

On Saturday, October 4, a capacity crowd of more than twenty-seven thousand, and a full press box, were on hand to watch Army relaunch its "Space Man," as *The New York Times* had dubbed Carpenter. Penn State was not as highly regarded as South Carolina. The Nittany Lions had blown a 7–0 fourth-quarter lead in a loss at Nebraska in their opener but come back the next week to smash in-state rival Penn 43–0. They were not going to be surprised by the Lonely End, but coach Rip Engle refused to promise that they would be able to stop it. "We think we have the defensive theory necessary to stop Army's offensive," he told reporters a few days before the game, "but I'm not sure we have the speed." When asked if his scouting staff had given him any recommendations for how to handle the attack, Engle had deadpanned, "Yes, they've helped a lot. They've advised us to stay home." Nevertheless, upwards of four thousand fans accompanied Penn State on the more than four-hour road trip from State College to West Point. A large portion of the Nittany Lions' out-of-town rooters were female students—there were so many that Jim Tarman, the Penn State sports publicity director, told *The New York Times*, "An unusually large number of unescorted coeds will be going to the game. Many of them, I think, are more interested in meeting a future general than in watching the game."

It's almost certain that the ladies enjoyed that night's dance (or "hop" in academy parlance) more than that afternoon's contest. As the *Times*'s Allison Danzig described the game, "No West Point football team, not even the renowned Blanchard-Davis championship elevens of the Nineteen Forty's [*sic*], has put on a more terrifying display of offensive striking power than did the Cadets from their new 'lonely end,' unbalanced line wing-T formation for the first thirty minutes." Army took the opening kickoff and drove sixty-four yards in eight plays for its first touchdown, which came on a six-yard run by Dawkins one play after he'd hauled in a nineteen-yard pass from Anderson. The Cadets' second drive began at the Nittany Lions' 47 when nose tackle Bill Rowe hit fullback Andy Moconyi and forced a fumble that Rowe himself recovered. It took just four plays for Army to score from there, with Anderson running for his first touchdown of the season from a yard out. The quick drive included a pass from Caldwell to Carpenter for thirty-three yards that saw the end leap high to steal the ball from the hands of Penn State defensive back Fran Paolone. There was a brief cessation of the onslaught while Blaik rested his regulars before sending them back into the game late in the first quarter.

Army needed just two plays to score again. On the first play of the second quarter, Dawkins carried over the left side behind a terrific lead block from Anderson—who took out three Penn State defenders—for eleven yards to the Army 45-yard line. Caldwell then took a shot downfield. Faking a handoff first to Walters and then to Anderson, he dropped back three steps and looked to his right, where Carpenter was streaking all alone along the sideline. With three pass rushers bearing down, Caldwell uncorked a beautiful arcing pass that Carpenter caught in stride at the Nittany Lions' 23, and the end galloped across the goal line untouched.

Caldwell was like a new man. Blaik had suspected his quarterback's confidence would benefit from the victory over South Carolina and all the hoopla that came with it. "[He] hardly fits the description of Danzig," he wrote to MacArthur, "but he did come out of the Syracuse haze and I'm certain some acclaim will do much to give him assurance." Caldwell only threw three passes in the first half, but he connected on all of them, each more spectacular than the one before. The last came late in the second quarter, when he took a five-step drop from the Cadets' 28-yard line, patted the ball once, and loosed a bullet to Dawkins, who was running a crossing route over the middle from right to left. The halfback caught the ball at the Army 47 and, twisting back to his left, wrenched free from two defenders. Running with his by now familiar choppy stride, he easily outraced defensive back Don Jonas to the goal line. His six points increased Army's lead to 26–0, which is where it stayed after Monk Hilliard missed the extra point.

Penn State center Steve Garban had been thrilled to get the chance to play in Michie Stadium. Like most of the Army players—like most American boys—he used to lie on the floor of his living room and listen to the radio call of the Army–Notre Dame contests of the 1940s. In the locker room, with his head hanging from equal parts shame and exhaustion, he waited to hear Engle tear into the team for its poor play. Instead the coach began by saying, "Guys, you just haven't been playing football." The problem, he explained, was not in the defensive scheme but in the defensive execution. Preparing to play Army in 1958 was in many ways similar to preparing to play Army in 2012. Today, in the age of the wide-open spread passing game, the offensive attack at West Point is a ground-based option scheme. The Cadets' opponents have, in most cases, only a week to prepare for an offense that will be like no other they will see for the rest of the season. Forty-two years ago, when three-yards-and-a-cloud-of-dust was the dominant offensive theory in college football, the Black Knights of the Hudson were throwing more passes than just about every other team in the land.

With Engle's words ringing in their ears, the Nittany Lions buckled down in the second half. "I think we came out and just played a little tougher," says Garban. The Cadets, after putting on the most awesome aerial display in team history over the first thirty minutes of the game, failed to complete any of their eight passes in the third and fourth quarters. They did not score a point. They lost three fumbles and committed a surfeit of penalties. Dawkins, who was not nearly as good at throwing the halfback option pass as Anderson, tossed an interception. The game ended in a 26–0 Army victory, but the Cadets had been far from perfect.

Blaik felt that the second-half letdown was a good dose of humility for his boys. "After all," he wrote to MacArthur on October 6, in his customary Monday morning report, "it showed that this is a strictly ordinary team which is capable of playing both good and bad. It seems odd that everyone should be going overboard on the Army team, especially in view of the fact that this is probably the most inexperienced group of varsity players representing a major team ranked in the first twenty-five." Better that the Cadets should peak one week later, he believed, when Army traveled to South Bend, Indiana, to take on Notre Dame.

Chapter 6

JUGGERNAUT

AFTER EVERY ARMY HOME GAME, Blaik and his wife, Merle, hosted a party at their quarters, which were nestled in a densely wooded housing area across Lusk Reservoir from Michie Stadium. The guest list typically included most of the Bull Pond campers, along with their wives, as well as whichever friends or former colleagues of Blaik's happened to be visiting West Point for the weekend. Among the revelers who mingled at the jovial gathering following the win over Penn State was Joseph Byrne Jr., a successful New York businessman and second-generation Notre Dame graduate who billed himself as the eastern representative of Fighting Irish football. It was Byrne, perhaps more than any other man, who had built the Army–Notre Dame rivalry into the greatest in college football. He was one of the founders of the Notre Dame Club of New York in 1915, the university's most influential alumni organization, and with his connections both on Wall Street and in Tammany Hall, he had arranged for the special trains from Grand Central Station to West Point every fall for the Irish's annual game against Army. In 1923, Byrne negotiated the game's change of venue to Ebbets Field, an agreement sealed when he signed the contract on behalf of his alma mater. He also sold and distributed tickets for the games every year, even after the venue was famously moved to the Polo Grounds in 1924, which increased the seating capacity to sixty-five thousand.

Whenever the Fighting Irish visited New York, Byrne provided players and coaches with theater tickets and restaurant reservations. He became such a confidant of the football program that in 1928 he had been on hand in Notre Dame's locker room at Yankee Stadium to witness Rockne's legendary "Win one for the Gipper" speech that spurred the underdog Fighting Irish to a 12–6 victory over undefeated Army.

Blaik and Byrne had known each other for a long time, and if Blaik's rivalry with Notre Dame had often been a bitter disappointment—he had beaten the Fighting Irish only four times in thirteen tries as both a head and assistant coach at Army—the two men had nevertheless remained on friendly terms. So it was with a smile that Blaik allowed Byrne to lead him by the lapels of his brown tweed jacket down to his basement laundry room. For the better part of the next hour, he and Byrne discussed the upcoming date in South Bend. Byrne warned him that Notre Dame was itching to play Army. The Lonely End was no longer a secret, and Byrne predicted that the Fighting Irish would win convincingly, going so far as to forecast a final score of 21–0.

If Byrne was trying to make Blaik nervous, he needn't have bothered. The Cadets' coach already knew more than enough to be anxious. The Notre Dame lineup, after all, consisted of many of the same players who had beaten his boys 23–21 in Philadelphia one year earlier.* The Fighting Irish were significantly bigger than Army along the line—center Robert Scholz outweighed Bill Rowe by a full fifteen pounds—and in the backfield, bruising 215-pound fullback Nick Pietrosante had five pounds or more on every one of Blaik's players save for tackle Ed Bagdonas, who weighed in at 220. Blaik wrote to MacArthur that Notre Dame was "a far better team than the one we met the year before." He and his coaches felt that, for the most part, the Black Knights' superior speed canceled out any size advantage for their opponent, but what they were unsure of

---

* The winning points had come on a late field goal by junior end Monty Stickles, who had been denied admission to West Point in 1955 because of poor eyesight. It was one of only two field goals he would kick in his Notre Dame career.

was how long the first-teamers would be able to endure the physical punishment that the Fighting Irish seemed sure to inflict.

Blaik confided to MacArthur that he had been troubled during the win over Penn State by the way his starters seemed to tire anytime they had been left in the game for more than seven minutes. Intuitively, it didn't make sense—the physically active lifestyle of the Corps of Cadets usually saw to it that Blaik's teams were in outstanding condition, and he and his coaches did what they could to sharpen their players' fitness each day at practice. Blaik's training sessions almost always included full-contact drills. In an effort to reduce the chance of early season injuries, he had eased back on the intensity of practices before both the South Carolina and Penn State games. But on the Tuesday and Wednesday before Army left for South Bend, Blaik drove his team hard. He wanted his players battle-ready.

Based on painful experience, he did not intend to use his reserves much against the Fighting Irish. Blaik had tried to rest his starters early in the 1957 game, inserting his second string late in the first quarter with Army leading 7–0. But the unit had promptly surrendered an eighty-yard touchdown march. With Army up 21–7 in the third quarter, Blaik had again tried to rest his starters, only to see the second-team defense let Pietrosante loose up the middle for a sixty-five-yard touchdown run on the first play from scrimmage. This time, it was going to be up to the first team to avenge that bitter defeat.

For all the fuss over the Lonely End, the Cadets had actually been using an unbalanced line since that 1957 game against Notre Dame. The formation's sole purpose then had been to maximize the effectiveness of halfback Bob Anderson, whom Blaik had praised as Army's "best sophomore since Glenn Davis." A gifted athlete, Anderson stood a strapping six-two, but he was surprisingly nimble for a big man. Army's coaches loved the way he patiently waited for holes to open in the line before slashing into the secondary. And once he was in the open field he ran with a long, graceful stride that helped him

pull away from outclassed defensive backs. Anderson was also strik-
ingly good looking. In an article for *Sport* magazine in November
1958, the cartoonist and writer Murray Olderman positively gushed
over him: "He is full-lipped, dark-eyed and huskily handsome. A
bashful smile plays around his lips, and his young, smooth forehead
wrinkles when he concentrates."

Anderson's grandfather had come to America from Czechoslo-
vakia, where the family name had been Andruczy. Bob's father, John,
a printing press operator in Linden, New Jersey, had moved the family south in 1948 to Cocoa, Florida, after Bob was diagnosed with
rheumatic fever, a condition that caused him so much pain he
would awake each morning unable to walk. In Cocoa, John purchased a Dixie Cream Donut shop on U.S. Route 1, and he would
rise early every morning to make all of his donuts by hand—rolling
out the dough, shaping the donuts and flipping them one by one
onto his thumb before laying them out on a tray to go into the oven.
At home, Bob's mother, Mary, ran a tight ship, and it was a family
rule that everyone had to be home at six every evening. That was
when his father returned from work, and Mary made clear that anyone who wasn't home by six would not eat. "She would never let me
get a big head," Anderson says. "Never."

Aided by Cocoa's warmer climate, Anderson had recovered from
his rheumatism within a year and soon began pursuing athletics. He
earned fifteen letters in four sports at Cocoa High and was a prep
All-America in football. He received a raft of scholarship offers and
verbally committed as a junior to Georgia Tech, where his brother,
John Jr., who was older by five years, was a senior. Bob used to visit
John every weekend in the fall in order to attend the Yellow Jackets'
football games. In the summer, Anderson worked odd jobs in construction and earned extra money in the afternoons by umpiring
Little League games at a park three blocks from his home. It was
after one of these games, when he was hustling to be home by six,
that the father of one of his schoolmates stopped him and asked if
he had ever considered attending West Point. "He said, 'I have a
friend who's a lawyer down in West Palm Beach and his brother is
a recruiter at West Point, and they called and West Point is interested

in you,'" says Anderson. "Then he said, 'Don't give me an answer. Go home and talk it over with your folks and think about it.'"

Anderson knew that his brother's tuition at Georgia Tech had cost his parents nearly two thousand dollars a year, and John Jr. had still been forced to work in order to have enough money to get by. West Point, of course, was free, and the more Bob thought about it, the more he liked it. The academy had a tough reputation, and he had been less than impressed with the way that civilian colleges tended to coddle their football players. Anderson came from a family in which hard work was the ultimate virtue. If he was going to be a college football player, he decided, he would rather do it the hard way. "Neither of my parents graduated high school," he says. "I don't know what would have happened at Georgia Tech, but I knew enough about West Point to know they were going to pay me to go and it wouldn't cost my parents anything."

Around his Army teammates, Anderson was hardly bashful, but he did, in the words of Blaik, "have a tendency to play himself down" to both his coaches and the press. Knowing that the boy was his own harshest critic, Blaik would motivate him not by shouting or criticizing, as he would to make Harry Walters angry, but by pulling Anderson aside and telling him how much the team needed him, or how well he was doing. On the morning of the 1957 season opener at Michie Stadium against Nebraska, Blaik had asked Anderson to stay behind after he'd delivered his pregame remarks to the team at Trophy Point. It was a sunny, crisp fall day, and as Anderson's teammates headed for the mess hall, Blaik, in his brown tweeds and fedora, stood silently with his hands behind his back, looking north up the Hudson River. Anderson stood behind him at attention. But after waiting for what seemed an eternity, he relaxed and began to shuffle his feet impatiently. His teammates were by now sitting down to lunch. Finally, Blaik turned, put his left hand on Anderson's right shoulder, and looked him in the eye. "Son," said Blaik, "I want you to know that you're starting at halfback for me this afternoon because you're the best I have at that position. I want you to hold your head up high, and lift your knees up high, and run like a stallion."

Anderson barked back, "Yes, sir!" Blaik nodded, patted him on the shoulder, and dismissed him. "I could have run through a wall," says Anderson. "I could have run through the whole stadium, he had me so charged up." Brimming with fire, the halfback tore through the Cornhuskers in his collegiate debut, running for eighty-three yards and a touchdown on thirteen carries in a 42–0 rout.

Two weeks later, on the eve of the 23–21 loss to Notre Dame in Philadelphia, Blaik tweaked Anderson again. Addressing the team, he announced his plan to open the game. On the first play, he said, Dawkins would run off tackle. On the second, Anderson would sweep around left end, a play called Bazooka Eighty-one. "Then," Blaik said, "we're going to kick the extra point."

And that was exactly how it happened. From the Army 19-yard line, Anderson took the pitch, cut inside a block from fullback Vin Barta that took out two Fighting Irish defenders, and dashed into the open field. As he sprinted toward the end zone, he could hear nothing but the sound of his feet hitting the turf and his breath coming in quick, rhythmic pants. "All week long our coaches had told us that their slowest guy was faster than our fastest guy," says Anderson. "I was waiting for somebody to jump on my back. I was struggling hard, I was going to carry somebody with me if I had to. It was a weird sensation. And when I crossed the goal line it was like somebody took a radio and turned it all the way up. One hundred thousand people. Oh my goodness. But how did Blaik know? I still have no idea."

The rivalry between the Black Knights and the Fighting Irish had for many years been the most important, and the most rancorous, in college football. Army's yearly meetings with Navy had seen their share of bad blood—the Midshipmen had refused to play the Cadets in 1928 and again in 1929 in protest of Army's reliance on open recruiting—but the series, especially after the shared hardships of the Second World War, was much more about fellowship and bragging rights than it was about bitter vengeance. Not so for Army–Notre Dame. The feud had begun in 1913 as an eastern stage upon which a small Indiana Catholic college had hoped to earn national recognition, but it had grown bitterly out of control by the time both schools put an end to it after the 1947 season.

It was the opinion of Red Blaik that the rivalry had enriched the Fighting Irish program far more than it ever had his own. Notre Dame had become a national sensation by upsetting the powerful Cadets 35–13 in that first game and had proceeded to build its reputation as a titan with a string of wins over powerful Army teams.* Indeed, the Fighting Irish had made beating the Cadets an almost annual rite—Army won only five times in the series through 1943. But in spite of Notre Dame's lopsided advantage, both teams usually entered the contest ranked among the country's very best, and there were few more highly anticipated dates on the college football calendar. The demand for tickets was so great that the game had been played in major-league stadiums in New York City since 1923.†

But the 1946 game, which was played on November 9 at Yankee Stadium, was something different. Blaik's national championship squads of 1944 and '45 had swamped the Fighting Irish by a combined score of 107–0, the Cadets' first victories in the series in thirteen years, and Army came into the game ranked number one in the country and riding a twenty-five-game winning streak. The Cadets' roster still included several of the stars from the '44 and '45 teams, including running backs Doc Blanchard, the reigning Heisman Trophy winner, and Glenn Davis (who would win Army's second straight Heisman later that year). Second-ranked Notre Dame, on

---

* Notre Dame's 1913 victory over Army is widely considered to be the moment when the forward pass—which had been legalized in 1906 but was not widely used—revolutionized college football. Using the tactic, the Fighting Irish and end Knute Rockne showed how a smaller team could beat a bigger one, and throwing the football soon came into vogue.

† The only game not played at either Ebbets Field, the Polo Grounds, or Yankee Stadium (the usual venue) was held at Chicago's Soldier Field on November 29, 1930. Pregame expectations were that the game would smash the stadium's—and college football's—attendance record of more than 123,000, but miserable rainy conditions kept the crowd to around 100,000. The dreary contest ended after three hours in a 7–6 Notre Dame victory, and the day was further marred by a stampede for the exits that resulted in numerous injuries.

the other hand, had bolstered its lineup with a raft of ex-servicemen from prewar Fighting Irish squads. The matchup of the country's top two teams, coupled with Notre Dame's desire to avenge their lop-sided wartime losses—suffered when many of their best players had been fighting in Europe or the Pacific—built anticipation for the game to an unprecedented pitch. The Army–Notre Dame rivalry had been a marquee event for years, a sporting phenomenon comparable to the World Series or a heavyweight championship bout. Now it was something beyond even that. So the mythmakers of the press dubbed the contest the Game of the Century, the first time that de-scription had ever been used.

The schools handled ticket sales themselves, either directly or through connected supporters like Joe Byrne, with each getting an allotment of thirty-nine thousand seats. Face value for the tickets ranged from one dollar for general admission to four dollars and eighty cents for seats on the 50-yard line. Though the game sold out almost immediately after tickets went on sale August 1, thousands of people continued to send money directly to both schools, which resulted in more than a million dollars in refunds—and almost as many disgruntled fans. A bustling black market soon sprang up and quickly grew beyond the control of either school. Both institutions felt that they had been prudent in how they distributed their allot-ment of tickets—Notre Dame limited even its most prominent alumni to four seats apiece, while Army restricted sales to those who had graduated from the academy before 1932—but a *New York Times* report noted that officials at South Bend and West Point were "considerably upset over the fact that speculators had got hold of tickets in large numbers." Scalpers were openly charging up to two hundred dollars a seat, which infuriated people who had been shut out at the box office in favor of well-connected alumni. Both schools liked to hold the game up as emblematic of the college football ideal, a meeting between two of the country's most esteemed programs. Instead, they had been embarrassed by the naked greed of their own alumni.

For Notre Dame's legion of New York–based fans, also known as the subway alumni, this was a chance for retribution. In the year leading up to the game, Blaik received at least one postcard a day from South Bend. One of them, from an organization calling itself the Society for the Prevention of Army's Third National Championship, read:

> *Dear Coach Blaik:*
>   *This is to remind you that the day of retribution is fast approaching. Might I advise that you make the most of the short time that remains, for as the poem has it, "Gather ye rosebuds while ye may." I trust that you have not severed all affiliations with Dartmouth College—any port in a storm, you know.*
>   *There are but 205 days left until Nov. 9 . . .*
>   *SPATNC (ND Chapter)*

All the vitriol led to some ugly incidents on game day. Some in the crowd of seventy-four thousand taunted Blanchard, Davis, and the other Army players with shouts of "Slacker!" and "Draft dodger"— the same jeer that the Corps of Cadets had heard a few hours before, during its march into Yankee Stadium. The cadets had also been set upon outside the stadium by scalpers offering to buy their tickets. When the men in gray refused, the scalpers heaped further abuse on them.

The game itself was memorable primarily for the hype that had preceded it. Concerned more about mistakes and field position than with scoring touchdowns, Blaik and Frank Leahy, his Notre Dame counterpart, both chose to play it safe. The result was a desultory defensive struggle and a monumental anticlimax. The Fighting Irish crossed midfield just three times, Army nine. Neither team scored, and the game ended in a disappointing 0–0 tie. The sportswriters who had so relentlessly built the game up tried to make the outcome palatable by praising the players for their terrific blocking and tackling, but few among the thousands on hand that day—or the twenty-five million more listening on radio—had come for that.

Officials from both schools regarded the 1946 game as a tawdry fiasco. Besides the ticket-selling mess, wagering on the game had also gotten out of hand. Bookies had offered half a point on either team, and their take was estimated at an astonishing eight to ten million dollars. On December 31, academy superintendent General Maxwell Taylor and new Notre Dame president Father John J. Cavanaugh put out a joint statement: The series between the Cadets and the Fighting Irish would end after the 1947 game. "Two reasons led to the decision," read the statement. "The first was the conviction of the authorities of both schools that the Army–Notre Dame game had grown to such proportions that it had come to be played under conditions escaping the control of the two colleges, some of which were not conducive to wholesome intercollegiate sport." Blaik felt that the rivalry was an important one for college football but chose not to protest. "The game," he said, "was generating a form of psychological hate detrimental to the best interests of the United States Army . . . A long cooling-off period was not only advisable, it was inescapably urgent."

The 1958 Army–Notre Dame game was the last in a two-year agreement between the schools. Officials in South Bend were eager to continue the series into the next decade and lobbied the West Point administration for more games in the future. But nobody at the academy was eager to restart the rivalry. That March, Blaik had written a letter to Davidson informing him that the athletic board had voted four to one against a renewal of the series after the 1958 game. "Other than an unusually large financial return," wrote Blaik, "there is little reason to play Notre Dame. It is again obvious that the pressure of this game on the Corps of Cadets is disproportionate to any possible benefit the service may receive from playing Notre Dame." That sentiment hit home with Davidson, who was already concerned about the amount of emphasis the academy placed on football. In his reply to the athletic board, he stated that, in order to keep football in its proper place in the lives of cadets, no more than three "pressure games" per season should be scheduled. With the annual date against Navy and the upcoming appointment in 1959 with new rival Air Force—as well as the academy's desire for West Point to be seen as a national institution—this left room, said Davidson, for only one more such game, which "we are to rotate around the country." Going forward, the academy intended to schedule games against

Notre Dame only periodically. Beyond 1958, nobody knew when, or if, the Cadets and the Fighting Irish would play again.

One of Notre Dame's heroes from that 1946 game had been sophomore halfback Terry Brennan. In addition to making several long runs, he had also intercepted an Army pass at the Fighting Irish goal line after the Cadets had advanced to the Notre Dame fourteen. In a 27–7 victory over Army the next year, Brennan had twice run back kickoffs for touchdowns. Affable and handsome, he remained popular in South Bend after he graduated in 1949, and when head coach Frank Leahy resigned in 1954, Notre Dame promoted the twenty-five-year-old Brennan from his job as the freshman coach. Even in 1958, at the age of thirty and already in his fifth season on the sideline, he was still the youngest varsity football coach in school history.

Brennan had gotten off to a fast start in South Bend, going 17–3 in his first two seasons with many of Leahy's players on his roster. But in 1956, the Fighting Irish stumbled to a 2–8 record that included defeats against rivals Navy and USC and an ugly 40–0 home loss to Bud Wilkinson's Oklahoma Sooners. The amiable Brennan had been an electrifying player, fast and dashing, but as a head coach, he struggled to connect with his players, who were less devoted to him than they had been to his emotional predecessor. Where Leahy had been a dramatic speaker, capable of inspiring locker-room orations, Brennan—who as a player used to steal naps during Leahy's tearful monologues—left his players flat. His finest moment on the Notre Dame sideline, in fact, had come when he'd decided not to say anything at all. In 1957, the Fighting Irish had traveled to Norman, Oklahoma, for a rematch with the Sooners, who were then riding a forty-seven-game winning streak. The week of the game, Oklahoma was the subject of a *Sports Illustrated* cover story that bore the loaded headline WHY OKLAHOMA IS UNBEATABLE. During the flight to Norman, the Notre Dame players passed the issue around on the plane, and in the locker room before the game, Fighting Irish center Ed Sullivan, one of the team's co-captains, held up the magazine and began railing against the "unbeatable" Sooners. Brennan had been preparing his pregame remarks in an office next to the locker room, but when he heard his players carrying on, he wisely scrapped his speech. Appearing at the dressing-room door to take his boys out onto the field, he simply said, "Let's go." The room exploded in cheers, and Notre Dame dropped Oklahoma 7–0 in one of the most famous upsets in college football history. The report on the game in the following edition of *Sports Illustrated* ran under the headline REASON TAKES A HOLIDAY.

By 1958, Brennan was locked in a struggle over control of his program with school administrators and Father Theodore Hesburgh, who had been named Notre Dame's new president in 1952 at the age of thirty-five. Dark-haired and handsome, Hesburgh was one of the most charismatic college presidents in the country. He was a protégé of Father John J. Cavanaugh, the departed school president, who had labored mightily to clean up college sports in the aftermath of the scandals in college basketball and at West Point. Cavanaugh advocated the elimination of all athletic scholarships and the elevation of eligibility requirements, going so far as to decree that Fighting Irish players maintain a seventy-seven average in academics in order to play football on Saturday. Hesburgh maintained that policy, and while Cavanaugh hadn't been able to do away with scholarships—one of his policies was that he would never put Notre Dame at a competitive disadvantage—his successor had cut back on them after the departure of Leahy in 1954. Like Red Blaik, Terry Brennan was being forced to try to win the hard way.

The entire West Point community, which hadn't seen a victory over Notre Dame since 1945, was keenly interested in the 1958 game. And within the Corps of Cadets, which had been on hand in Philadelphia the year before, anticipation had built to a fever pitch. The prevailing sentiment among the members of the corps was that Army should have beaten the Fighting Irish in 1957—and both the Army team and Red Blaik, who called the defeat "the hardest I had to take in twenty-five years as a head coach," shared it.

There was by now no chance that the Lonely End would catch the Fighting Irish by surprise. So Blaik asked his coaches to add some new plays to the Army offense. Terry Brennan had told Arthur Daley of *The New York Times* that very week that he was not worried about the mystery surrounding Blaik's far flanker. "I don't care how he gets his signals," said Brennan. "It's really unimportant. It's Bob Anderson and Pete Dawkins who have been giving me sleepless nights."

Blaik put the Cadets' offensive game plan in the hands of backfield coach Tom Harp and line coach Bill Gunlock. Both men had been drawing up additions to the playbook ever since the scrimmage against Syracuse one month earlier, and they had been pleasantly surprised to find that their new attack was remarkably adaptable. The most significant change they made in advance of the Notre Dame game was a play that sent Dawkins in motion wide to the left side when Army was lined up with Carpenter split wide right. Against South Carolina and Penn State, Army had experimented with starting Dawkins in motion for a few steps to his left before having him reverse field on the snap of the ball and run either a short out or a sideline route. The play had so far been fabulously successful—Dawkins had caught six passes for 144 yards and three touchdowns in the first two games with both Caldwell and Anderson throwing him the ball. "When I saw that, and I was seeing the reaction of the defense, then I started thinking about, What if we let Dawkins just keep going?" says Gunlock. "We'd get people stretched from one sideline to the other."

Tom Harp was cautious about adding the play to Army's offensive arsenal. His concern was that it would be too much to learn, that the Cadet players, already overloaded and sleep-deprived by the rigors of academy life, would have a hard time absorbing any new plays. Gunlock, with less experience at West Point than his colleague, felt that the additions weren't so rigorous. Besides, blocking assignments on the line, already simplified by his version of zone blocking, would not be affected. Blaik talked it over with both men after watching film with the team the day after the Penn State game. After asking a few questions, he thought silently for several seconds before saying, "On Monday, I'll take the B Squad and experiment with it, just to see what it looks like."

The assistant coaches ran Monday's varsity practice while Blaik worked with the B Squad at the other end of the field. Both Gunlock and Harp occasionally stole glances down the field at Blaik and the JV, but neither could clearly discern what was happening. At the conclusion of practice, as the Cadets trotted across the Plain toward the gymnasium, Blaik slowly crossed the field to meet with both men. He stopped only briefly and offered no explanation, simply saying, "We're going to put it in." And that was the end of that.

With the new play, the Army offense would not only be spreading the field from sideline to sideline, but it would also be attacking defenses with four receivers. ("That," says Gunlock, "was just unheard-of.") At the end of his run in motion to the left, Dawkins would simply turn back to Caldwell and look for the ball. Anderson, the halfback on the left side, would release on a pass route into the flat beyond Dawkins, angling toward the sideline. The weak-side end, Don Usry, would break from the line of scrimmage and run a short hook route about twelve yards downfield. Caldwell would choose his hot receiver based on how the defense responded to the man in motion. If a defender had shadowed Dawkins across the field, the quarterback would throw to Anderson. If the defensive back stayed with Anderson, Dawkins would get the ball and Anderson would become a downfield blocker. Usry was the safety valve. Carpenter, all alone on the right side of the formation, was primarily a decoy.

Army went through its final drills at West Point on Thursday afternoon. That night at dinner, members of the team were paraded through the mess hall on the shoulders of their fellow cadets during a pep rally. The next morning broke warm and cloudy, and the academy was shrouded in a thin mist of fog that had settled into the river valley. After Blaik's boys stood for an inspection from a tactical department officer, they boarded two buses parked on Thayer Road, the academy's main drag, which runs parallel to the Hudson River and between the barracks and the main cluster of academic buildings. As Bob Anderson waited to board the bus, he marveled at the

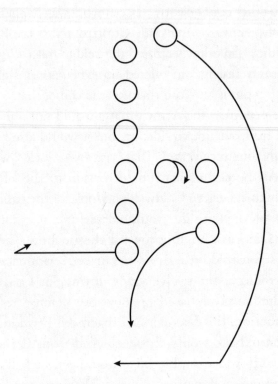

scene. The corps always sent the team off for big games in style, with the Rabble Rousers, West Point's all-male spirit squad, leading cheers from atop the buses as cadets crowded around them and sang "On, Brave Old Army Team." This time, however, the atmosphere was more spirited than usual. The corps wasn't just singing and cheering, it was *rocking* the buses back and forth. Anderson can remember today looking out his window at the gray-clad, roiling crowd and thinking, *How can we let these guys down?* As the Cadets' caravan headed south on Thayer Road, the corps led the way, many of them walking arm in arm. Those walking next to the buses pounded on the vehicles' sides and kept up a steady stream of song, including a pair of lesser-known West Point fight tunes, "Slum and Gravy" and "Gridiron Grenadiers." After a few hundred yards, the buses began to accelerate, but the cadets, some with stacks of books under their arms, kept pace by breaking into a run.

The rousing sendoff from the Corps of Cadets and the practice-field success of the new play gave a tremendous boost of confidence to the already optimistic Army coaches and players. But the exhilaration was short-lived for some, most notably fullback Harry Walters. The players had packed their own gear after practice the night before their trip, and Walters, a superstitious soul, had left his lucky pair of jockey shorts—the same tattered, grungy pair he had been covertly wearing over his jock strap for the last three years—in his locker at West Point. Upon realizing his mistake before the team's departure Friday morning, he had immediately called trainer Ed Pillings, who had seen Walters in the training room many times and was the only other person on the team who knew about his peculiar talisman. Walters asked Pillings to make sure the lucky underwear got packed before the team charter departed from Stewart Air Force Base in Newburgh, New York. But the trainer forgot, a fact that became clear after the team arrived in South Bend and went straight to Notre Dame Stadium for a quick practice. When Walters discovered that his underwear was still missing, he began to reprove Pillings, asking, "How could you forget, Eddie?"

Blaik approached them and snapped, "What's this all about?" He betrayed no emotion—or apparent revulsion—as Walters sheepishly explained the situation. Fortunately for the fullback, Blaik was superstitious, too. It was Blaik, after all, who dictated that the pregame menu remained fixed, and it was Blaik who insisted on staying at the same hotels and country clubs whenever Army traveled. When Walters finished speaking, Blaik thought for a few seconds, then looked at Pillings and said, "Call the superintendent. Have him bring them out on his plane."

Gar Davidson was indeed flying to South Bend for the game on Saturday morning, along with several guests and at least one team manager; about four hundred members of the First Class were also making the trip. Pillings wasn't about to ask a three-star general to hand-carry a pair of dirty underwear. So after consulting with head manager John Bryer, he called assistant manager Terrence Rich and asked him to do it. Rich complied, and as Walters dressed for the game on Saturday afternoon, the pair of jockey shorts hung in his locker.

The morning of October 11 was crisp and clear in South Bend, with bright autumn leaves covering the staid Notre Dame campus. By noon, with a little over ninety minutes to kickoff, football supplicants had already been strolling the grounds for hours—many, including Stella Novogratz, the mother of Army lineman Bob Novogratz, stopped to say a prayer at the school's Grotto of Our Lady of Lourdes. Back at the team hotel in Michigan City, Blaik had begun the day by gathering his players together before their traditional pregame steak lunch. After dispensing with reminders to have confidence in the game plan and not believe anything printed in the papers, he had pulled a note from the breast pocket of his brown tweed suit and said, "I want to read you men a telegram from General MacArthur."

Along with his usual edict that there was no substitute for victory, the general alluded to the imminent ending of the Army–Notre Dame series by reminding the Cadets, "Today, you have an opportunity, which will not again be had by any of you." And he ended by telling them they also had a chance "to show that you are a great Army team." Blaik's voice caught on that last line, as he folded the paper and returned it to his pocket. MacArthur rarely failed to stir the emotions of the Cadets when he spoke, and this telegram had its intended effect. After a few seconds of somber silence, Blaik paused, cleared his throat, and dismissed his players to their lunch.

Once inside his office at Notre Dame Stadium, Blaik went over the game plan with his staff for the last time. The coaches had focused on the passing game during Army's first two victories, experimenting and tinkering with the playbook. Anderson, who had been the engine of the offense the year before, had so far been relegated

largely to the role of decoy while the Cadets put the ball in the air
and let Bill Carpenter and Pete Dawkins run wild. But against Notre
Dame, Blaik planned to make Carpenter the decoy and lean heavily
on his two halfbacks. Blaik felt even more certain of the soundness
of his plan after he stepped onto the field, where a gusty wind was
blowing. It was one more reason to keep the ball on the ground.

Alternating with Dawkins, Anderson carried three times for
twenty-five yards on Army's opening drive, which covered fifty-four
yards to the Fighting Irish 13-yard line. It was there that the Cadets'
attempted their first pass, with Anderson taking a pitch from
Caldwell and rolling right on the halfback option. But Fighting Irish
safety Bob Williams stepped in front of Dawkins and picked off the
throw at the 4.

Williams, now under center at quarterback, led Notre Dame out
to its own 14-yard line. But with less than a minute and a half to go
in the first quarter, he was slow with a handoff to Jim Just as the
halfback headed over right tackle. Williams reached with the ball to
try to put it into Just's hands, but it bounced off his left hip, careering forward beyond the line of scrimmage and into the waiting arms
of Bob Novogratz at the 20-yard line.

The Black Knights needed only two plays to score from there.
The first was a run by Anderson, who nearly gave the ball back
when he fumbled at the Fighting Irish's 15. But center Bill Rowe
saved the halfback from his second turnover of the quarter by falling
on the ball at the 16. On second down, Army tried out its new play,
sending Dawkins in motion left. Jim Just, the Notre Dame safety,
tracked Dawkins as he crossed the field—but Just was playing extremely deep, more than ten yards off the line of scrimmage, and
linebacker Nick Pietrosante covered Anderson in the left flat. With
Carpenter split wide to the right, the middle of the defensive secondary was wide open. Caldwell spun left on the snap and dropped
four steps, as though he were going to keep rolling to his left. But he
stopped abruptly, turned upfield, and threw over the middle to reserve end Jack Morrison, who had come into the game for Don Usry.
Morrison, now in the space vacated by Just, had turned back toward

Caldwell at the 5 but was still drifting toward the end zone as the ball arrived. Caldwell's pass was a little short, and Morrison had to reach back and stoop to corral the ball as he crossed the 3. He gathered it into his belly and took another step before tumbling forward into the end zone. Nobody had touched him. Monk Hilliard missed the conversion kick, and Army led 6–0.

Morrison was a burly, round-faced first classman from the Youngstown, Ohio, suburb of Austintown. He had been recruited by Notre Dame out of Austintown High but refused the offer of a football scholarship because of his contempt for rival Ursuline High, Youngstown's prestigious Catholic high school, which sent several players a year to South Bend. Morrison went so far as to tell the Fighting Irish assistant coach who was recruiting him, "I don't want to play *for* Notre Dame. I want to play against you."* The coach— today, Morrison cannot recall his name—chuckled and said he'd heard *that* before. After his touchdown had given Army the first lead of the game, Morrison lined up along the Notre Dame sideline for the kickoff. As he waited for the end of a television time-out, the same assistant coach reached out and tapped him on the arm. "Nice catch, Morrison," he said. "You finally got your wish."

Army mounted another drive in the second quarter behind the running of Anderson and Dawkins, marching sixty-one yards to the Fighting Irish 5-yard line. There, on fourth down, Blaik chose to go for the touchdown rather than kick a field goal. Again Dawkins went in motion to the left. Caldwell tried to hit Anderson in the flat with a short pass, but Notre Dame halfback Norm Odyniec, who had been on the sidelines for the Black Knights' first touchdown, recognized the play immediately. He had come forward to cover Don Usry, who was back in the game at tight end. But Usry ran the wrong route, turning to the outside instead of the inside, and was too close to Anderson. Odyniec followed Caldwell's eyes and then

---

* Like so many of his future teammates, Morrison was attracted by West Point's free tuition and the fact that he would not lose his scholarship if he was unable to play football. He had also already received a visit from Doc Blanchard, who took Morrison and his mother to a screening of the just-released John Ford movie *The Long Gray Line*.

jumped in front of Anderson, stumbling to the ground as he batted the pass away. Had Odyniec caught the ball, he would have had a clear path to the Cadets' end zone.

Army went to the locker room at halftime still leading 6–0. The Cadets had dominated the action in the first thirty minutes, driving deep into Notre Dame territory on three occasions while holding the Fighting Irish to zero points. But Blaik was worried. His team had wasted two opportunities in the first half, and his starters had been forced to play nearly the entire thirty minutes. His strategy with substitutes had been to work them in along with the first-teamers, as he had done with Usry and Morrison in the first half. But he felt certain that Notre Dame was not going to be kept at bay forever. The bigger and more physical Fighting Irish were hitting hard, attempting to pound Army into submission—Blaik wrote to MacArthur later that his opponent's intent was apparently "to destroy us physically in order to win."

Army began the second half on its heels. Anderson fumbled the kickoff, which the Cadets recovered at their own 21-yard line. Two penalties set them back to the 1, where Blaik elected to punt on third down. Rowe's short snap was high, and Caldwell, who doubled as the punter, had to jump for it. When he came down, Notre Dame end Monty Stickles, the man who had kicked the field goal to beat the Cadets in Philadelphia the year before, was in his face. Caldwell sprinted right, but Fighting Irish guard Myron Pottios had joined the pursuit from that side. Stickles grabbed Caldwell around the waist from behind, missed his grip, and latched on to the quarterback's left forearm, spinning him around. As Pottios prepared to hit him, Caldwell flung the ball forward like a man hurling a discus. But the ball hit the ground short of the line of scrimmage, and the referees penalized Army for intentional grounding and ruled the play a safety. Notre Dame had cut the lead to 6–2, and the Cadets had to kick the ball back to the Fighting Irish from the Army 20-yard line.

For the first time all afternoon, the crowd sensed a chance for the home team to seize control of the game. The Notre Dame players felt it, too, and Pietrosante spearheaded an advance down to the

Army 19. A holding penalty effectively ended the drive, forcing the Fighting Irish to turn the ball over on downs, but later in the quarter, they got the ball back on their own 10-yard line. Working out of a spread T formation, with an end split wide on one side and a back split wide on the other, Notre Dame began a deliberate advance, running Pietrosante up the middle and Just and Odyniec around the ends on the toss-sweep. The drive stretched into the opening minutes of the fourth quarter, and the Fighting Irish again reached Army's 19-yard-line. But on fourth down, Bob Williams overthrew a wide-open receiver in the end zone. (Notre Dame completed just four passes for eleven yards on the day.) The Cadets began their last drive from their own 33-yard line with four minutes remaining, still leading 6–2.

On first down, Dawkins sprinted out into the right flat on a sideline route, filling the space vacated by Carpenter. But Bob Williams jumped the route and stepped in front of the pass with nothing in front of him but open field. Glory would have been his, and victory would have belonged to Notre Dame, if only he could have held on to the ball. ("By that much," wrote Blaik later, "went Terry Brennan's job.") Army now faced second-and-ten. Blaik's starters had played most of the game—Anderson and Novogratz, who finished with eighteen tackles, would ultimately play all sixty minutes—and they had stood the Fighting Irish up on three second-half drives deep into Army territory. They were tired. They were sore. But in one of the defining moments of the season, they nevertheless summoned the resolve to mount one final, gritty drive.

It all began with Pete Dawkins. Blaik adored his right halfback for his ability to see the entire game, to recognize immediately the positioning and movements of each player on the field. Despite the near-disaster on first down, Dawkins wanted to give the play another shot. When he returned to the huddle, he looked at Caldwell and said, "I can get away from that guy. I'll just cut the other way." Caldwell agreed and called the adjusted play in the huddle. On the next play, Dawkins cut to the middle instead of toward the sideline, and Caldwell hit him in stride for a twenty-three-yard gain and a first down at the Fighting Irish 43. Army downshifted into its running game from there. Dawkins carried three more times on the drive for nineteen yards, including a six-yard sweep around left end for the final touchdown of the game and a 12–2 lead. He wrapped up the scoring by throwing to Anderson for the two-point conversion. When the final gun sounded on the Black Knights' 14–2 victory, the 450 cadets in attendance stormed out onto the field and bore the Army starters off on their shoulders.

In the dressing room, Dawkins presented Blaik with the game ball, telling the coach, "You should have gotten this a year ago." ("A nice speech," recalled Blaik. "So good, in fact, it was evident he had practiced it for a year.") Blaik wrote later that the victory made him feel young again. And why not? He knew now that he had more than just a good team. For the first time in nearly a decade, he had a great one.

Chapter 7

MR. WONDERFUL

BOB ANDERSON WINCED as he sank into his seat on the team bus outside Notre Dame stadium. The Cadets had used the Lonely End primarily as a decoy in their victory over the Fighting Irish, and Anderson and fellow halfback Pete Dawkins had borne the brunt of the offensive burden, combining for forty carries and 150 rushing yards. Dawkins had scored the pair's only touchdown, but Anderson had put in the more bruising afternoon. Again and again, he had plunged into the heart of the Notre Dame defensive line. He was physically exhausted and sore. But he was also deeply satisfied. He and his teammates, stung by their narrow defeat to the Fighting Irish in 1957, had been pointing toward this game for an entire year. As Anderson slumped back into the corner of his seat and looked out the window, a smile spread across his face. Below him, standing outside the stadium tunnel, a young lady stood in the deepening autumn chill, wrapped in an overcoat and clutching a Notre Dame pennant. She was clearly waiting for somebody. As she looked up and down the tunnel, her gaze swiveled upward and her eyes locked with Anderson's. She returned his smile, and as Anderson waved from behind his window, he flashed an even bigger grin and said under his breath, "You're probably the most unattractive girl I've ever seen."

The bus was only partially full. Blaik usually brought the team back to the hotel as a group after a road game, but this time he had decided to give his players an evening pass, along with a gentle admonishment: "Remember, gentlemen, that we have a game next Saturday." Many of the Black Knights, rather than return immediately to the team hotel in Michigan City, had decided to go out for the evening in South Bend with friends or family. Only a handful of players were spread out in the seats on the bus, and, being careful not to face the window or look at the girl who had smiled at Anderson, they began to break into laughter, stifled at first, and then roaring. Then a single voice silenced them all.

"Andy! Come sit with me!"

It was Red Blaik. He was sitting, as was his custom, in the front row directly behind the driver. Anderson cast a nervous glance at his now-silent teammates, stood up, and stepped into the aisle. Everybody knew about Colonel Blaik's frosty formality—his detractors called it priggishness—and Anderson's remarks to the unaware girl had been particularly loutish. He thought he might be in for a scolding. But Blaik had also called him by his nickname, Andy, rather than by his surname, which was almost unheard of. Warily, Anderson slid into the seat next to the man he revered, and feared, more than any other on earth.

Blaik, sitting with his fedora in his lap, complemented Anderson on his play and then paused for a few seconds. With his eyes fixed on his hat, he said quietly, "You know, Andy, my wife came down to Pershing Hall on Friday to see the team off."

"Yes, sir." Anderson had only met Merle Blaik once, a few years before. He knew what she looked like, but he did not know her well.

"You know, she always used to come see us off, but she stopped a long time ago," Blaik said, before looking Anderson in the eye, "after what happened in Fifty-One. But she came back for this game."

Anderson did not reply. He was fully aware of what had happened in 1951—everybody was—but nobody had ever heard the Colonel mention it. "You know what happened in Fifty-One, don't you, Andy?" said Blaik.

"Yes, sir."

Blaik recounted both his after-hours meeting with the Third

Class football players in the film room and his visit later the same night with General Irving, the superintendent. The supe had assured him, Blaik insisted, that if his boys came forward and told the truth, they would not be automatically dismissed. He told Anderson about Bob Blaik, and about how he had been unceremoniously turned out of the barracks and forced to sleep at home the night of his dismissal. He told the story of how he had directed his longtime secretary, Harriet Demarest, to type up his letter of resignation, and of how MacArthur had ultimately convinced him to stay. "Blaik said MacArthur told him that you don't quit when you're down," says Anderson. "You quit when you're on top."

Blaik fell into silence as the bus rolled west through the fading light, and both coach and player drifted into their own private reveries, staring out the window, or forward into the glow of the headlights. Anderson had been emotionally moved—how awkward and embarrassing it must have been for Bob Blaik to come home that night!—and more than a little confused by the entire story. *Why is he telling me this?* For a man who kept people at such a remove, the story seemed at once intensely personal and more than a little random. But Anderson did not dwell on it for long. He was after all, tired and sore and longing for his bed.

More than fifty years later, Anderson would look back on this encounter with Blaik and wonder how had he missed the obvious. "Had I been smarter," he says, "I would have realized that he had just told me that he was thinking about retiring."

On Monday morning, two days after Army's victory over Notre Dame, the Associated Press released its weekly poll of the top college football teams in the country. For the first time since November 1950—less than six months before the catastrophe of the cheating scandal—the Cadets held the number-one ranking. Army was a national sensation, easily the most written-about team in the game, though the ninth-ranked Louisiana State Tigers were beginning to attract a measure of hype for their unique three-platoon system, which featured a defense-only unit that coach Paul Dietzel referred to as "the Chinese Bandits." Dietzel was a former Blaik assistant, having coached the Black Knights' offensive line in 1953 and '54. Handsome and media-savvy, he had devised the politically incorrect nickname as both a motivational tool for his defense and a public relations tactic for his team after reading in the comic strip *Terry and the Pirates* that Chinese bandits had been feared for their vicious nature.* But LSU, which had begun the season unranked in the national polls, was still a footnote to the season. With West Point just a little more than fifty miles up the Hudson River from New York City, the media capital of the world, the hype around Red Blaik's mysterious offense had been intense.

Luckily for Joe Cahill, Army's veteran sports publicity director, he had a fresh and glamorous face to put forward as the team's and the academy's representative. Through the first three games, senior halfback Pete Dawkins had scored six touchdowns and was leading the country in scoring. Opponents had begun the season focusing their defensive game plans on stopping Bob Anderson. The resulting lack of attention, coupled with Blaik's quirky spread formation, had cleared the field for Dawkins, who was averaging more than four yards per carry and more than twenty-two per reception.

Dawkins's athletic exploits were not limited to football. He was also one of the top defensemen on the Army hockey team—a starter for the varsity since his Third Class year despite the fact that he had no prior experience in ice hockey before he came to West Point (though the Michigan native did know how to skate). He led the plebe team in scoring, was named the outstanding sophomore in the East, and as a junior was the highest-scoring defenseman in the country, with twenty-five goals and thirty-eight points. That same year he had led the Cadets to their first-ever defeat of powerful

---

* The Chinese Bandits captured the imagination of fans in Baton Rouge, where the locals were inspired to compose this rather discourteous chant:

> *Chinese Bandits on their way,*
> *Listen to what Confucius say!*
> *Chinese Bandits like to knock,*
> *Gonna stop a touchdown, CHOP! CHOP!*

Boston College, a 5–4 overtime victory in which he carried the puck the length of the ice to score the winning goal. "Offensively, he possessed a very hard shot and had good straightaway speed, and [he] was capable of consistently playing sixty minutes," said Army coach Jack Riley, who was soon to be named the head coach of the 1960 Olympic team.*

But Dawkins was more than just a superlative athlete. He was a superlative cadet, the most accomplished at West Point since Douglas MacArthur. He had been appointed First Captain of the Corps of Cadets and had been elected both captain of the football team and president of the Class of 1959. A gifted student, he ranked eighth out of 499 first classmen and wore gold stars on the collar of his dress gray uniform that designated him as a member of the top 5 percent of his class. He also played six musical instruments. "There has not been a cadet like Dawkins in fifty years, and in some respects there has never been anyone like him," wrote *Life* magazine's Marshall Smith on the eve of the clash with Notre Dame. "In the 156-year history of the Military Academy, only 53 first captains have also been star men. Only 11 have been class presidents. Only two have been football captains. Peter Dawkins is the only cadet to be all four." One of the jokes making the rounds at West Point during that golden autumn of 1958 was that it was a shame Dawkins and MacArthur were not classmates, since MacArthur would have made a fine adjutant. Another paraphrased the book of Matthew: "Did you hear about Dawkins? He just opened up a tin of sardines and a loaf of bread, and fed dinner to the entire First Class."

A skinny towheaded boy from the Detroit suburb of Royal Oak, Dawkins was the son of a dentist. Henry Dawkins had commanded military field hospitals in the Pacific during World War II, and his mobile commands had moved, like the war itself, from island to island, taking him to Guadalcanal, Saipan, and Tinian, where he had been on hand to witness the takeoff of the *Enola Gay* when the plane departed for its atomic mission over Hiroshima. Pete's mother, Fran-

---

* Riley led the 1960 team to a semifinal upset of the Soviet Union at the Squaw Valley Games en route to Team USA's first hockey gold medal.

ces, was a homemaker with a B.A. from the University of Michigan. Known to his family as "the squirt," Pete tagged after his big brother, Dale, competing with and against older boys in daily games of baseball, basketball, and football, the game he loved best. He dreamed of playing quarterback. A natural lefty, he often practiced throwing right-handed in order to make himself a more versatile passer.

Pete used to practice jump-passes by throwing balls through a tire slung from a tree in a vacant lot. One day when the boy was eleven, Henry Dawkins noticed that his son's right arm had become extremely weak. Henry also noticed that Pete had begun to carry his head to one side and forward of his shoulders. A closer examination revealed a curvature in the boy's spine, and doctors diagnosed him with a slight case of polio.* Rather than put him in a brace, the doctors prescribed intensive physical therapy. Under the close attention of Frances, Pete began weekly treatment sessions at a clinic operated by the Sister Kenny Foundation.† His physician was Dr. Ethel Calhoun, and she showed Frances and Henry how to lay their son out on a table every night and exercise his muscles by pushing on his legs and arms. She also urged Pete to use barbells to further strengthen his weakened body. Dawkins, who was never completely disabled by the disease, needed less than two years of treatment to fully recover.

His bout with polio was like catnip for the mythmakers of the press, and there were indeed some writers who did everything but put Dawkins in an iron lung. During his magical senior season, he begged a scribe for *The New York Times*, "Please don't make a big thing of it. It has been overplayed. It is all out of perspective." But while the tale had been frequently overblown, it also had an unmistakable and resonant significance in the story of his life. For starters, the aggressive physical therapy Dawkins endured spurred in him a lifelong devotion to weight training, a pursuit that would play a

---

* Jonas Salk's vaccine for polio was not introduced until 1955.
† Former Australian Army nurse Elizabeth Kenny, who established the Sister Kenny Institute in Minneapolis in 1942, disdained the conventional use of braces and splints to treat polio in favor of "retraining" muscles—a groundbreaking method of treatment at the time.

crucial role in his athletic development. More importantly, when his doctors told him he would probably never play football again—though they also told Frances that if she were to keep the intensely competitive boy off the field, it might be a devastating blow to his morale—Dawkins took their words of caution as a direct challenge. It was an attitude he had learned early, and through hard experience, while trying to keep up with Dale and his friends. *I'll show them.* "Everything," Dawkins said, "stemmed from football."

Nevertheless, for much of his youth, Pete's mind and will were far ahead of his frail body. By the time he was a senior at Cranbrook School, a small preparatory academy in nearby Bloomfield Hills, Dawkins stood about six feet but weighed only 170 pounds. He was a good passing quarterback, though his lack of size kept him from being heavily recruited to play college football. An excellent student, he had already been accepted at both Michigan and Yale, and he had only mild interest in West Point. At the end of his junior year his football coach, Fred Campbell, a former marine and a vocal booster of the academy, had taken Dawkins to West Point for a visit. Campbell had also taken it upon himself to contact Red Blaik on the boy's behalf, going so far as to send still photos and film of Dawkins in action.* Pete had eventually submitted an application to the academy but heard nothing until June of 1955—about two weeks before new cadets were supposed to report for Beast Barracks—when he received a telegram informing him that his application for admission had been denied. Dawkins had until then been leaning toward attending Yale, where he had been offered a spot on the football team. But when West Point turned him down, Dawkins changed his mind. *I'll show them.*

Blaik had not been impressed by what he had seen in Dawkins's film clips, and he suspected the boy was just another "silk stocking" prep school athlete—one who could certainly benefit from a year spent bulking up at Manlius. Dawkins, however, did not want to go to prep school. He and Campbell lobbied Blaik for help, ultimately

---

* Doc Blanchard would later tell Dawkins that the films had been a source of great amusement to the Army coaching staff.

convincing the coach to secure an alternate appointment for Dawkins from his congressman.* Blaik did not see much of Dawkins during his plebe year until spring practice of 1956. "I knew the first half hour of the first day he wouldn't make it," Blaik told *Sport* magazine in 1958. "He wasn't a natural enough passer to play quarterback in the T. But he could run."

Dawkins—who had not yet turned eighteen in the spring of '56—remained buried on the depth chart into the fall. And he might have stayed buried if he had not taken the field as a punt returner during the Cadets' annual scrimmage with Syracuse. As he backpedaled to field his first kick, two would-be tacklers converged on him from the left and right. Dawkins caught the ball and, with a few quick steps forward, split the two defenders and burst into the open field, where he feinted past a third and sprinted into the end zone, easily pulling away from the Syracuse pursuit. Blaik converted him into a varsity halfback on the spot. The only trouble was, Dawkins had only ever been a quarterback. Blocking and tackling techniques were unknown to him. For the rest of the season, he worked before and after every practice to master those skills with Tom Harp. To the chagrin of some of the other backs, including Harry Walters, Harp used them as Dawkins's blocking and tackling dummies.

In October, deep into the fourth quarter of an ugly 48–14 loss at Michigan, Blaik inserted his reserves to finish the game. Army had the ball on the Wolverines' 22-yard line when Dawkins took a pitch on a sweep around left end, slipped a tackler, and sprinted into the end zone for a touchdown. Years later, his brother Dale told an interviewer, "You could sense the intensity that was there, the single-mindedness—this kid was determined that he was going to score."

As a second classman the next season, Dawkins had averaged well over five yards a carry and combined with Bob Anderson to form one of college football's most dangerous backfield tandems. Though

---

* Even though he had no experience in ice hockey, the academy had used Dawkins to fill one of the admission slots set aside for Jack Riley's club.

Dawkins's blocking and tackling improved, they never reached the point where he was considered very good at either, a fact he has always acknowledged. "Bob was a much better blocker than I," he said years later, "a consummate blocker." When Bill Gunlock was hired on the eve of spring practice in 1958, he spent many extra hours in the film room getting up to speed on his new team. Blaik joined him one day, and as the two men sat alone in the room watching film of Dawkins on the run he said to Gunlock, "I'm not sure Pete Dawkins is a full-contact football player."

"Colonel," said Gunlock, who had been especially impressed with Dawkins's abilities as a receiver, "we better figure out how to make him one because when he's got the ball in his hands, he might be the best player we have."

As the legend of Pete Dawkins grew during the autumn of 1958, the press requests for interviews flooded into the Army sports publicity department. Most of the interrogations were completed during what little spare time Dawkins had between academics, athletics, and his responsibilities as commander of the Corps of Cadets. Coordinating all of the media requests for Dawkins was the job of Joe Cahill, who farmed most of the grunt work out to a young army specialist named John Underwood. After Underwood left the service in 1960, he would go on to work as a sports reporter for the *Miami Herald*— where he'd begun working while he was in college—and later for *Sports Illustrated*, where he was a mainstay of the writing staff for more than twenty years. But in 1958, he was Cahill's assistant and spent much of his time churning out copy for the Army game programs. Several days a week, Cahill would send him down to New York City with copies of stories that Underwood had written, to be run in newspapers without a byline in case any of the dailies needed to fill space in their sports pages. Dawkins was in almost constant demand from the press, and he was a frequent visitor to the sports publicity office, sometimes stopping by even when he had no interviews scheduled. "I accused him of flirting with Joe Cahill's secretary, Anita," Underwood says, "but the truth was he just liked to sit around and share opinions." Dawkins, one of the most well-spoken athletes of his or any other day, was almost instantly likable, and his thoughts frequently seemed to come out fully formed. Reporters believed Blaik when he told them, "I can practically prophesy that if he stays in the army, Dawkins will be chief of staff."

With all the demands on his time—Dawkins was one of several first classmen working on a Rhodes Scholarship application—nobody, not even his classmates, seemed to know just how he managed to get everything done while still maintaining his lofty academic standing. He was, first and foremost, a tireless worker, who even as brigade commander regularly violated the academy's lights-out regulations, which dictated that all members of the corps not on duty were to be in their bunks with the room lights turned off after taps sounded at ten fifteen. There was no formal strength and conditioning program for the Cadets in 1958, but Dawkins kept up with his weight training by stashing a contraband set of dismantled barbells under his mattress. "When you've got a lot to do, you get it done," was how he explained his achievements to *Life* magazine. Aiding him in his efforts was a keen mind and a remarkably powerful memory. Peter Stromberg, a classmate, remembers walking with Dawkins to class on days when it was obvious he had not been able to complete the assigned reading. "He was able," says Stromberg, "simply by listening, and reasoning, I think, to acquit himself okay when called on in class."

It has to be tough watching one of your schoolmates turned into a Frank Merriwell hero, and to some cadets, the hype for Dawkins was overblown. Even today, a few of his former Army teammates caution against buying into it, insisting that Bob Anderson was by far the better all-around football player. There really isn't much debate about that fact, even among Dawkins's admirers, or from Dawkins himself. But Dawkins *was* a talented runner, shifty, aggressive, and determined, if not overly quick, as well as a marvelously gifted receiver. Blaik admired Dawkins most for his ability to see the whole field from his position at left halfback—a talent that had already played a crucial role in the victory over Notre Dame. On the train back to West Point after the 1957 loss to Navy, his teammates had voted overwhelmingly to make him the team captain. "It wasn't even close," says team manager John Bryer, who counted the votes.*

"I don't know when Pete slept, frankly," says Harry Walters. "He had so many irons in the fire that guys like me—rugged fullbacks with quick tempers—I was trying to find extra sleep every year I was at West Point. I'm not so sure Dawkins did any of that. He was just an icon in a lot of ways. He had so many gifts: intellectual, athletic, leadership. He had it all."

Of all Red Blaik's former assistants who had left West Point to take over programs of their own—the number was up to thirteen by October of 1958—none had ever coached against him in a game. This was remarkable since nine of the thirteen were still active in college football, with all but one having held his job for at least four years.[†] Only Virginia's Dick Voris, who had been the offensive line coach and top assistant at West Point from 1955 to '57, was in his rookie year.

Voris had graduated in 1948 from San Jose State, where he played center and linebacker for the Spartans. Like many other college players of the time, he had gone to school only after serving in World War II—he spent four years with the marines in the Pacific theater. Genial and intelligent, he had risen quickly through the coaching ranks, going in just six years from high school to junior college to the NFL, where Blaik found him as the line coach for the Los Angeles Rams. Voris was a sharp student of football, and during his time at West Point he had displayed such enthusiastic confidence in his ideas and convictions that he was often able to carry the day in the debates over technique and strategy that Blaik relished. But the Cadets were only available to the Army coaches for a few hours at

---

* Dawkins cast his vote for center Bill Rowe.

† A tenth Blaik protégé, Sid Gillman, was in his fourth season as coach of the NFL's Los Angeles Rams. The other eight college coaches were Paul Amen, of Wake Forest; George Blackburn, of Cincinnati; Clarence "Chief" Boston, of New Hampshire; Paul Dietzel, of LSU; Bobby Dobbs, of Tulsa; Andy Gustafson, of Miami; Murray Warmath, of Minnesota; and Bob Woodruff, of Florida.

most each day, and Voris had wanted to work at a school where he would have more time to spend with his players. When he left for Virginia, he was just thirty-six.

A sturdy, florid man with thinning red hair, Voris took over a program in Charlottesville that was in need of rebuilding. The Cavaliers, after winning at least seven games every season from 1949 to '52 under coach Art Guepe, had fallen to the bottom of the Atlantic Coast Conference under Ned McDonald, who won just five games in three years before giving way to Ben Martin, a former Navy halfback. Martin did a bit better, with seven victories in two seasons before he left to take over the fledgling program at the United States Air Force Academy. In Virginia's first game under Voris, the Cavaliers had lost to Clemson 20–15, but they had come back the next week to surprise Duke 15–12. The new coach pronounced the victory "the most important of my career." It would also be the only victory of his career. Though Voris kept assuring fans that the program would turn itself around, Virginia went on to lose its next twenty-eight games, tying an NCAA record for futility and costing Voris his job at the end of the 1960 season. Besides the numbing string of defeats, he left behind in Charlottesville a trail of irate alumni and a team whose apathy was so pronounced that it was the subject of a story in *Sports Illustrated*.* Voris, who loudly complained about the paltry number of scholarships the university allotted to football—just sixteen in his last year—never had enough early success to buy himself time with impatient fans or school officials. He returned to the NFL as an assistant and never again wore the mantle of head coach at any level.

Voris had tried to copy the Blaik model in Charlottesville, right down to hiring a pair of former Army assistants to fill out his staff. Voris had also hired a rookie coach out of the NFL, a twenty-eight-year-old defensive back named Don Shula. Shula had spent the 1957 season with the Washington Redskins, his third team in seven pro seasons, and he felt that his playing days were nearing an end.

---

* The piece quoted one Cavalier advising his teammates on the eve of the final game of the 1960 season, "One more loss and then we can get drunk."

He had come to the attention of Voris at the annual convention of the American Football Coaches Association, held that January at Philadelphia's ornately Gothic Bellevue-Stratford Hotel.* The AFCA convention has long been the most important networking event for coaches in college football, and it was at a reception there that Shula approached Army defensive line coach Frank Lauterbur. Shula had played four of his seven NFL seasons for the Baltimore Colts, and he and Lauterbur, the Colts' former defensive line coach, had remained friendly. Shula told Lauterbur that he was looking for a job and asked if he knew of any openings. Lauterbur told him that his good friend and former colleague Dick Voris had just taken over at Virginia, and that he would call Voris on Shula's behalf. A few weeks later, in February, Voris called Shula and offered him a job as the Cavaliers' defensive secondary coach over the phone. Shula accepted immediately.

Among the duties of the Cavaliers' rookie assistant was the job of advance scouting. Instead of traveling with the team on the weekends, Shula would head to wherever Virginia's opponent for the next game happened to be playing. When Voris led his team onto the field at West Point on October 18 to play the Cadets, Shula was scouting Vanderbilt in Gainesville, Florida, where he would watch the Commodores play to a 6–6 tie with the University of Florida.

Back at West Point, on a sunny and unseasonably warm day, Shula's defensive backs intercepted reserve Army quarterback Tom Blanda once, but they were otherwise overmatched by the Cadets' passing game, which soared for 141 yards on just seven completions. Before a homecoming crowd of 27,250, Army dominated from the opening kickoff in a 35–6 victory. For most of the game, the Cadets made it look easy. They went seventy-three yards on eight plays in the opening quarter to score their first touchdown, then zipped sixty-eight yards in two plays for their second—a drive highlighted by a sixty-one-yard catch-and-run by Bill Carpenter, who hauled in a rainbow from Caldwell down the right sideline at the Virginia 35

---

* The AFCA was founded in New York City in 1922 by Army coach Charles Daly, West Point class of 1905 (and Harvard, '01).

and twisted through two tackles before he was brought down at the 7-yard line. The Cadets went sixty-six yards for a touchdown in the third quarter, then scored twice in the fourth, first on a six-yard run by Caldwell to cap off a ninety-five-yard drive, and then on a twenty-four-yard interception return by reserve fullback Don Bonko, playing at Monster back in place of Harry Walters. Bonko broke into the Cavaliers' backfield on a blitz up the middle along with middle linebacker Bob Novogratz. Quarterback Arnold Dempsey, backpedaling furiously, tried to unload the ball to the right, but Novogratz leapt and batted the pass high into the air. Bonko settled under it and took off for the end zone. On the day, Army ran up 457 yards of total offense, 316 of which came on the ground. Bob Anderson had his best day of the entire season, catching a touchdown pass from Caldwell and rushing for 124 yards on seventeen carries.

But the gaudy numbers hid the fact that the performance was something of a letdown for Blaik's boys after their emotional victory over Notre Dame the week before. In addition to Blanda's interception, the Cadets fumbled the ball away four times, three in the first half alone. The first led to the Cavaliers' only touchdown; the second came after Army had driven eighty-three yards to the Virginia 2. Against the Fighting Irish a week earlier, the Cadets had put the ball on the ground three times, only to recover possession on each occasion. The fumbles brought Army's turnover total through four games to a whopping thirteen. Add in the seventy yards' worth of penalties that the Cadets had committed against the Cavaliers, and it was apparent that Blaik's best team in years was far from perfect. The Black Knights weren't just prone to mistakes; they were prone to bunches of them. Writing to MacArthur on the Monday after the win over Virginia, Blaik noted all the miscues—explaining away the fumbles as a by-product of Army's "fast-breaking offense," and the penalties as a result of the team's "young, inexperienced personnel" at some positions. Still, he concluded, "We can't afford those mistakes against better teams."

Pittsburgh, whom the Cadets were to face on October 25, was one of those better teams, a big bruising club with a quarterback in Ivan Toncic who was a superior passer to Notre Dame's Bob Williams. The

Panthers were "better in many ways," said Blaik to MacArthur, than the Fighting Irish, and they would be the Cadets' second major road test in the last three weeks. And if that wasn't enough of a challenge, his team would also be dealing with its first major injuries of the season.

Pete Dawkins had fallen during an eighty-three-yard drive in the second quarter. His first two carries of the possession had gone for thirteen and thirty-eight yards. His third went for ten, but as he was blocking for Anderson on the next play, a Virginia defender's helmet had struck him squarely on the left thigh. "It was just a routine play," says Dawkins, "but as soon as I got hit, I thought, 'That's going to be a problem. That's not good.'" Blaik held him out through halftime. At Dawkins's urging, Blaik put him back on the field for the second-half kickoff. The pain, however, was so great that Dawkins was unable to run, and he spent the rest of the final thirty minutes of the game watching from the bench. Harry Walters had gone down early in the fourth quarter following a thirty-two-yard sprint into Virginia territory. He had been playing one of his best games of the season—scoring Army's first touchdown and making all three of his conversion kicks (he had taken over the job from Monk Hilliard after the Notre Dame game). Walters, with his quick burst off the snap, had sprinted through the line and into the defensive secondary, but his speed didn't last, and he had been run down by Cavaliers safety Sonny Randle, a standout sprinter on the Virginia track team.* Randle, who had scored Virginia's only touchdown of the game in the second quarter on a seven-yard pass from quarterback Fred Russell, caught Walters from behind and rode him to the ground. As he fell, Walters felt a sharp pain in his left ankle. Randle stood up, taunting him for being so slow. Walters had the energy to retort but not to continue in the game.

In a single afternoon, Blaik's offensive backfield had been re-

---

* Randle, whose first name was Ulmo, had already been selected by the Chicago Cardinals with the first pick of the nineteenth round of the NFL draft on January 28, 1958. In an eleven-year pro career, spent mostly in St. Louis after the Cardinals moved there two years later, he played in four Pro Bowls, including in 1960, the year he led the league with fifteen touchdown receptions.

duced to Bob Anderson, Joe Caldwell, and two question marks. It was immediately apparent after the game that both Dawkins and Walters would miss the next Saturday's date with Pittsburgh. Though the injury to Dawkins was reported as a "muscle pull," it was in fact a hematoma, a deep thigh bruise. Walters had a severely sprained ankle. Throughout the following week, neither injury made much progress. Dawkins's left thigh was gradually turning black and purple, making it painful to walk, and so severely impairing his stride that he was unable to run at full speed. Walters was on crutches.

Blaik did not have full confidence in their replacements. The backup to Dawkins at right halfback was second classman Steve Waldrop. A Dallas native and record-setting high school sprinter, he had come to West Point after playing freshman ball at Mississippi State. "[Waldrop] has never played well or as well as he should," Blaik wrote to MacArthur, "but with the pressure of filling Dawkins's position he may rise to the occasion." The coach was more worried about the fullback position. His number-one reserve, third classman John Eielson, had been out for two weeks after his palm had been stepped on and ripped open by a pair of cleats during practice the week of the Notre Dame game. The third-string fullback, his classmate Don Bonko, was "far below Walters," in Blaik's estimation, not nearly as quick or as intelligent. He assured MacArthur that "Gibson, the defensive quarterback, will be made second fullback."

Lessening his team's susceptibility to injury had been the impetus behind Blaik's invention of the Lonely End. His new offense had keyed Army to a spectacular start. More importantly, it had helped the Cadets make it through the first third of their schedule without a major injury to a single member of their starting eleven. Now, for the first time all year, they were at less than full strength. Army had held its number-one ranking for the second week in a row after the win over Virginia, but its status as college football's top team was suddenly in serious jeopardy.

Chapter 8
THE END OF PERFECTION

So SPECTACULAR HAD THE ARMY offense been through the first four games of the season that it had taken until the week of the Pittsburgh game for the Cadets' defense to receive some recognition from the sporting press. Most of the coverage focused on middle linebacker Bob Novogratz—the weak-side guard on Blaik's unbalanced offensive line—who was proving to be as valuable to the team as Anderson or Dawkins. Novogratz had made fifty-eight tackles through four games, and had recovered four fumbles. Blaik described him as the "sword and flame" of an Army defense that had surrendered just two touchdowns and sixteen points, two of which had come on a safety after the bungled punt attempt against Notre Dame. With one half of the Cadets' backfield sidelined with injuries, Blaik would be counting on Novogratz and the rest of the defense to shut down a dangerous Pittsburgh team. "In a relative sense, Dawkins and Walters will not be missed nearly as much when Pitt has the ball," wrote Lawrence Robinson of the *New York World-Telegram*, who mused that the game could very well turn into a defensive stalemate.

Novogratz was hardly an unknown entering the fall, though he had usually been singled out during the preseason because he was the lone returning starter on Army's offensive line. At six-two, 210 pounds, he was quick, aggressive, and prodigiously strong. Novogratz, in fact, might have been one of the most powerful players, pound for pound, in college football. A soft-spoken former wrestler, he had skinny legs and long, muscular arms that were, in the words of Harry Walters, "like two axes."

In the win over Notre Dame, Novogratz's teammates had marveled at the way he had physically dominated offensive tackle Bronko Nagurski Jr., the son of legendary fullback Bronko Nagurski. The elder Nagurski had been an All-America at Minnesota in the late twenties before going on to a storied pro career for the Chicago Bears from 1930 to 1943. At six feet and 225 pounds, he had been mammoth for his day, and his son was built to almost exactly the same specifications. Nagurski Jr. wasn't a giant by 1958 standards, but he still had at least fifteen pounds on Novogratz. The Army linebacker had nevertheless knocked him to the ground time and again with his powerful arms. "Nagurski grunted on every play," says Walters. "But every time he went after Novogratz, there was a double-grunt, because the second would come when Bob knocked him to the ground. It became a joke for us on the field."

"As far as his position," says Bill Rowe, "Bob was better than Anderson or Dawkins." And defensive line coach Frank Lauterbur says that Novogratz was "probably the best all-around defensive player I ever coached."

Like Dawkins, Novogratz had risen from obscurity. In the winter of his Third Class year, he had been wrestling as a heavyweight for the Cadets when Blaik spotted him during a practice and ordered Frank Lauterbur to "get that kid out for football." Thus began Novogratz's meteoric rise to the top of the depth chart: He made the A Squad during spring practice a few months later, and supplanted Bill Rowe as the starting left guard after Army's opening 42–0 victory over Nebraska in the fall of '57.

The son of Austrian immigrants, Novogratz grew up in eastern Pennsylvania's Lehigh Valley in the mill town of Northampton, home of the Universal Atlas Cement Company. His father, Frank, was a gruff, taciturn laborer for Universal who spent his days filling bags of cement in the mill's pack house, and when Bob was a boy, Frank would arrive home after work covered in the gray dust that hung in the air at the place. Frank Novogratz, with his thick Austrian accent, was a passionate believer in the American ideal, and along with his wife, Stella, he raised six children to trust in the virtues of hard work and representative democracy. He had been a loyal member of the local chapter of the Democratic Party since the early years of the Depression, when, to earn extra money, he had driven voters to the polls in his Essex Super Six sedan—a car he had bought with money saved from his very first Universal paychecks. Bob worked throughout his childhood and held down three jobs when he was in high school, delivering newspapers in the morning, shining shoes for a local cobbler in the afternoon, and setting up pins in the evening at the bowling alley attached to the Liederkranz, Northampton's bustling German social club. During the summer, he earned extra money delivering ice.

Novogratz desperately wanted to go to college—a goal that was also important to Frank—but he needed a scholarship in order to afford school. As a skinny, undersized defensive end at Northampton High, he had not been recruited to play college football. But he loved the game, and with his eyes on earning his way into a top-flight university, he set his sights on Blair Academy, a prep school in northwestern New Jersey. Two of Bob's older brothers had been good high school players, and two of his cousins who had spent a year at Blair had ultimately earned football scholarships to Virginia. Novogratz worked as a day laborer on the Northampton and Bath Railroad the summer after his high school graduation and scraped together about $3,500, enough to cover most of his tuition. The school also provided him with a small financial aid package when he was admitted in the fall of 1954.

That year at Blair turned out to be everything Novogratz had hoped for. Playing offensive tackle for coach Steve Koch, he put forty pounds on his skinny frame. He also hit the books, and by the spring had scholarship offers from Penn and Virginia. But Frank, through his political contacts, had secured an appointment to West

Point for his son.* Bob had not been recruited to play football at the academy, and the appointment was a surprise to him. "My father had a real cement worker's mentality," says Novogratz. "He was not a very communicative guy, but I knew this was a very big thing to him. Not until later in life did it really occur to me why that was: He was an immigrant, he worked in the mill, and this was an important opportunity for me from his perspective. Him getting my appointment to West Point was probably his proudest achievement."

Novogratz had wrestled for the first time at Blair, where he found that his long arms and powerful upper body made him a natural grappler. But two surgeries on his right knee in his first eighteen months as a cadet had interrupted his mat career—his orthopedic surgeon, Lieutenant Colonel Robert W. Parvin, was known at the academy as "Carvin' Parvin" for the frequency with which he put cadets under the knife. Novogratz enjoyed wrestling, but he loved football more than anything else, and he jumped at the opportunity when Lauterbur offered him a chance to try out for the team. He earned All-East honors in 1957, but a right ankle sprain had hampered him during the bitter loss to Navy at the end of the season. In addition to being one of the strongest players on the team, Novogratz was an anaerobic marvel and rarely failed to give Blaik more than fifty minutes a game. He had played fifty-six against Notre Dame in an eighteen-tackle performance that Army would likely need him to duplicate against Pitt.

The sense had been growing that something special was happening at West Point—an awareness that Red Blaik and his boys, and especially their mysterious offense, were creating a unique legacy. By the time Army beat Virginia, Stanley Woodward, the man who had named the Lonely End, had already taken to the pages of the *Newark Star-Ledger* to denounce what he saw as the corruption of his creation.

---

* Frank's contact was Earl Gachenbach, the warden at the Northampton County Prison. Gachenbach obtained Bob's appointment from his congressman, Francis Walter.

Sports Illustrated had called Carpenter "Lonesome George" after the Penn State game, and many newspapermen had begun to refer to Blaik's far flanker as the "Lonesome End." In response, Woodward pleaded, "Though we don't get full backing from *Webster's Un-abridged,* we assume that 'lonely' indicates a proud, self-confident solitary state while 'lonesome' suggests self-imposed and mawkish isolation. To back up this view we cite a couple of quotations from literature: 'The ship, a fragment detached from the earth, went on lonely and swift like a small planet'—Joseph Conrad. 'Be good and you will be lonesome'—Mark Twain." Blaik, for his part, sided firmly with Woodward, disparaging the alternate labels as "come-lately mis-nomers" and insisting that "lonely" implied "a dignified stoicism."*

The Cadets had maintained their hold on the number-one rank-ing in the Associated Press poll after their win over Virginia, leading second-ranked Ohio State, LSU, Texas, and 1957 national cham-pion Auburn. Army was no longer a fluky surprise team but was instead punching with the heaviest hitters in college football. And as long as the Cadets remained undefeated, they were a target for every team left on the schedule—a daunting prospect with less than half the season gone and tough road games remaining against Rice, Navy, and, in less than a week, Pittsburgh. As if to drive that point home, some students at Pitt singled West Point out for an ambitious prank that would move the game between the two schools, briefly, from the sports pages to the front pages of newspapers around the country.

Two weeks before the teams were to meet, at about the same time Army had reached number one with its victory over Notre Dame, a handful of Pittsburgh fraternity brothers met for lunch at their usual campus hangout, a restaurant located on the ground floor of the school's massive Cathedral of Learning, a forty-two-story minaret in

---

* For what it's worth, Carpenter, who was never anything less than the epitome of digni-fied stoicism on the field, has always preferred "the Lonesome End." As do, apparently, most of the Army players and coaches—almost all of them used the term repeatedly dur-ing interviews for this book.

the geographic center of campus. It was there that Bruce Coine, Herbie Dodell, Manny Gabler, Mike Gerber, and Harvey Wimmer—all sophomore members of Pi Lambda Phi eager to write their names into frat-house lore—hatched a plan to steal the Army mule. Picked as the Army mascot to counter Navy's goat, mules had been on the sidelines at West Point since 1899, when they were still widely used in the service as beasts of burden, hauling everything from ammunition to military ambulances. "Navy tried to steal the mule every year," says Wimmer. "We thought it would be possible to go up to West Point and be successful." Wimmer, the only one of the five with a car, would drive the group to New York, where they planned to rent a U-Haul trailer and use the Yonkers home of Dodell's parents as their base of operations.

But the group needed a man with inside knowledge of the academy, somebody who knew the location of the mule stables and the quickest route into and out of the post. For this job, the boys recruited a sixth member named Paul Knaus, a junior who had left West Point at the end of his plebe year in 1956. Knaus, a member of Sigma Chi who was known to one and all at Pitt as Knobby Knaus, had been able to tell his fellow ring members that a tall cyclone fence surrounded the mule pens at the academy, and Wimmer, whose family was in the scrap metal business in Pittsburgh, secured a pair of wire cutters. The group left town on the Monday morning before the game, making the nearly four-hundred-mile journey to Yonkers in Wimmer's white 1958 Pontiac Bonneville convertible. It was a gorgeous machine, but it was hardly inconspicuous. The car measured over nineteen feet long fender to fender, and came equipped with a 370-cubic-inch V-8 engine, four headlamps on the front end, and a pair of slick fender skirts over the rear wheels.

When the brothers from Pi Lambda Phi had conceived their caper, the Panthers were coming off a bitter 22–8 loss to ninth-ranked Michigan State. Pittsburgh had entered the game unbeaten and ranked tenth, but the loss sent them plummeting out of the top twenty. A 15–8 win the next week over rival West Virginia improved the Panthers' record to 4–1 heading into the Army game. Coach John

Michelosen, whose teams were typically big and physical, if not altogether fast, usually favored a Power T formation. But in an opening-day 27–6 beatdown of UCLA in Los Angeles, Pitt had begun the game in a pro-style spread, with a balanced line and an end split seven to eight yards wide. It was a formation that made it easier for the Panthers' quarterbacks to throw the ball, and the final touchdown of the game had come on a fourth-quarter pass to a hulking sophomore tight end named Mike Ditka. Against West Virginia on October 18, Michelosen had added another wrinkle by introducing a no-huddle scheme he had dubbed the Panic T. Pittsburgh had beaten Army twice in three meetings since 1952, and with Michelosen's creative coaching complementing a deep, physical roster, the Panthers would be a major test for Blaik's team.

Such concerns were of only passing interest to the aspiring Pittsburgh mule thieves, whose lives had been overtaken by concerns more immediate than football. With Wimmer at the wheel, they rolled north through Westchester County early on Tuesday, October 21, and crossed the Hudson River via the sweeping expanse of the Tappan Zee Bridge before heading north on the Palisades Parkway. They pulled into the still-sleeping town of Highland Falls sometime before dawn and entered West Point through the post's south gate, about a quarter mile south of the squat redbrick barn in which the mules were stabled. Wimmer parked outside the mule pens and, using his wire cutters, snipped a hole in the links of the fence.

Things quickly began to go awry. Once inside the stables, Knaus found three mules, not just one, and he had no idea which was the right animal. Outside, Wimmer and Dodell—figuring that a non-military car parked outside the barn so early in the morning might arouse suspicion—had departed. The plan was for them to drive into Highland Falls and rent a U-Haul horse trailer, while those inside the stable would lead the mule on foot to a wooded area in Highland Falls along the Hudson River, where the two groups would reunite. But shortly after Knaus and his friends had made off with the placid, sleepy mule, a passing soldier had spotted the hole in the fence outside the barn and called the military police. At about the same time, an early-rising town resident had seen the mule being led down a side street and promptly notified police. As Wimmer and Dodell drove through Highland Falls, a fleet of police cars sped past them toward the academy.

Within minutes, some of those same police cars reappeared in Wimmer's rearview mirror. Panicked, he turned off the road, pulled in behind a café, and shut off his lights. The maneuver did not fool police, who easily spotted Wimmer's gleaming white Pontiac and arrested the boys after a brief and evasive interview. Academy officials waited until all six ring members were in custody and the mule was returned to its home before notifying the New York press, including *Look* and *Life* magazines and *The New York Times*. The story quickly made national news, which reported that the thieves had not actually absconded with the Army mule—they had instead grabbed a small burro in its dotage that had been retired after the 1957 season, an animal named Pancho.*

Released by the military police later that day, the boys drove straight back to Pittsburgh. On Friday, Wimmer received a message directing him to report to the office of Edward Litchfield, the chancellor of the university. Wimmer was certain that he was about to be expelled from school. But Litchfield surprised him by shaking his hand and saying that he wanted to cover the expenses for the excursion out of his own pocket. As he handed the cash to a stunned Wimmer, Litchfield said, "That was the best advertisement Pitt has had for an awful long time."

Sports Illustrated described the upcoming game between Pittsburgh and Army as a battle for "eastern supremacy." The Panthers were deep at almost every position, especially at end, where Michelosen and his assistants felt comfortable using up to seven different players. Pitt also had three capable quarterbacks in starter Ivan Toncic and backups

---

* Pancho, or Skippy, as she was also known, was presented to the academy in 1939 by Ecuador's ambassador to the United States, Colon Alfaro, who had two sons in that year's graduating class. Pancho was the second official mascot in West Point history, following the original Army mule, Mr. Jackson, who served from 1936 to 1948. Before 1936, mules were picked at random to roam the sidelines, usually from local stables.

Bill Kaliden and Ed Sharockman. A few days before the game, Panthers assistant Walt Cummins had told reporters that, because most of Army's first-teamers had played at least forty-five minutes against Notre Dame, he didn't believe Blaik had much confidence in his second string. When a Pittsburgh writer asked whether Michelosen and his staff thought that the Cadets might be susceptible to the pass—they had, after all, allowed Virginia quarterback Reece Whitley to complete eighteen of his thirty-three passes in the previous game—the coach was noncommittal. Oddsmakers had installed Army as a seven-point favorite, but Blaik made no secret of his concerns the week before the game. "At full strength, I think we could take them," he told reporters. "Now I can only hope."

Walt Cummins had been spot on in his evaluation of the amount of faith Blaik had in the Cadets' second string. Army's most oft-used reserves were Jack Morrison—the senior backup at tight end to Don Usry—and Glen Adams, the quarterback who replaced Joe Caldwell when Army was playing defense. But Blaik depended on the rest of his substitutes for at least a few valuable minutes every game. Now he would be leaning on two of them, sophomore fullback Don Bonko and junior halfback Steve Waldrop, to play major roles in the offensive backfield. Between the two, Waldrop certainly had the most talent. A record-setting sprinter at Central High in Jackson, Mississippi, he had played freshman football at Mississippi State in 1955 for head coach Darrell Royal and had far better football credentials than Pete Dawkins, for whom he was the backup. But where Dawkins's success was a function of desire, of application and hard work, Waldrop's failure to crack the starting lineup seemed to Blaik the result of a lack of drive. For his part, Waldrop thought that the reason he was a second-stringer was obvious. "Coach Blaik *loved* Pete Dawkins," he says. Waldrop, almost alone among his teammates today, draws little inspiration from Blaik, whom he remembers as a man who "knew your number but didn't know your name."

Waldrop had played in high school for Doss Fulton, a single-wing guru who bore more of a resemblance to the nebbishy title character from the 1950s sitcom *Mister Peepers* than he did to a football coach. "Fulton had never played football, and he was always really fair with everybody," says Waldrop. "He listened." Playing for Fulton had been fun, but playing for Red Blaik, in Waldrop's estimation, was like being sentenced to hard labor. And he used to roll his eyes whenever Blaik would compare football to combat. "He had that big picture of MacArthur above his desk," says Waldrop. "He saw himself as the Douglas MacArthur of the gridiron. But I never saw football as going into battle."

Waldrop was also put off by Blaik's imperiousness. When Waldrop had landed in the hospital after suffering an injury at practice one day during his sophomore year, his parents called Blaik at home to find out if their son was all right. Before Waldrop's first practice following his discharge from the hospital, Blaik had confronted him in the locker room and, in front of the entire varsity team, told him angrily, "Waldrop, you tell your parents never to call me at home again." Fifty years later, Waldrop remains bitter about the confrontation with his coach, saying simply, "He was a prima donna."

On Friday, October 24, the Cadets had a short walk-through of their game plan at Pitt Stadium, a massive bowl just off the Pittsburgh campus. Of immediate concern to Blaik was the condition of the field. The Panthers shared the stadium with the Pittsburgh Steelers, who had moved from their old home at Forbes Field after the 1957 season, and the venue had hosted a game every weekend in October. Where the turf had not been churned loose, it was worn down to dirt. The overnight forecast called for rain, and Blaik worried about the possible impact of a muddy, sloppy field on his team, which relied so heavily on its superior speed and quickness—qualities that had already been compromised by the injuries to Dawkins and Walters. Army had beaten South Carolina in the rain, but that game had been played on a Michie Stadium field that was in pristine condition and that had been covered with a tarp until just before game time. If Pitt was looking to slow his team down, could Blaik be so sure that the Panthers' athletic department would take similar precautions?

At two o'clock on Saturday morning, Red Blaik awoke to the sound of heavy rain against the window of his suburban hotel room.

He immediately picked up his phone and dialed the room of head manager John Bryer. Typically when Bryer's phone rang, it was for one of the players—he was the only person that Blaik allowed to receive telephone calls when the team was on the road. Usually, Bryer took messages from family members or friends of players. Occasionally, there were inquiries from amorous female callers who were eager to meet a West Point football player. Already that night, Bryer, a senior, had fielded an unusually large number of requests from young ladies who wanted to speak to Pete Dawkins, whose notoriety had increased exponentially after *Life* magazine profiled him on the eve of the Army–Notre Dame game. Propping himself up on his elbow, Bryer lifted the receiver of his phone and mumbled a sleepy and slightly perturbed, "Hello."

He sat up straight at the sound of Blaik's voice. "Bryer, make sure there's a tarp on the field." Bryer responded with a sharp, "Yes, sir"—the only acceptable answer to a command from Blaik—then hung up the phone. He was used to dealing with the sometimes odd and difficult demands of his job. One of the head manager's unofficial duties on the road was to field the Saturday morning phone calls from Merle Blaik, who would always ask how her husband was doing and if he was taking his daily vitamins and medication. Says Bryer today, "There was no way in hell I was going to remind the Colonel to take his pills." Rather than lie to Mrs. Blaik, he enlisted the help of Dr. Parvin, who traveled with the team, to check up on the Colonel. But in the matter of the tarp, Carvin' Parvin could be of no help to him, and Bryer wasn't sure how he was going to be able to fulfill Blaik's request. Pitt Stadium was more than twenty miles away.

Bryer phoned Roy Cooper, Blaik's longtime equipment manager, who traveled separately from the team and stayed in a hotel closer to the stadium. Cooper agreed to check the field, dressed quickly, and called for a cab. It was still raining when he arrived at Pitt Stadium, where the entrance gates were barred by a padlocked, twelve-foot-high chain-link fence. With the cab waiting for him outside the stadium tunnel, he scaled the fence and walked down to field level, where he found the turf exposed to the elements. By the time a dripping-wet Cooper got back to his hotel and called Colonel Blaik, it was three thirty. The Army coach nevertheless immediately telephoned the Pittsburgh athletic director, Tom Hamilton. A halfback at Navy in the twenties, Hamilton had returned to Annapolis as the head football coach from 1934 through 1936 and again in 1946 and '47. In his only two meetings on the field with Red Blaik, Hamilton had been beaten by a combined score of 42–18. Now Blaik was livid, and as he raged over the phone Hamilton assured him that the missing tarp was a mistake, that he didn't see how such an error could have been made, and that he would take care of the problem right away.

Nobody from West Point's traveling contingent returned to Pitt Stadium to see if Hamilton had followed through on his promise, but the answer seemed apparent when Army took the field to warm up. The conditions were so sloppy, and the footing so poor, that the Cadets lost a third player to injury in the moments before kickoff: Reserve tackle Bill Yost, a third classman, suffered a badly sprained ankle during pregame drills. In the locker room, Frank Lauterbur sidled up to Monk Hilliard, the inside tackle on Army's unbalanced offensive line. Yost was Hilliard's backup, and Lauterbur said, "You're probably going to have to play the whole game. Can you do it?" The way Hilliard saw it, there wasn't much choice.

Hilliard played all sixty minutes that day, every one of them a soggy, slippery, punishing ordeal. Despite intermittent showers, warmer temperatures in the upper forties had encouraged a crowd of more than fifty thousand to show up, while millions more tuned in on NBC, which broadcast the game throughout the East. The Cadets' offense started rolling early, driving all the way to the Pitt 15-yard line on its first possession of the game before stalling and turning the ball over on downs. Army got the ball back in the final minutes of the first quarter, and Caldwell hit Carpenter for twenty yards down the right sideline to the Panthers' 30-yard line. As time in the quarter ran out, Waldrop—a right-hander—took a pitch to the left and completed a downfield toss to Anderson, who took the ball to the Panthers' 6. On the second play of the next quarter, Waldrop took another pitch left and, sprung free by a lead block from Don Bonko, outsprinted two Pitt linebackers to the end zone.

Later in the second quarter, with Army leading 7–0, Waldrop came through again, intercepting a pass from Pitt halfback Dick Haley and returning it down the sideline to the Panthers' 24-yard line. A penalty pushed Army back to the 34, but on first-and-twenty, Waldrop caught a quick pass from Caldwell that moved the ball to the 22. Two plays later, he took a pitch around the left side down to Pitt's 7-yard line. On the next play, Caldwell faked a handoff up the middle to Waldrop and pitched to Anderson, who was sprinting to his right. Throwing off his back foot, Anderson lobbed the ball to Don Usry in the back of the end zone for the Cadets' second touchdown of the second quarter. The scoreboard read 14–0, and Army seemed to have the game in hand.

But the Cadets were hardly dominating play, and Pittsburgh's physical style was starting to take a toll. Bob Anderson had gotten his helmet knocked askew attempting to lay a block on Mike Ditka in the first quarter. "He hits me with a forearm and my chinstrap pops off," says Anderson. "He broke my nose *and* he made the tackle. And as I'm lying there on the ground in pain, I hear this voice over me, 'Hey, kid'—I'm a junior and he's a sophomore and he's calling *me* 'kid'—and he says to me, 'Here's your chinstrap, kid.'"

Even down by two touchdowns, the deep and physical Panthers were a dangerous team. Contrary to Michelosen's caginess before the game, the Panthers showed early that they intended to beat Army with the pass, and with two minutes left in the first half, that's exactly what they did. After Joe Caldwell punted the ball out of bounds at the Panthers' 13-yard line, Blaik—desperate to get his first-teamers a rest with his opponent pinned deep in its own territory—inserted several of his reserves along the defensive line and at linebacker, leaving starters only in the secondary. On first down, halfback Curt Plowman ripped off right tackle for six yards. On the next play, quarterback Bill Kaliden rolled right, pump-faked, and, with second-string tackle LeRoy Greene closing in from his blind side, launched a pass downfield. The ball floated nose-up for over thirty yards before settling in the arms of Ditka, who was dragged down from behind by Waldrop at the Army 45. Plowman carried for two more yards on first down. Only sixty-two seconds remained in the half. In the words of *The New York Times*'s Joseph M. Sheehan, "The situation screamed 'pass.'"

Years later, Blaik would confide to Harry Walters that he had never seen himself as a good sideline coach. There's a logic to this assessment: Blaik's entire coaching philosophy was based on controlling variables and forcing his players to forget the tactics of the sandlot. If a play was run to perfection every time, success would follow as a matter of course. He drilled all of his plays relentlessly and won most of his games before Army ever took the field on Saturday.

But Blaik got fidgety against Pittsburgh and let the Panthers back into the game with a calamitous decision. Watching from the press box, Tom Harp had called down to the sidelines after Kaliden's completion to Ditka and implored Blaik to insert Pete Dawkins into the game at safety in place of Waldrop, who had been beaten by Ditka on the play. It was an exceedingly odd call to make; Harp was the offensive backfield coach, and Dale Hall had thus far in the season done excellent work with the defensive secondary. But Harp worried that Waldrop's lack of game experience might leave Army exposed to another long pass—never mind that Waldrop had so far played superbly. Dawkins had also been agitating to get into the game. "I was very analytic about it," he says. "I remember the conversation—the stupid conversation. I said, 'Look, Steve hasn't played defense in games, yet. And the only way Pittsburgh can hurt us is a long touchdown pass. Put me in. I'll lay back twenty yards to make sure they don't score a touchdown.' Blaik was very reluctant to put me in, for good reasons. But I was pretty adamant about it."

Blaik finally relented. The Army coaches recalled a baffled Waldrop to the bench and sent Dawkins, with his pristine white jersey, into the game. He cut a dangerously conspicuous figure in Army's otherwise muddy secondary, and Bill Kaliden spotted him immediately. After taking the snap from center, he dropped back five steps, then backpedaled a few more yards and unloaded a deep pass down the middle of the field. Left halfback John Flara, who had lined up as a wingback, was running a fly route between the hash marks, and he split the two deep defenders—Glen Adams to his left and Dawkins to his right—as he raced toward the end zone. In the parlance of defensive football, Dawkins was the free safety on this play. The one man, in other words, who was not supposed to get beaten deep. "I knew exactly what they were going to do, and I laid back," says Dawkins. "This guy ran, and I said, 'I'll just move along.' And I literally could not accelerate. My legs just had no strength in them. It was like a slow motion nightmare." Flara caught the pass on a dead run, hauling it in at the 7, three yards in front of both Dawkins and Adams. Army's commanding lead had been cut to eight points.

Pitt went for the two-point conversion, but Kaliden's pass into the end zone fell incomplete. It hardly mattered. As the two teams headed for their locker rooms, the Panthers had all the momentum. To make matters worse, Army guard Al Vanderbush, who played on the strong side in the Cadets' unbalanced line and at linebacker on defense, was out of the game with a concussion. He had intercepted a pass from Kaliden in the first quarter, only to get knocked cold during the return on a blindside hit from Pitt tackle John Guzik. Senior Charlie Lytle was a more than capable replacement for Vanderbush—the first classman had actually held the starting job in the spring until he dislocated an elbow, giving Vanderbush an opportunity to impress the coaches—but Blaik's depth chart was now dangerously shallow. The Panthers had so far played their first and second teams on an almost equal-time basis and had been rotating as many as three players at some positions.

Army spent the second half just hanging on. Pitt, fully in command of events now, seemed to come at the Cadets in waves. Behind quarterback Ivan Toncic, the Panthers mounted a drive on their first possession of the third quarter. On a nifty, bang-bang double reverse—a play that exploited the tendency of Army's aggressive defense to overpursue—right halfback Joe Scisly spurted over left tackle for twenty-one yards to the Cadets' 39. With the home crowd in full cry, Toncic dropped straight back, drifted to his left, and lofted a long pass down the left sideline to Dick Haley, who jumped to bring it down at the 11-yard line. On third down from the 7, Toncic again went back to pass. With Bill Carpenter bearing down on him from the left, he threw off his back foot past Carpenter and over the outstretched arms of a leaping Bill Rowe. In the end zone, Panthers end Jim Zanos was cutting toward the sideline in front of Glen Adams. The ball came in chest-high and slightly behind Zanos, who tried to stop and wound up catching it as he fell backward to the ground. The touchdown cut Army's lead to 14–12, and the Panthers once again went for the two-point conversion. Toncic dropped back, then turned and completed a shovel pass to Haley, who was cutting toward the line just in front of him. Haley crashed into the end zone over the right side and the game was tied, 14–14.

Though Pittsburgh's passing attack kept the Cadets off balance all afternoon, the Panthers' chance for an upset was scuttled by several untimely pass interference penalties. And their run-first offense's inexperience with throwing the ball turned their attack into a boom-or-bust enterprise. Besides the interceptions by Waldrop and Vander-bush in the first half, Army's defense forced two more turnovers in the game's final thirty minutes. The last came late in the third quarter, with Pitt at the Cadets' 24-yard line, when Bill Carpenter stepped in front of a pass from Kaliden.

The Cadets mounted one final long drive in the fourth quarter, taking the ball all the way to the Pittsburgh 5-yard line. But here again, Blaik's sideline decision-making cost his team a chance at victory. On fourth-and-two from just inside the 5, he called time out and discussed with his coaches whether or not to kick a field goal. Harry Walters, whose ankle sprain did not prevent him from performing his placekicking duties, had already booted two extra points from almost the same distance, and he was pleading with Blaik to let him kick. "I was standing next to Blaik, looking at him mournfully," says Walters. But Blaik—with his fullback's injury, with the condition of the field, and with his feeling that Army would need at least a touchdown to win the game—chose to go for the first down. He sent Bob Anderson up the middle, but the halfback was stuffed for no gain. The Cadets held on to preserve the 14–14 tie, but with all the mistakes and missed chances, the game felt uncomfortably close to a defeat.

Anderson, who picked up forty-two yards on eleven carries, finished the day as Army's top rusher. Pitt outgained the Cadets' high-powered attack—which began the afternoon leading the country with an average of over 440 yards per game—by nearly 150 yards, and the Panthers' quarterbacks outpassed their Army counterparts 187 yards to 61. Among the few bright spots for the Cadets was Bob Novogratz, who, as expected, bolstered the defense with another eighteen-tackle performance, matching his total at Notre Dame. Blaik's team had also, for the first time all season, not fumbled the ball once. That alone had not been enough to earn the Cadets a victory, but on an afternoon that saw them pushed all over the field, it may have helped to save them from defeat. Their linemen were spent. Hilliard collapsed in the end zone as he was walking off the field toward the locker room. "I lost fifteen pounds that day," he says. Peeling off their muddy uniforms in the dank, steamy locker room, the players said little to each other. Some, including Hilliard, had family and friends waiting outside. But most were headed back to the hotel to brood. "My remembrance of the locker room," says Dawkins, "was that we were lucky. That could have been a lot worse."

The nonvictory put Army's number-one ranking in jeopardy. Number-two Ohio State had tied Wisconsin 7–7 that same afternoon, but number-three LSU had squeaked out a 10–7 win over Florida to improve its record to 6–0, and seventh-ranked Iowa, led by senior quarterback Randy Duncan, had outscored coach Ara Parseghian's scrappy Northwestern team to move to 4–0–1. The only blemish on the Hawkeyes' record had been an early-season 13–13 tie against Air Force, which was playing just its third season of varsity football. The Falcons, led by standout tackle Brock Strom, might have been the country's most surprising team, having jumped out to a 4–0–1 start following their 16–14 defeat of Utah on October 25. The fledgling academy had not yet begun its annual series with both

Army and Navy, but the Falcons were due to meet the Cadets for the first time in 1959.*

Blaik's shorthanded team earned respect for playing a very tough and deep Panthers club to a stalemate on the road in horrible conditions, but the voters for the Associated Press poll could not discount how thoroughly Army had been outplayed. On the Tuesday after the game, the AP's new rankings elevated LSU to number one, followed by Iowa at number two. Army dropped to number three. The Cadets' reign at number one had lasted only two weeks. They were still in the hunt for the national championship, but there could be no more slipups.

---

* Air Force would not play Army again until 1963 and had to wait until 1966 to meet the Midshipmen on the fields of friendly strife. The three teams did not begin their annual round-robin rivalry until 1972.

Chapter 9

THE CRUCIBLE

ON SUNDAY, OCTOBER 26, Red Blaik and his team returned to West Point battered and exhausted. The Cadets' nine-game season was now a little more than half over and the physical toll had begun to add up, especially along the offensive line: Tackle Monk Hilliard was still wobbly one day after he had collapsed on the field at the end of the tie with Pitt; so was guard Al Vanderbush, who had suffered a concussion while returning an interception in the first half; and center Bill Rowe had begun to struggle with an inflamed rotator cuff, which prevented him from raising his right arm over his head or out to the side. "Bill Rowe was one tough kid," says Bill Gunlock. "His shoulder had atrophied down to about half the size of the left one, but he never said a word to anybody."* Blaik held all three linemen out of contact drills during that week's practice. Fortunately, both Pete Dawkins and Harry Walters, who had missed the worst of the muddy struggle in Pittsburgh, seemed to be on the mend. Dawkins returned to practice on Wednesday, and Walters, whose ankle sprain had been more serious than Dawkins's deep thigh bruise, was also making progress.

---

* Says Rowe of the injury, "I could move it behind me just fine, which as a center was really all I needed to do."

The week was an ideal time for Blaik to give his players a breather. Army's next opponent was Colgate, who had beaten the Cadets just twice in sixteen tries, the last time in 1936. So far in 1958, the Raiders had won just once in five games—a 7–0 victory over lower-division patsy Bucknell—and been outscored 88–27 by the unimposing quartet of Cornell, Rutgers, Princeton, and Yale. The only drawback to the game from Blaik's perspective was that his team would have to play it at all. Army's opponent on November 8, Rice University, would have the Saturday off, and so would have an extra week to prepare for the Black Knights' visit to Houston. The Lonely End scheme had so far protected Army from devastating injuries, but the Owls would be the Cadets' third tough opponent in a five-week stretch. Rice was a big, rugged Southwest Conference (SWC) outfit and was coming off an impressive 34–7 thumping of fourth-ranked Texas on October 25. In order to be ready for the Owls, Blaik's team needed an easy victory over Colgate that would allow the first-stringers to rest for long stretches.

On November 1, the Raiders did their best to cooperate. With President Dwight Eisenhower in the stands as part of a sellout crowd, Army galloped over Colgate 68–6. The Cadets led 19–0 at the end of the first quarter and held the Raiders to two first downs in the first half, at the end of which they led 41–0. In just two quarters of work, Bob Anderson carried thirteen times for seventy-six yards, ran for two touchdowns, and caught a two-point conversion pass. Dawkins made just one catch all afternoon, but it had been good for a seventy-four-yard score. With victory more or less assured by halftime, Blaik benched his starters for the game's final thirty minutes and played every man on his bench, including sophomore guard Jim Miller, who, according to the Associated Press, wasn't even listed in the program.

The Colgate game had been played under sunny skies, but when the Cadets returned to practice the following Monday, the weather was overcast and temperatures had dropped from the upper fifties into the forties. Conditions in Houston, meanwhile, were in the balmy upper sixties, with even warmer weather forecast for the weekend. To prepare his team to play in the heat, Blaik moved practice indoors to the field house, where the coach kept the thermostat cranked up above eighty degrees. He also, to the amusement of his players, ordered everyone to wear long underwear. "I looked at the guys in the locker room," says Al Vanderbush, "and with the white legs of the long underwear coming down below the knees of our football pants, we all looked like sheep or goats, you know, with these skinny white legs—especially Novogratz, who was strong upstairs but had the skinniest pair of legs. The long johns hung all the way to his shoes and just flapped around his ankles."

For the second week in a row, Blaik limited the scrimmage time for all of his starters and held Dawkins and Walters out of contact drills altogether. Both players were going to be available to play against Rice, and the bulk of Blaik's concern had now shifted to quarterback Joe Caldwell, who was in an extended funk. In thirty minutes against Colgate, he had completed just four of his ten throws—his second straight inconsistent game. Against Pitt, Caldwell had connected on only three of eleven passes, with two costly interceptions. Though Blaik noted to MacArthur that Caldwell looked sharp in the Cadets' field-house practice sessions, the coach worried that his quarterback's confidence had slipped.

There were other, more promising signs for Army. Chief among them was the emergence of Don Bonko. The Cadets' backup fullback had carried a team-high fourteen times in the Pittsburgh game and had also made several impressive tackles on defense. A powerful, attacking runner from Lorain, Ohio, Bonko had so impressed Blaik, in fact, that the coach planned to continue to work him into the lineup even after Harry Walters had returned to full health. "Don was one tough guy," says Walters. "And frankly, in some ways, he was a better fullback than I was. He was more of a straight-ahead guy and I had more speed." Bonko was actually the same age as Walters and most of the rest of the first classmen. He had entered Manlius in 1955, in the same class with Bill Carpenter, but the prep school had done little to prepare him for West Point. Carpenter says that Bonko "was at the Dick-and-Jane-Went-Up-the-Hill reading level." At the end of his plebe year at West Point, Bonko had been "turned back," in the parlance of the academy—dismissed from school—for deficiency in English. He had been readmitted in 1957 with the Class of '61. Some of the sting of having to repeat his Fourth Class year was taken away when he was made a "recognized" plebe, meaning he was spared another year of the hazing and hassle endured by new cadets. "Bonko could barely add and subtract and read . . . and he got through West Point," says Carpenter. "He's the gold standard I hold and say, if you want to get through the academy, you can get through."

Blaik knew all about Bonko's struggle with schoolwork because he kept close tabs on the academic performance of his varsity players. Monk Hilliard was on pace to be the lowest-ranked man in the Class of 1959—the "goat" in cadet slang—and since his sophomore year he had been required to visit Blaik's office once a week. Climbing the stairs of the gym's south tower to Blaik's sanctum "was exactly like going to see God," says Hilliard. Once inside the office, with its bright burnt-orange carpet and darkly paneled walls, he would take a seat across the mahogany desk from both Blaik and the enormous portrait of MacArthur that hung behind him. "Maurice," the coach might say, "we've reviewed your grades and you're having trouble in chemistry. Now, what kind of help do you need?"

"The next day in class," says Hilliard, "some instructor would be there and he'd say, 'Stop and see me at your break.' He'd give me some things to review and make sure I covered everything."

Hilliard, who was from Milan, Tennessee, had not come to West Point from a strong school system. Indeed, he had graduated from high school without ever having taken a course in world history, a hole in his curriculum vitae that had forced him to regraduate from Manlius, where world history was a requirement—he is the only member of the 1958 team with two high school diplomas. But Hilliard's struggles at West Point were less a function of his narrow secondary education and more the result of an undiagnosed reading disability. "I never really learned to read," he says. "In first grade, we *did* learn to read, but I never really liked it and so I just never did it that much. I was so slow that in a regular two-hour exam, I never got it finished."*

Seven times during his cadet career, Hilliard had been "turned out" after failing an end-of-semester exam. Three times the turnouts were for English or literature exams—his best grades at West Point almost always came in math courses. Every cadet who was turned out was, after a few days set aside for additional study, given a retest that he had to pass in order to satisfy the course requirement. Cadets who failed retests were dismissed from the academy, so the pressure for the exams was intense. But where the normal test period was two hours, the time allowance for the retest was four, which was a godsend to Hilliard. "I maxed four of the seven turnouts I took," he says. "By the end of my senior year, they were sending guys over to me to tutor and coach them through their turnout exams."

Throughout Hilliard's four years at West Point, his mother received twice-monthly calls during each academic year from Red Blaik, who would let her know how her son was doing. He would also remind her, says Hilliard, that she should "give Maurice all the encouragement you can. He needs it up here." Hilliard did not know about the calls and only learned about them years later from his mother. "That's just the way Colonel Blaik was," he says. "He helped a lot of guys who were having trouble."

Red Blaik never had to worry about Don Usry's schoolwork. The man dubbed by the press the "Friendly End," or sometimes the "Gregarious End," because of his position at the opposite end of the Army line from Bill Carpenter, excelled at the math and engineering courses that made up the core of the curriculum at West Point, and he had entered the 1958 season as a Dean's List student, ranking in the top 15 percent of his class. Usry had been recruited to Texas A&M by Bear Bryant in 1955 and spent one year playing

---

* Hilliard suspects he suffers from dyslexia, but he has never sought help for his reading trouble from doctors. "I still have that problem," he says. "I just have to concentrate really hard when I read."

Red Blaik in his office beneath a portrait of his idol, General Douglas MacArthur, in October 1958. The two men had known each other for nearly forty years, since Blaik's days as a cadet, when MacArthur had been the academy's superintendent. Their personal correspondence centered on war, politics, and, most importantly, Army football. It was MacArthur who convinced Blaik to remain at West Point after the humiliation of the 1951 cheating scandal. *(Courtesy of United States Military Academy)*

Bob Blaik, Army's starting quarterback, and his father during a break in spring practice, March 1951. Within two months, both men would become enmeshed in the cheating scandal that shocked the country and devastated the academy's powerful football team. By the time it was over, thirty-seven varsity football players had been expelled, including Bob Blaik. *(George Silk/Time Life Pictures/Getty Images)*

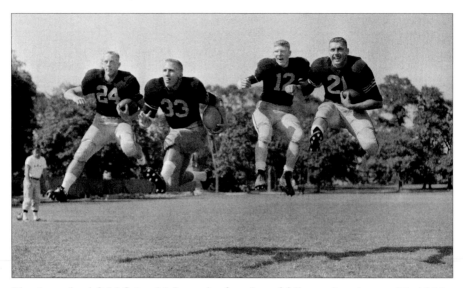

The Army backfield flying high on the first day of fall practice, August 29, 1958. From left to right: halfback Pete Dawkins, fullback Harry Walters, quarterback Joe Caldwell, and halfback Bob Anderson. Of the four, Caldwell was the most inexperienced, having seen action in only one varsity game. *(© Bettman/Corbis)*

Red Blaik poses with his 1958 coaching staff. Back row, left to right: Tom Harp, Blaik, Frank Lauterbur, Dale Hall. Front row, left to right: Chuck Gottfried, Barney Gill, Bill Gunlock. *(Courtesy of United States Military Academy)*

An earlier Army coaching staff, from the mid-1930s—led by Blaik's rival, Gar Davidson (center). Blaik and Davidson had been assistant coaches together at West Point from 1927 until 1932, when Davidson was promoted to head coach. They were reunited in 1956, when Davidson returned to the academy as superintendent, and their enmity bubbled over into a struggle for control of the football program. One of Davidson's assistant coaches, Blackshear "Babe" Bryan (third from left), preceded him as superintendent. *(Courtesy of the Davidson Family)*

After getting a block from Harry Walters (33), Bob Anderson (21) completes his first pass of the year to Pete Dawkins on the halfback option early in the opening quarter of Army's 45-8 blowout of South Carolina on September 27. More than any other play, the halfback option was the bread and butter of the Cadets' offense in 1958. *(© Bettman/Corbis)*

Bill Carpenter (87), stands outside the Black Knights' huddle between plays during the victory over Penn State. Blaik's decision to have his far flanker stand apart at all times was purely utilitarian—he did it to conserve Carpenter's energy—but the mystery of how the "Lonely End" knew what play to run captivated the nation. Carpenter's habit of putting his hands on his hips and affecting a relaxed pose only enhanced his mystique. *(Edward Hausner/*The New York Times/*Redux)*

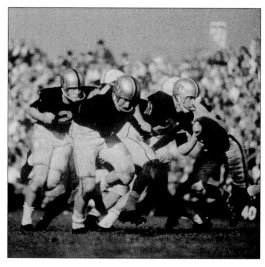

The Army backfield on the move against Penn State. From left to right: Pete Dawkins, Harry Walters, and Bob Anderson. *(Hy Peskin/*Sports Illustrated*)*

Pete Dawkins runs to daylight against Notre Dame. The victory over the Fighting Irish was Army's first in the series since 1945 and elevated the Black Knights to the number-one ranking in the AP college football poll. After the game, Dawkins, who scored Army's final touchdown, was carried off the field on the shoulders of his fellow cadets. *(Francis Miller/Time Life Pictures/Getty Images)*

Guard and linebacker Al Vanderbush (64) returns an interception against Pittsburgh behind the blocking of Bill Carpenter (87) and Bob Novogratz (61). Vanderbush had begun the season as a starter, but he was knocked out cold on this play and never returned to the game. Charlie Lytle replaced him in the starting lineup for the remainder of the season. *(Ed Morgan/Sports Illustrated)*

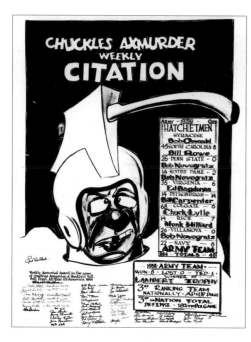

The work of New York illustrator, and Red Blaik confidante, Willard Mullin, the Chuckles Axmurder award was presented weekly to the outstanding defensive player of the previous game. Bob Novogratz, who played guard on offense and linebacker on defense, earned the award three times during the season, more than any other Army player. Blaik referred to Novogratz as, "the sword and flame of a remarkable defensive team." The Cadets' defense allowed two rushing touchdowns all season and gave up just 5.4 points per game. *(Used by Permission from the Estate of Willard Mullin; Shirley Mullin Rhodes)*

Don Usry, Army's "Friendly End." The native Texan was a gifted student and an outstanding football player, but a complicated personality. Off the field, it was Usry, and not Bill Carpenter, who held himself aloof from his teammates. *(© Bettman/Corbis)*

Backup quarterback Glen Adams comes down with a crucial late interception in front of All-America end Buddy Dial during the dramatic victory over Rice. (Houston Chronicle)

Don Usry (89) pulls in a Joe Caldwell pass for a twenty-yard completion in the second quarter against Navy. Usry was open all day against the Midshipmen, and played perhaps the finest game of his career. He caught five passes for eighty yards and returned an interception for the final touchdown of the day in the fourth quarter. (© *Bettman/Corbis*)

Pete Dawkins and LSU halfback Billy Cannon prepare to sample a slice of watermelon at the *Look* magazine All-America dinner, December 5, 1958. In 1959, Cannon would succeed Dawkins as the winner of the Heisman Trophy. (*John Lent/AP Images*)

Army's starting lineup on the field at Philadelphia's Municipal Stadium the day before the game against Navy. Front row, left to right: Bill Carpenter, Monk Hilliard, Charlie Lytle, Bill Rowe, Bob Novogratz, Ed Bagdonas, Don Usry. Back row, left to right: Pete Dawkins, Harry Walters, Joe Caldwell, Bob Anderson. *(Bill Achatz/AP Images)*

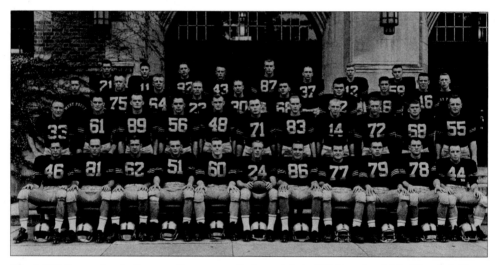

The 1958 Army football team. Front row (left to right): Gil Roesler, HB; Chuck Millick, E; Don Tillar, G; Bill Rowe, C; Charlie Lytle, G; Pete Dawkins, HB; Jack Morrison, E; Monk Hilliard, T; Ed Bagdonas, T; LeRoy Greene, T; Jim Kennedy, HB. Second row (left to right): Harry Walters, FB; Bob Novogratz, G; Don Usry, E; Bob Oswandel, C; Steve Waldrop, HB; J. Scott Brown, T; Russ Waters, E; Bob Rudesill, QB; Gerry Clements, T; Mike Jezior, G; John Corby, C. Third row (left to right): John Bryer, Mgr.; Bill Yost, T; Al Vanderbush, G; Henry Minor, HB; John Eielson, FB; George Joulwan, G; Jim Dougalas, HB; Tom Blanda, QB; Frank Gibson, QB; Tom Munz, Mgr. Back row (left to right): Bob Anderson, HB; Glen Adams, QB; Otto Everbach, E; Roger Zailskas, HB; Bill Carpenter, E; Don Bonko, FB; Joe Caldwell, QB; Dick Buckner, C. *(Courtesy of United States Military Academy)*

freshman ball for the Aggies before transferring to West Point. At six foot three and pushing 215 pounds, he was one of the biggest players on the Cadets' line, with massive hands, good speed, and a demeanor that was, in the words of his backup, Jack Morrison, "all business." Usry was a proud Texan, and contrary to his nickname, he came across to most of his teammates and classmates as aloof, arrogant, and driven to succeed. "Don," says Steve Waldrop, "liked to be right."

Usry had been born to play football. His father, Donald W. Usry, had been a small, wiry high school running back in Midlothian, Texas, in the early 1930s. Donald was so in love with the game that he had broken up with his high school sweetheart because he felt she was too petite to bear him the kind of big, strong boys who could grow into great football players. A few years later, he married Ruth Rogers, whom he prized for her sturdy frame and large hands. Don was born in Midlothian in 1937, and the family, along with Don's older brother, Kenny, moved in with Ruth's parents in the tiny central-Texas town of Venus for the duration of the Depression. During World War II, when Donald and Ruth had moved to Long Beach, California, to build bombers for Douglas Aircraft, both Don and Kenny stayed behind in Venus with Ruth's parents. But when Donald and Ruth returned after the war, hard times followed. The best work Donald could find consisted of knocking around town doing odd jobs, while Ruth worked in the tiny general store owned by her father. The family remained dirt poor until 1952, when Donald moved the household to Cleburne, thirty miles to the west.

Football, and not the prospect of a new job for Donald or Ruth, was what sparked the relocation. Kenny, a senior quarterback, and Don, a rangy freshman end, had led Venus's six-man team to a district championship in 1951, and boosters from the bigger, and more prosperous, town of Cleburne had begun to pay calls on the Usry household soon after. For a poor family, the boosters' pitch had been impossible to resist: Move to Cleburne and receive not only a house to live in, but also jobs and a $125 monthly stipend. Ruth worked in a dress shop. Donald, whose father had owned a movie theater in

Midlothian, was installed as the projectionist at the town cinema. For Don, a gifted student who excelled at mathematics, football was now a job—one that would ensure he could eventually get a college degree. His father devoted himself to his sons' athletic careers, gearing the family's life around making sure his boys were fit to play. Donald went so far as to transform the family dinner table into an athletic training table, with high-protein meals and no sweets, and he was on the sidelines at every Cleburne practice and game throughout Don's high school career. As a senior in the fall of 1954, he caught twenty-one passes for 423 yards and nine touchdowns and was named first team All-State.

When the time came for Don to choose a college, he followed the same utilitarian principles that had brought his family to their new home. In the early spring of 1955, Usry spurned an offer from Doc Blanchard to play at West Point and began telling people he planned to enroll at Southern Methodist University, in Dallas. But in late April, at a track meet on the SMU campus, he met with a recruiter from Texas A&M. Under the bleachers of Owenby Stadium, with his high school sweetheart watching, Usry signed a letter of intent to A&M and accepted a check from the recruiter, who told him he would be paid five hundred dollars per game.* Don liked the idea of entering the military, but West Point had offered him nothing more than admission to the academy and a chance to play football for Red Blaik. Usry had thought that A&M's renowned ROTC program would give him the chance to pursue a military career at the same time he was earning money for playing football. But he quickly grew disillusioned with life as an Aggie. "He thought he would be treated like every other freshman in the ROTC program," said Usry's then-girlfriend Mary Hogan, who had seen him sign with the Aggies. "But he said it was a joke. Since he was a football player, he could get a senior to shine his boots." Usry, who had already passed West Point's entrance examination as a high school senior, left Texas

---

* Coach Bear Bryant's infamous 1955 recruiting class is rife with similar pay-for-play stories. Shortly after Usry signed his letter of intent, the SWC slapped the Aggies with two years of probation.

A&M after one semester and entered the academy with the Class of 1960. There is no evidence that his transfer to Army involved a financial transaction, but after his appointment, his father went to work at the first high-salaried job he'd ever held, as an inspector at the Dallas-based Texas Engineering & Manufacturing Company, which had an aircraft-construction contract with the Department of Defense.

By the time Usry arrived at West Point, he had been playing football as a de facto professional for four years. For him, the game was a vocation, a fact that goes a long way toward explaining an attitude that many of his teammates describe as detached and unemotional. He kept his feelings to himself, which may explain why he was a regular sleepwalker. His West Point roommates grew accustomed to his late-night excursions, when Usry would often jump out of bed and stalk into the hallway, only to return a few minutes later mumbling incoherently about Texas A&M and Bear Bryant. "He probably seemed all business because football *was* business to him," says Usry's son, Don. "And growing up dirt poor I am sure was also a catalyst for his drive."

On the field, Usry was one of Blaik's most polished and dependable players. He was also one of the fastest and most physical members of the Army line. Usry had played more minutes than any other third classman besides Bob Anderson in 1957, starting seven of nine games. And his offensive role had expanded in the new offense. After catching six passes for all of forty-five yards in '57, he had already caught four for forty-nine yards and two touchdowns in '58. He was one of only two players from Texas on the Army roster, and his notoriety as the "Friendly End" made him a focal point for media scrutiny in the buildup to the Rice game—the Cadets' first in the Lone Star State, where expectations were high.

The clash with Army was a high-profile opportunity for Rice—a chance to beat a powerhouse opponent in a game with national rankings on the line. The Owls had opened the season by losing two of their first three games, with the pair of defeats coming courtesy of Purdue, then ranked fourteenth, and LSU, which was now the number-one team in the country. But Rice coach Jess Neely's club had followed up its slow start by beating, in succession, Arkansas, sixteenth-ranked Southern Methodist, and fourth-ranked Texas by the combined score of 71–14. Though the Cadets would be the Owls' third straight ranked opponent, Rice was on a roll, having climbed to thirteenth in the AP poll, and was fresh coming off a bye week. The weather at game time was forecast to be sunny, with temperatures in the upper seventies, and a sellout crowd of close to seventy thousand was expected on homecoming Saturday.

Red Blaik was less concerned with the Owls' momentum and the prospect of a large crowd than he was with the heat. Army's manpower disadvantage, in terms of both the size of its players and the depth of its roster, would be all the more acute if the weather was as hot and humid as Blaik expected it to be. When the Cadets went through a quick run-through at Michie Stadium on Wednesday afternoon, a light snow had been falling, and temperatures had been in the thirties when their TWA charter had departed from Stewart Air Force Base on Thursday, November 6.

The flight to Houston was quiet and uneventful, with most of the players engrossed in their academic studies. On standing orders from Blaik, Monk Hilliard and fellow tackle Ed Bagdonas, who was a strong student, were sitting together going over Hilliard's coursework. If Hilliard had any questions his linemate could not answer, he could always seek help from the team's academic counselor, a young air force officer named Frank Borman, who was assigned to the academy as an instructor in the Department of Engineering. Captain Borman, whose next assignment would be as an astronaut in the Gemini and Apollo space programs, had graduated from West Point in 1950—he had been Blaik's manager as a first classman in 1949, the last time Army had gone undefeated—and he was a constant presence on the sideline at every practice and game.

Upon landing in Houston, the players peered out of the airplane's windows and shielded their eyes against the glare of bright sunlight on concrete. It was seventy degrees. Blaik was standing at the exit as the jetway stairs were wheeled to the plane's side and a stewardess swung the door open. He had been prepared for the weather to be warm, but he was taken aback all the same by the blast of heat that swept over him—a scorching wind whipped up by the propellers of the airplane. "It was like a punch in the face," says John Bryer, who was standing right behind the coach. Blaik turned to him immediately and said, "I want oxygen on the field tomorrow." Bryer turned to Dr. Parvin, who was standing nearby, and in response to the manager's nonplussed expression, the surgeon said he would put in a request with San Antonio's Brooke Army Medical Center once the team reached the hotel.

A small contingent of local press was on hand to meet the plane. As the Cadets stood on the runway, blinking against the sun, a reporter sidled up to Hilliard, who had been the last man down the jetway stairs. "Are there any players still on the plane?" asked the sportswriter.

"No, sir. I'm the last one," said Hilliard.

"Which ones are the linemen?"

"I'm one of the linemen, sir," said Hilliard to the bemused reporter. "In fact, I'm the second-biggest man on the team."

The Cadets' hotel might have provided relief against the heat, but it was hardly of much comfort to Red Blaik's spartan sensibilities. Traveling in unfamiliar environs, far removed from the informal eastern network of suburban country clubs and hotels that he had haunted for more than two decades, Blaik had been coaxed by the Rice athletic department into staying just three miles from downtown Houston at the opulent Shamrock Hotel, a massive eighteen-story monument to excess. The Shamrock had been built less than a decade earlier by wildcatting oilman Glenn McCarthy, the inspiration for the character Jett Rink in the novel *Giant*, by Edna Ferber— who rechristened the hotel the Conquistador in her book. For the Shamrock's grand opening on St. Patrick's Day in 1949, McCarthy had brought in a raft of Hollywood stars, including Errol Flynn and Ginger Rogers. In addition to its eleven hundred air-conditioned guest rooms, the hotel boasted an opulent lobby trimmed in burled mahogany, a grandly manicured garden, and an enormous swimming pool capacious enough to host water-skiing exhibitions. *Time* magazine called the Shamrock "less a hotel than a kind of Versailles," and its interior design was eclectically lurid. The hotel claimed that its motif represented "the best of all periods," but the layout quickly earned the scorn of America's architectural community. Frank Lloyd Wright, who stayed at the Shamrock not long after it opened, once dismissed the lobby's garish ceiling design as "the effect of venereal disease on architecture." Despite its owner's extravagance, the hotel struggled to fill rooms and it quickly became a financial albatross. McCarthy defaulted on his loans in 1952, and Hilton Hotels acquired the property two years later.

The Shamrock nevertheless rolled out a Texas-sized welcome for the Army team. Players were given white cowboy hats at check-in and were invited to a debutante ball at the hotel on Saturday night. "On the top floor, they had a bull staying in its own suite," says Bill Carpenter. "Typical Texas." Adamant about keeping to his routine, Blaik took the players to a movie after their Friday night dinner. His cinematic taste was for Westerns and war films, and the Cadets had grown used to sitting through shoot-'em-ups. But this time, some of the first classmen had suggested the film *Damn Yankees*, a musical retelling of the legend of Faust, set in the world of Major League Baseball and starring Tab Hunter, Ray Walston, and, in a vamping performance as the temptress Lola, Gwen Verdon. To the players' surprise, Blaik agreed—though some speculate today that he may have been duped by the movie's title into thinking it was a war picture.

On the bus after the show, the players were silent with anticipation as Blaik, the last man to board, mounted the steps. He was not known for his sense of humor—or for his taste in show tunes—and nobody was sure how he would respond to being taken to a sex-charged musical comedy. But as Blaik's smiling face appeared above the first row of seats, he began to croon the chorus to Verdon's purring, showstopping song of seduction, "Whatever Lola Wants, Lola Gets." After the laughter died down, Blaik raised his arms and waved his fingers as if he were casting a spell. Then, paraphrasing a line from the movie he said to his players, "I want . . . *touchdowns*."

Red Blaik was clearly having fun—more fun than he'd had coaching football in a long time. He liked this Army team, and it liked him back. He had lately begun to encourage Bill Rowe's motivational schtick on the bus rides to Michie Stadium by asking his center, "What do you see, Rowe?"

"Before '58, I never heard him say a thing on the bus," says Rowe. "He always just sat there. But we joked around with him a lot, which you would *never* do with Colonel Blaik. We used to talk Jake, the bus driver, into taking us past the crowds so we could look at the girls rather than going up the back way to the stadium. We'd say, 'Hey Jake, let's take the scenic route.' So one day Blaik got on the bus and said, 'OK, Jake, take the scenic route.'"

"He used to tell me he ranked us as the smartest team he ever coached," says Harry Walters, who later became close friends with Blaik. "Those offenses on his great teams of the forties were *handoff-handoff-handoff*. We were certainly asked to do more—asked to do things that those teams didn't do. That was his measuring stick."

Saturday morning was warm and humid in Houston, with the city shrouded in a light fog. By kickoff at two o'clock, temperatures had risen to eighty degrees and the fog had been burned off by the warmth of the sun, which beat down with unrelenting severity on the turf at Rice Stadium forty feet below ground level, and shielded from any cooling breezes by the surrounding lower bowl. Blaik described the gametime conditions to MacArthur as a "steaming inferno," before adding, "Two minutes after the game started our team looked like it had been playing for hours." John Bryer and Dr. Parvin had secured a dozen canisters of oxygen from Brooke Army Medical Center, and along with two medics, they stood ready on the sidelines. By the end of the game, every canister would be empty.

The offenses for both teams started slowly. The Owls' defensive line, led by 235-pound senior tackle J. D. Smith, dominated the Army running game.* Blaik had been worried about the readiness of his banged-up offensive line, and the Black Knights' performance

---

* The Owls' other tackle was Don Rather, whose older brother, Dan Rather, was then the news director at KTRH radio in Houston.

in the first quarter, which ended with both teams deadlocked at zero, saw his worst fears realized. Neither Anderson nor Dawkins had any room to run. The Cadets' defense, at least, was holding its own, keyed by the sparkling play of Bob Novogratz and Don Bonko. (Harry Walters had started the game, but his ankle was still not 100 percent, and Blaik tried to rest him when Army was on defense.) From the Monster linebacker position, Bonko showed good instincts and a remarkable knack for breaking into the offensive backfield. The Cadets' aggressive style suited him perfectly. Rice did reach the Army 23-yard line on one early drive, but Bonko and Bill Rowe disrupted a handoff from quarterback Jon Schnable to halfback Larry Dueitt, and Rowe recovered the fumble on the 28.

Early in the second quarter, the Owls finally broke through behind the deft passing of backup quarterback Alvin Hartman, who connected with senior end Buddy Dial on a pair of big plays. From the Rice 44-yard line, Hartman found Dial down the left sideline for an eighteen yard completion to the Cadets' 38. At six-one, 185 pounds, Dial was neither as big nor as fast as Bill Carpenter, but he was a preternaturally gifted receiver, having led the SWC in 1957 with twenty-one catches for 508 yards. A few plays later, from the Army 27, Dial sprinted straight down the center of the field, cutting toward the left corner of the end zone inside the 20. Hartman, after faking a handoff, lofted a beautiful pass toward Dial's outside shoulder. The end had about a step and a half on safety Glen Adams, who had hesitated momentarily when he saw Hartman fake the handoff. Dial leapt into the air to gather the ball in at the 3-yard line. Adams dove desperately as the pass arrived but could only grab at Dial's ankle as the receiver staggered into the end zone. Halfback Bill Bucek kicked the extra point, and Rice led 7–0.

With Army trailing for the first time all season, Joe Caldwell abandoned the running game on the next series, completing six straight throws in the face of a furious pass rush to drive the Cadets from their own 30 down to the Owls' 8-yard line. The Rice ends, copying a tactic used by Pitt to great effect two weeks earlier, were slanting inside on nearly every down in an effort to get into the Army backfield and disrupt both running and passing plays before they had a chance to develop. The ploy had seemed to baffle Caldwell against the Panthers. But he shed his indecision on this drive, getting rid of the ball quickly and accurately—though his receivers saved him on more than one occasion. On third down from the Rice 48, Caldwell threw over the middle to Carpenter, who leapt high in the air to catch the ball in traffic at the Owls' thirty. On the next play, Caldwell threw a short pass to Anderson in the left flat and watched as his halfback cut up the field to the 16. After another completion took the ball to the Rice 8, Caldwell called for the halfback option to the right. Taking the pitch, Anderson rolled toward the sideline as Dial sprinted to cut him off. Harry Walters dove to roll-block Dial, giving Anderson enough time to lob the ball to the back of the end zone where Carpenter was drifting toward the goalpost, covered in front by Bucek and from behind by defensive back Hart Peebles. The pass came in high, and all three players leapt for it. Bucek's momentum, however, carried him back into Peebles, knocking the latter out of the play, and Carpenter, who had an inch or two on both defensive backs, caught the ball cleanly for the touchdown. It was his third reception of the drive. When Walters hit the conversion kick to tie the score 7–7, there were just under seven minutes remaining in the first half.

All this time, Glen Adams had been quietly fuming at the end of the Black Knights' bench. He had done little in the previous week but prepare to face Buddy Dial and defend the very play on which he had been beaten for the first six points of the game. Now he burned with humiliation. Adams was from Texas. His hometown paper, the *El Paso Times,* was on hand to see him play. Defense was his specialty. And when Blaik turned to him after Carpenter's touchdown and said, with a meaningful look, "You think I ought to put you back in there?" he snapped.

"I never would have ordinarily talked back to Colonel Blaik," says Adams, "but I was so mad I looked at him and said, 'Colonel, they pay you to make those decisions. I'm here to play football.'"

Blaik's eyes narrowed and he stared at Adams for a moment before saying, "Get back in there."

The half ended with the two teams still deadlocked at 7–7, but

Blaik was encouraged by the fact that he had been able to give most of his first-teamers a breather late in the second quarter. His linemen certainly needed it. Bill Rowe had wrenched his knee, aggravating an injury that had been bugging him for a few weeks. Monk Hilliard, meanwhile, had been playing most of the afternoon opposite J. D. Smith, who outweighed him by twenty-five pounds. On Army's first running play of the game, an inside handoff to Dawkins, Smith had knocked Hilliard backward into the halfback for a three-yard loss. In the huddle afterward, Dawkins had scolded his tackle for the block, prompting Hilliard to retort, "I'll tell you what, Pete. I'm gonna *stop* him, and you pick which side you want to run around." Hilliard had also taken a knee to the helmet, which left him briefly disoriented. As the Cadets lined up for the next play, Dawkins had had to grab his tackle by the belt to guide him to his position. Inside the Army locker room, trainer Ed Pillings had filled the sinks with crushed ice, and Joe Caldwell cooled off during the halftime break by sinking his head deep into one basin.

The game remained tied through the third quarter. One early Rice drive ended with a fumble, and Caldwell, playing his finest all-around game of the season, snuffed out two more with interceptions of Hartman. Blaik, meanwhile, readied his team for the final fifteen minutes by relieving Caldwell and the rest of his starters just before the end of the third quarter. Army had so far played disciplined football, and the Black Knights' only turnover had come on a fumble in the first half. But with the ball inside Owls territory, backup quarterback Tom Blanda dropped back and looked into the left flat for reserve halfback Gil Roesler. Rice defensive back Gordon Speer, the fastest man on the team and an All-SWC sprinter who had been clocked at 9.7 seconds in the 100-yard dash, stepped in front of the pass and took off down the sideline accompanied by a coterie of blockers. Speer appeared to have a clear path to the end zone, and the sixty-nine thousand inside Rice Stadium rose to their feet with a roar. But reserve Army guard Don Tillar, coming from across the field, had a good angle. The Owls' speedster had outrun his blockers, and Tillar, a six-foot-three senior who had begun the season on the injured list—he'd taken a finger in his right eye during an early

September practice and suffered a scratched cornea—closed the gap with every stride. After a forty-yard chase, Tillar ran Speer out of bounds at the Army 25.

Tillar had been in the game because Bob Novogratz was completely spent. Throughout the second half, Novogratz continually looked to the Army bench, trying to make eye contact with Blaik in the vain hope that the coach would signal him over to the sideline for a breather. But whenever he had been able to get Blaik's attention, the coach had responded by imploring Novogratz to keep fighting. "He'd give me one of these," says Novogratz, holding up a fist and shaking it. "And every time he did that, I just thought, 'Shit.'"

Rice moved to the 21 after Speer's interception, from which point Hartman attempted to reconnect downfield with Dial. Once again, the end sprinted down the middle of the field at Adams, the safety, before breaking toward the left corner of the end zone. But Adams had not bitten on the play-action fake this time. He drifted back and to his right with Dial, and as the ball began to descend, Adams went after it. Hartman had not been as accurate with this pass—the ball, rather than dropping over Dial's outside shoulder, came in slightly behind him. The end and the safety jumped together, but Adams had position, and he caught the ball against his chest at the 5, where Dial dragged him to the ground. The game remained tied at 7-all.

There were more close calls to come for the Black Knights. Late in the fourth quarter, Steve Waldrop, who led the team in rushing on the day with nine carries for forty-six yards, positioned himself deep in Army territory to receive a punt. But he lost track of the yard lines—standing at the Army 10, he instead believed he was at the 5. After retreating a few steps to field the kick from Rice punter Bill Bucek, Waldrop stepped backward over what he thought was the goal line and waited for the referees to blow their whistles and signal for a touchback. But the whistles never came, and he was tackled just short of the Cadets' 5-yard line. The Owls took over at the Army 40 following a Caldwell punt, with the crowd once again in full cry.

Rice mounted its final drive of the game behind quarterback Jon Schnable. On first down, he rolled right and threw to halfback

Sonny Searcy for eight yards. Consecutive gashing runs by Schnable and Speer took the ball eighteen yards down to the 14. Blaik, saving his starters for a final offensive push, kept his second-string defense on the field. The Army reserves gave ground all the way to their own 9-yard line before stiffening. On fourth down with less than two minutes to play, Rice coach Jess Neely decided to attempt a field goal. Schnable, the holder, positioned himself at the fourteen, and Bucek prepared to kick.

The Owls' line was tightly bunched, supported on the wings with blockers stationed behind the outside hips of the ends. The Cadets were in a seven-man front, with linebackers filling the gaps between the guards and tackles. The wing blocker on the left side of the Rice line, fullback Raymond Chilton, was playing directly across from Army end Otto Everbach. Don Bonko positioned himself behind and to the right of the end, slapping Everbach on the outside hip to let him know what direction he planned to go. On the snap, Everbach drove to Chilton's inside, turning him away from Bonko, who was charging around him to the outside and taking dead aim on Schnable and Bucek. The snap to Schnable had been perfect, but Bucek's three-step approach took a beat too long. Bonko leapt into the air with his arms outstretched, and the kick bounced off his right forearm. He sprinted after the bouncing ball, attempting to scoop it up at the Cadets' 24-yard line. But he lost his hold, and Rice downed the play there. The ball belonged to Army. One minute and forty-four seconds remained in the game.

Writing in his autobiography, Red Blaik explained his strategy for his team's final possession:

> *There was no time for a long march. Even if there had been time, we were not up to it physically. If we were to pull it out, we had to do it with a pass play that would go all the way. Everybody in the stadium knew it. There was time for three more plays. The first two would have to be passes. They would serve three purposes. Either could conceivably bring a score. If incomplete, they would stop the clock. Both would set up a third pass.*

Caldwell had thrown the ball sparingly—and not particularly well—since the Cadets' second-quarter touchdown drive. He had, in fact, not completed another pass. But starting in the long shadow cast by the western grandstand, he took the snap, faked a handoff to Bonko, and zipped a pass to Anderson in the left flat. The ball came in low, and Anderson, in one motion, reached down to catch it and spun to the outside, shaking a tackler and breaking into the open field. He sprinted up the left sideline to the 34, but rather than step out of bounds, he cut back to the inside, where Hart Peebles finally corralled him at the 36. The play had taken more than ten seconds off the clock.

Caldwell then tried to hit Pete Dawkins along the right sideline, but Peebles jumped the play and nearly intercepted the ball. When Dawkins returned to the Cadets' backfield, he grabbed Caldwell by the arm. His route on the previous play had sent him into the flat along the right sideline, filling the space behind the Lonely End—in this case Russ Waters, who was in the game for an exhausted Carpenter. Peebles was playing Dawkins to the outside, guarding the sideline to keep him from running out of bounds and stopping the clock. The Owls, having missed their late field-goal attempt, were playing for the tie. Not Dawkins. "By this point, we had a sense of mission about this team, that we could not lose a game," he says. "I wanted to win."

He looked Caldwell in the eye and said, "Joe, this guy is playing me way off my right shoulder, so let's just do a post route off that. You hit me down the middle and we'll score." It was almost exactly the same call Dawkins had made late in the game against Notre Dame, when Caldwell had hit him over the middle for a twenty-three-yard gain that had helped to clinch the victory. Dawkins had, by this point in the season, earned a reputation among his teammates for, as Blaik called it, "his destiny-conscious leadership," and Caldwell quickly assented to the audible. But before the huddle broke, Dawkins addressed his weary teammates: "We've got to give Joe an extra second," he said. "This is it. We can do it. One second."

Sixty-two seconds were left on the clock when Caldwell took the snap from Bill Rowe. Once again he spun and faked a handoff to Bonko. Anderson stayed in the backfield to block, and he absorbed the rush from Don Rather as Caldwell dropped back and drifted to his right. He had more than an extra second to work with, and he planted his feet on the 30 and threw high and long down the middle of the field. Dawkins had feinted to the outside, as if to break toward the sideline again, before cutting back to the inside and dashing upfield. He had a couple of yards on Peebles as he raced under the ball and cradled it into his chest at the Rice 40-yard line. With the ball tucked into the crook of his left arm, Dawkins sprinted away from Peebles on his way to the end zone. But Bill Bucek, who had been covering Waters on his fly route down the sideline, was angling quickly toward Dawkins from the right. At the 15, Bucek dove for the halfback's ankles. His right arm swept down and caught Dawkins on the right heel, knocking him off balance. He staggered, putting down his right arm in an effort to stay up. For an agonizing five yards, Dawkins seemed about to fall, but he never stopped churning his legs. He righted himself just inside the 10 and galloped across the goal line, his head tipped back slightly in exhaustion and exaltation. Flipping the ball behind him as he turned to jog to the Army bench, he was finally caught from behind—in a bear hug from a jubilant Waters.

As the exultant Cadets lined up for the extra point that would make the final score 14–7, Anderson looked across the line of scrimmage at Rice end Gene Jones and flashed a sympathetic smile. "Tough luck," he said. "We got the cheap one that time." The defeat was a bitter pill for the Owls. "Anybody who says we didn't have a better ball club than Army is crazy," Dial said after the game. "We gave the game away. I'm not the type to take anything from a club that beats us—but Army better thank the Lord they won today, because we tore 'em up. Every Southwest Conference line we've played blocked more efficiently than Army's line. But we just don't see many backs like Anderson and Dawkins."

The Owls had been undone by their four turnovers, as well as by Caldwell, who threw for 166 yards. "It was his best day as a passer,"

Blaik told MacArthur. "His throwing arm was completely knotted immediately after the game. He was a pathetically contorted and an exhausted figure."

Rather than fly home that evening, Blaik and the Cadets returned to the Shamrock. The debutante ball would soon be in full swing.

Chapter 10

GOLDEN DAYS

RED BLAIK AND HIS PLAYERS had a few hours following their pulsating victory over Rice to celebrate at the Shamrock Hotel. Nothing serious, of course—there was still a curfew, and the team's return flight to West Point early the next morning. But several players attended the debutante ball that the hotel was hosting, including Bob Anderson and Bill Carpenter, who caught an elevator to the lobby along with three or four teammates. The group had only descended a few floors, however, before the doors slid open to reveal Red Blaik, who was also on his way to the ground floor. The players, who had been chatting casually just a moment before, fell silent. "Normally nobody spoke to the Colonel unless he spoke to us," says Carpenter. Tonight, though, Blaik broke the tension almost immediately by asking one of the players how he was feeling. The coach was smiling, happy, and relaxed. He asked them about their plans for the evening. Would anybody else be joining them? Did they need any extra money? "Before we got down to the lobby, he gave everybody two dollars and said, 'Go have a good time,'" says Carpenter, adding that he and his teammates had been so stunned by the exchange that nobody really considered how exceedingly difficult it would be, even in 1958, to have much of a "good time" on two dollars. "When we got out, we all just looked at each other, and it was like, *Man, that's a first.*"

A celebration was under way at West Point, too. Around two thousand members of the Corps of Cadets had watched the Rice game on a closed-circuit broadcast in the auditorium of one of the academic buildings. The transmission had gone off without a hitch until late in the fourth quarter, as Dawkins raced toward the Owls' goal line with his only reception of the afternoon. The cadets in the theater had risen to their feet and begun to cheer when the screen suddenly went blank—the closed-circuit feed had been lost. The shouts of joy abruptly turned to shrieks of anger and frustration. For seven long minutes, confusion reigned as the cadets, unwilling to leave, waited to watch the rest of a game that had already ended. At last, a young captain burst into the rear of the hall shouting for everybody's attention. The auditorium grew quiet as the officer explained that he had just gotten off the telephone with a friend in Texas who told him that Dawkins had scored and Army had won. The cadets erupted in cheers, none louder than those of the plebes, who after every football victory were given permission to relax, or "given a fallout" in cadet slang. There would be no pulling in of chins and throwing back of shoulders in an exaggerated "brace," no eating meals at silent attention, and, most importantly, no hazing until Monday morning.

The rigors of plebe year were familiar to the men of Army football, who had endured them like everybody else. There was little difference between the life of an Army football player and that of the rest of the Corps of Cadets—their days were ruled by the clock. Every morning, cadets rose at reveille, ten minutes before the first formation of the day at six o'clock, where they stood at attention for a quick head count before returning to the barracks to shower, shave, and dress for breakfast at six-thirty. By seven, they were back in their rooms cleaning up and getting ready for the first class of the day at seven fifty-five. There were two eighty-minute class periods in the morning, with a third eighty-minute period set aside for study. Lunch was at ten minutes after noon, and the first of two hour-long afternoon classes began at one. The final academic period ended at three fifteen, and football players had to be dressed and ready for practice at four, by which time those cadets who were not members of corps-squad teams were participating in either intramural athletics (two days every week) or the daily regimental parades on the Plain that served as close-order drill training—both 1st and 2nd regiments passed in review together on the Saturday mornings before home football games. The day's fourth and final formation was at twenty minutes after six, when the corps marched back to the mess hall for supper. For football players, dinnertime represented their only break of the academic day. To accommodate the end of practice, they were allowed to arrive late for the evening meal, though they still had to be done like everyone else at ten minutes to seven.

"The football team was part of everyone's life, but it didn't intrude on our lives in any way, and there was very little talk about football, from what I can recall," says Peter Stromberg, a classmate and friend of Dawkins's, as well as a fellow member of Company L-2.* "We all went to the games—no one made us. But if you played lightweight football, and you had a game that conflicted with the A Squad game, you still played. There was no special treatment for anyone, except that occasioned by necessary travel to away games. Football players had the same curriculum. They took the same examinations. Football was just something they did."

The only real respite in any cadet's day came after supper, when there were thirty minutes of free time before the three-hour evening study period began at seven fifteen. Most of the football players were so tired and beat up from practice and the rigors of the season that it was all they could do not to spend that half hour in their bunks. "A lot of guys would get back to their room and take a nap, then study," says reserve end Jack Morrison. For those who had been recruited by civilian football programs, quiet moments like this were a reminder of the life they had foresworn—a life in which their only real concern would have been football. One of the members of

---

* That's L Company, 2nd Regiment. Both regiments of the Corps of Cadets were broken down into twelve companies of about one hundred men, which were identified by letters of the alphabet, from *A* to *M,* and not including *J*. Companies were sorted by height, with the tallest cadets in the "flanker companies" of A-1 and M-2, and the shortest in M-1 and A-2. The majority of Army football players were assigned to flanker companies.

the 1958 team had visited Tennessee on a recruiting trip. When he had told an assistant coach in a meeting that he wanted to study engineering, he was told flatly that he could do no such thing. Engineering students, the assistant said, met for two afternoon lab sessions every week, when he would be required to be at football practice.

Cadets were graded every day in every subject. Colonel Sylvanus Thayer, the academy's most influential superintendent, had instituted this practice more than one hundred years before. Thayer, who is referred to at West Point as the "Father of the Military Academy," presided over the school from 1817 to 1833, and his principles of discipline, study, and daily examinations have, for the most part, endured on the banks of the Hudson for the better part of two centuries. The cadets' regimen of daily tests enabled Thayer to academically rank each cadet every week. In 1958, these rankings, or "files," were posted every Monday morning on the walls of the two sally ports that allowed passage into the cadet barracks complex, which surrounds a pair of spacious, enclosed courtyards. The courtyards, called "areas" by the cadets, were the hubs of the school's daily life—with the 1st Regiment in Central Area and 2nd Regiment in North Area. When Albert Einstein died in the spring of 1955, just a few months before the Class of 1959 arrived for Beast Barracks, the joke making its way through both areas had been *Everybody just gained a file.*

Bob Anderson labored mightily to survive his Second Class year, which included difficult courses in both fluid mechanics and thermodynamics. "Andy had to study long after taps and would average less than seven hours sleep," wrote Blaik in his memoirs. "To get by on this amount and still play football is a trick nobody can appreciate who has not tried it." One of the ways that academy officials tried to help any cadet who struggled with academics was to have him share a room with classmates who were doing well in school. For the autumn semester in 1958, Anderson bunked with Don Usry. But the Cadets' Friendly End proved anything but accommodating, rarely offering assistance to his roommate. Instead, according to Anderson, Usry "spent most of his time writing letters to his girlfriend."

The academic rigors and rigid discipline of West Point life were the key components to Blaik's yearly attrition problems, and a big reason why he felt his program deserved more recruits. But while Army's chronic lack of manpower was at the heart of his dispute with academy superintendent Gar Davidson, there had been other issues nagging at the coach in the fall of 1958. For starters, Davidson had been proceeding with his plan to separate the positions of head football coach and athletic director. One memorandum written on this subject by Colonel Charles M. Mount, the academy's chief of staff, dismissively referred to Blaik as the "present incumbent," and noted that in September of 1952 then-superintendent Frederick Irving had approved the separation of the positions while stating "that the time and manner in which the duties of director of athletics are absorbed will be determined later." Blaik, according to Mount, had too much authority, and the result was an overemphasis on football. "Limited resources have been concentrated on football while the other sports have been required to get along to a considerable extent with the leavings or with the secondary efforts of the football men."

Another of Davidson's objectives as superintendent was the modernization of the academy's curriculum with the addition of elective courses. "Observation of people, non-graduates as well as graduates, in combat situations during World War II and Korea had convinced me," Davidson said, "that the monolithic nature of the Military Academy curriculum did not merit the sacred homage paid it." Blaik, like many other graduates of West Point, despised any change that he perceived as softening the sharp corners of cadet life, and he scoffed at the superintendent's "half-baked ideas and encouragement to the Lincoln (social science) thinkers."

But Blaik, somewhat ironically, had no disagreements with Davidson's most publically controversial check on Army football: his refusal to accept invitations to postseason bowl games. By the time the Cadets beat Rice on November 8, they seemed assured of receiving at least one such summons, and representatives from the Cotton

Bowl had been on hand in Rice Stadium to personally follow up with Davidson on the invitation they had extended to the academy on October 27. It was not the first time that officials for the event had approached the general—he had previously rebuffed an invitation from them in 1956. Now, citing West Point's "long-established policy concerning participation in postseason football games," he once again turned the Cotton Bowl down. Davidson went on to add, "Practice in preparation for a Bowl game would prolong the season at a time when the players should be recovering ground lost during the regular season and preparing for the term-end examinations in January." Blaik, who was usually sick by the end of the season anyway, wholeheartedly agreed. Whenever reporters grilled him about the possibility that Army would play in a bowl game, he would deflect the questions by noting that the academy had never before accepted such an invitation. He would usually go on to add—perhaps in an effort to ensure that Davidson bore the brunt of the popular scorn—that such a decision was not his to make, but instead "was up to the superintendent and the people in Washington."

Neither the Army players nor the assistant coaches shared Blaik's opinion. They wanted to play in a bowl game in the worst way, and they suffered in silence every time Davidson declined another postseason invitation. Besides the Cotton Bowl, Army had already turned down an invitation to play in Louisville on December 13 in what was to be the inaugural Bluegrass Bowl.* For the assistants, a bowl game would have been a perk, as well as a valuable opportunity to expand their networks within the small, tightly knit fraternity of college football coaches. The players, meanwhile, saw a bowl game as a chance to test themselves against the best teams in the country—most of the Cadets were itching for a chance to take on LSU, which had displaced Army atop the AP poll two weeks before. "We were

---

* As it turned out, the Bluegrass Bowl was played only once, with Oklahoma State defeating Florida State 15–6 in a game the Cowboys' players dubbed the "Froze Bowl." Temperatures of seven degrees above zero on game day held the total attendance to around seven thousand people—event organizers had managed to sell just over three thousand of the thirty-six thousand available tickets. The most noteworthy aspect of the game was that it marked the national broadcast debut on ABC of Howard Cosell.

better than them, we would have won," says Harry Walters. "No one could stop the Lonely End offense, no one."

More than a few people in Washington, D.C.—and in Louisiana— also felt Blaik's boys should be allowed to play in a bowl game. In late November, after the news of Davidson's Cotton Bowl decision hit the papers, his office received an angry letter from the Honorable F. Edward Hébert, the representative from Louisiana's First Congressional District. "I direct your attention to the report of the Board of Visitors to the United States Military Academy dated 11 February 1955," Hébert wrote from his office in New Orleans:

> *The Service Academies belong to the nation at large and the better they are known to the people, the wider will be their appeal to young men who may be considering a military career . . . The appearance of their students in athletic competition in different parts of the country is to be encouraged provided it does not make excessive demands upon their time. The Board therefore approves participation by the military Academy in intercollegiate athletics, including intersectional competition and recognized "Bowl" games.*

"Am I to assume," challenged Hébert, "that this statement is a repudiation of the policy set by the Board of Visitors in 1955 and signed and concurred in by the President of the United States who transferred the report to the Department of Defense with instructions to put into effect its recommendations?" He then added for good measure, "Navy has played in two Bowl games and the Air Force Academy is standing by right now to accept a Bowl bid if it is offered to them."

The Midshipmen had actually played in three postseason games, having tied Washington 14–14 in the 1924 Rose Bowl. But they had also accepted two bowl invitations in the previous four years: Navy had whipped Ole Miss 21–0 in the 1955 Sugar Bowl and thumped Rice 20–7 in the 1957 Cotton Bowl. As for Air Force, Hébert's analysis was exactly right. The academy was only three years old and was in no position to turn down the kind of free publicity that a bowl game would provide. And with its team undefeated at 6–0–1 and ranked tenth in the country, a bowl game seemed a near certainty.

Had Red Blaik not introduced the Lonely End, it's quite possible that 1958 would be best remembered for the miraculous rise of Air Force football. Construction of the fledgling academy, based in Colorado Springs, had not yet been completed, and the entire campus consisted of only three buildings and about thirteen hundred cadets. Both the field house and the gymnasium were unfinished, so the football offices were located on the first and second floors of the cadet barracks. Without a home field, the Falcons, as Air Force's athletic teams were known, hosted games at various sites around the state, playing most frequently at the University of Denver's Hilltop Stadium. The academy had admitted its first cadets in 1955 and was still more than six months away from awarding commissions to its inaugural graduating class—a situation that prevented it from becoming a member of the NCAA. As a result, Air Force was not yet subject to the association's rules.

One of the benefits of this official limbo was that the Falcons' players were not bound by the NCAA's eligibility restrictions, and there was nothing to prevent a cadet who had played one or more seasons at another college from playing four more at Air Force. Because the academy planned to join the NCAA in the fall of 1959, the Falcons' coaches concentrated most of their recruiting efforts on high school players who would not be ruled ineligible before they graduated, but when a former Big Ten lineman with the brawny name of Brock Strom walked on to the team in that first season of 1955, they welcomed him with open arms.

Strom hailed from Ironwood, Michigan, a remote mining community on the state's Upper Peninsula, just across the Wisconsin border. He had considered enlisting in the air force when he was a senior in high school, but with a handful of football scholarship offers he opted for college instead. A smallish, square-jawed tackle, he played for three years at Indiana, where he was also a member of the Air Force ROTC program. Throughout his years with the Hoosiers,

Strom closely followed the Air Force Academy's public search for a home—which by 1954 had eventually been narrowed down to Colorado Springs and Alton, Illinois—and when he learned that it would be taking applications for its first freshman class in 1955, Strom, an outstanding student, submitted his paperwork at the earliest opportunity. He walked on to the team during summer training, and soon after his teammates voted him their captain for the Falcons' inaugural season. By his senior season of 1958, he ranked seventh in his class academically, and he was again voted team captain.

The Air Force administration had felt that it was crucial for the new academy to field a competitive football team from the start in 1955. To that end, the school had lured Lawrence "Buck" Shaw away from his duties as the head coach of the San Francisco 49ers. A slender, gentlemanly figure with white hair and sharp features, Shaw had played across the line from Red Blaik as a tackle at Notre Dame in 1919, and had since enjoyed great success as both a college and professional coach. At Santa Clara in 1936 and '37, he led the Broncos to consecutive victories over LSU in the Sugar Bowl. He moved on to Cal in 1945 before jumping to the NFL to assume command of the 49ers the next year. Shaw had won 71 of 114 games in the pros by the time he arrived in Colorado Springs.

Air Force charted an ambitious course for its new football team. The Falcons would play freshman ball in 1955, move up to the junior college level a year later, and then play a mid-major schedule in 1957 that would consist primarily of teams from the Skyline Conference, including Wyoming, Denver, Utah, New Mexico, and Colorado State.* By 1958, Air Force intended to be ready for the big time. Today, such a plan seems worthy of Icarus, but this was a different era in college football. Army and Navy had both been powerhouse programs for the better part of the last fifty years, and the prospect of a service academy fielding a top-flight football team, one capable of beating the best teams in the country on any given Satur-

---

* The 1957 Falcons did play one traditional college powerhouse, opening the season against UCLA in the Rose Bowl—where the Bruins whipped them 47–0.

day, was anything but laughable. Besides, with the country in the midst of the Jet Age, there was nothing more modern, more cutting-edge and seemingly limitless, than the United States Air Force. On the occasion of the Falcon's gridiron debut, against the freshman team from the University of Denver, one enthusiastic scribe in the *Denver Post* positively gushed, "It will be an historic Hour . . . Forget the game, forget the score. Be there to tell your grandchildren that you witnessed the first game played by the school which in years to come will many times be national champion."

That the Falcons might be aiming a little too high was apparent to Strom on a chilly Wednesday afternoon in November of that first season, when Air Force played its final game at Hilltop Stadium against the freshmen team from Oklahoma. The Sooners brought seventy-seven players to Denver and were accompanied by varsity coach Bud Wilkinson, who was then in the midst of an undefeated campaign that would end in an Orange Bowl victory and a national championship. The Falcons, meanwhile, were drastically undermanned because two days before the game, the academy had ruled twenty-six members of the fifty-five-man squad academically ineligible. Oklahoma won going away, 48–12.

Despite the lopsided loss, Air Force wasn't half bad that first, frantic season. The Falcons finished 4–4 while running their offense out of a straight T formation, with at least one end regularly flanked out wide. Much like Blaik's boys, they were on the small side, a disadvantage they negated with their speed and their willingness to throw the ball. With a squad of sophomores in 1956, Air Force went 6–2–1, but Shaw returned to the NFL after the Falcons struggled to only three victories against better competition in 1957.* To replace him, the academy hired a handsome, dark-haired Naval Academy graduate named Ben Martin, a keen offensive thinker who had recently been fired after two losing seasons at Virginia. Martin had graduated sixth in his class at Annapolis in 1946 and earned three varsity letters as a halfback. At Air Force, he junked Shaw's straight

---

* Shaw's run of success in the pros continued with the Philadelphia Eagles. In 1960, he retired after leading the club to the only NFL championship in its history.

T and installed his Flexible T offense, which like the Lonely End featured wingbacks and split ends. Martin also put the Falcons in a base set that included an unbalanced line, giving his undersized team a blocking advantage to one side. Unlike Army's Bazooka and Bataan formations, only the Falcons' tackles changed sides when the call was for either unbalanced right or unbalanced left.*

On September 26, the day before the Lonely End formation made its debut, Air Force opened the 1958 season with an easy win over Detroit. The next Saturday, the Falcons stunned eighth-ranked Iowa, playing the Hawkeyes—who hadn't even bothered to scout them the previous week—to a 13–13 tie in front of forty-eight thousand in Iowa City. Air Force used misdirection, motion, and a devastating short passing game to keep Iowa on its heels all afternoon. Time and again, the Falcons rolled sophomore quarterback Rich Mayo out in one direction and then threw back the other way, usually to a halfback. The play was almost always good for five or six yards, and a modern football fan would probably recognize more than few similarities between the Air Force scheme and the West Coast offense. The Hawkeyes had entered the game as twenty-eight-point favorites, but they were lucky to escape with a tie after the Falcons missed a thirty-one-yard field goal attempt with nine seconds left. Throughout the fourth quarter, the one thousand cadets who had made the journey to Iowa City from Colorado Springs kept up a nearly constant chorus of the academy's fight song—*Off we go into the wild blue yonder, Climbing high into the sun!* After the final gun sounded, one ecstatic Air Force player told a reporter, "It seems like we won a hundred to nothing."

The rest of the season played out in similarly exhilarating fashion, as the Falcons pulled out victory after victory. They followed their "upset" of Iowa with easy wins over Colorado State and Stanford, then prevailed in a remarkable run of narrow victories. On October 25, Utah, led by quarterback Lee Grosscup, scored what seemed to be the winning touchdown with twenty-six seconds left, but the

---

* The formation had been added to the Air Force playbook by Martin's inventive rookie offensive coordinator, Pepper Rodgers.

play was called back for an illegal substitution penalty, and Air Force won 16–14. The following Saturday at Oklahoma State, the Falcons trailed 29–18 in the fourth quarter, but Mayo threw two touchdown passes—the last with just nine seconds to play—for a wild 33–29 victory. "We used to look at each other sometimes during the Sunday staff meetings and say, 'How do we keep doing this?'" says Jim Bowman, a young Air Force lieutenant who had joined Martin's staff that fall as the coach of the scout team. By the time Blaik was preparing his team to take on Villanova on November 15 in its last game before the annual clash with Navy, Air Force and Army both had identical 6–0–1 records, and the Falcons had climbed to tenth in the Associated Press poll, seven spots behind Army.

There was little reason to think that the ascendancy of the country's newest service academy would end anytime soon. In just three years, Air Force had gone from playing a freshman schedule and living in frame barracks at Denver's Lowry Air Force Base to the upper echelons of the college football pyramid. If Army wasn't going to accept a bowl invitation, there was little doubt in anyone's mind that the Falcons *would*. What better way to show the whole country what was going on in Colorado Springs than to put Air Force on national television on New Year's Day?

When Pete Dawkins scored the winning touchdown against Rice, he not only saved the Cadets' undefeated record and their lofty perch in the national rankings, but he also restored a good measure of the luster to his name—a luster that had faded slightly after his costly defensive gaffe against Pittsburgh. In Army's penultimate game against Villanova, Dawkins kept right on rolling. The Main Liners played Army to a 0–0 draw in the first quarter but lost control of the game in the second after Dawkins brought the twenty-seven thousand fans at Michie Stadium to their feet with a swerving eighty-yard punt return for a touchdown. Fielding the kick at the Cadets' 20-yard line, he sprinted to his left and faked a reverse to Bob Anderson, then slipped out of a diving, grasping tackle attempt and twisted upfield at the 24. A block from tackle Ed Bagdonas sprung him into the open, and he sprinted up the left sideline to the 50, where Bill Carpenter cut down another defender. Dawkins raced from there past the Villanova 30, where he made his final move by cutting inside Don Usry, who was driving the last defender into the Main Liners' bench.

Dawkins's second touchdown of the quarter, on Army's next possession, was even more of an individual effort. While running a crossing route over the middle of the field, he came back to catch a badly underthrown pass—Joe Caldwell's throwing arm had been hit by a rushing Villanova lineman—scooping it up at the Main Liners' 20 and turning upfield with defenders bearing down on him from the right and left. Demonstrating his remarkable vision, he stopped short and took one step to the rear as the defensive backs collided in front of him. Jumping to his left, he took off for the end zone and galloped untouched across the goal line to complete a forty-six-yard scoring pass. Harry Walters missed the conversion kick, and Army led 13–0 at the end of the first half.

The Cadets went on to win 26–0, as Dawkins scored three touchdowns and caught four passes for 125 yards. In the process he solidified his reputation as a big-play machine. Seven of his twelve touchdowns on the season had covered twenty-two yards or more, and he was averaging nearly thirty-one yards per catch, an astonishing number in any era. He was a shoo-in for the All-America team, as well as a favorite for the Heisman Trophy.

Watching it all happen with a kind of detached amazement was a first classman named Gene Mikelonis, the man Dawkins had replaced in the Army backfield. Both Dawkins and Mikelonis had arrived at West Point in the summer of 1955, but where Dawkins found himself buried on the depth chart at quarterback, Mikelonis proved himself to be not only the top running back on the plebe team but also every bit the equal of Pat Uebel and Bob Kyasky, the starting A Squad halfbacks. Shifty and fast, if a bit undersized at five foot eleven and 170 pounds, Mikelonis was so good that the following season, with Uebel lost to graduation and Kyasky having been shuffled to quarterback, Blaik made him a starter and publicly declared him the Cadets' best running back. In the 1956 home opener against the Virginia Military Institute, Mikelonis ran for ninety yards on his first eleven carries. But on his twelfth, a sweep to the right, he blew out his knee. He never played football again.

Mikelonis had come to West Point from the small town of Dubois, Pennsylvania, a coal mining and railroad town nestled in the foothills of the Allegheny Mountains, less than a hundred miles northeast of Pittsburgh. Other than an uncle who had served in World War II, his family had no connection to the military. Mikelonis was a marvelous high school football player, one of the top recruits in the nation—he scored fifty-four touchdowns in three years, including twenty-six as a junior—and he had scholarship offers from a raft of powerful collegiate programs, including Michigan, Michigan State, and Notre Dame. Army came after him, too, sending Paul Dietzel to meet with him during his junior year.* A scholarship was important to Mikelonis. His father was a foreman at Jackson China, a nearby plant that produced dinnerware for restaurants and hotels, and he did not have enough money to send his second-oldest son to college. Gene agonized over his decision for months, finally choosing to play for Red Blaik. In addition to the prestige of playing at West Point and the prospect of a superior engineering education, he liked the fact that, unlike at a civilian school, his scholarship would be safe if he got hurt and was unable to perform. "I went for the long-term perspective," he says.

Mikelonis had blown out his knee making a cut he had made hundreds of times before. The sweep was a bread-and-butter play of Blaik's T-formation offense, and few backs ran it as well as Mikelonis. After turning upfield, he liked to run straight at the nearest defensive back and then cut back to the inside, a move that, when successful, could turn a modest gain into a big one. But on his twelfth carry against VMI, the Keydets' defensive back hit him low on the side of the knee after Mikelonis had planted his right foot to make the cut. He felt no pain at first, not even when he tried to take

---

* Mikelonis was one of the last players Dietzel recruited for Red Blaik before departing to take over at LSU. Red Blaik once described Dietzel as the world's greatest recruiter, adding, "If he so much as gets his feet under the supper table with a boy, the boy is his."

another step with his right leg and crumpled to the turf. "It felt like I stepped into a ten-foot hole," he says. Dr. Parvin diagnosed his injury as a tear of the medial collateral ligament.* Two days later, Mikelonis underwent surgery to repair the damage.

The operation was a success, but Parvin had missed a crucial detail: a second tear, this one in the knee's anterior cruciate ligament. When Mikelonis returned for spring practice, he found that he could not cut or move as he used to. By the time Parvin, along with a surgeon visiting from Walter Reed Army Medical Center in Washington, D.C., diagnosed the second injury, the knee was beyond repair. Mikelonis's athletic career was over. It had lasted all of seven years, from his first days of Little League back home in Dubois to that sunny Saturday at Michie Stadium. He returned to the Corps of Cadets as an at-large member and refused to let himself wallow in self-pity and bitterness. "It was tough sometimes to sit there and watch wishing you could be out there," he says. "But I knew my football was done." He instead became an enthusiastic booster of the team. Blaik favored Mikelonis when the opportunities arose, taking him on the road to the Penn State game in 1957 so that he could visit with his family. Like everyone else at West Point, Mikelonis knew many of the men on the 1958 squad, and he rooted for them. "It wasn't going to do me any good to be bitter," he says. "Colonel Blaik wasn't one to dawdle over anybody, but he had a soft heart. And Pete's a good guy. I knew all along they were going to be a good team."

The victory over Villanova held a special significance for Red Blaik. The last time he had led a team onto the field against the Main Liners had been on September 29, 1951, in the first game after the cheating scandal had decimated his varsity squad. Villanova had beaten Army that day for the first time in thirty-six years, and it wasn't even close, with the Cadets on the short end of a 21–7 score. In the

---

* Without the ability to perform a magnetic resonance imaging test, Parvin made his diagnosis by manually manipulating Mikelonis's knee.

ten years that preceded that defeat, Blaik had experienced almost nothing but triumph, but the eight that followed had brought him only fleeting glimpses of glory. Until now.

Only Navy stood in his way.

Chapter 11

NO SUBSTITUTE FOR VICTORY

FEW DEFEATS IN HIS CAREER rankled Red Blaik as much as Army's loss to Navy in 1950. The Cadets had left for Philadelphia with an 8–0 record and were ranked second in the country by the Associated Press. Their defense, led by All-America linebacker Elmer Stout— and featuring an aggressive sophomore guard named Ray Malavasi— was the stingiest in college football, allowing just a little more than three points per game.* Blaik himself was enjoying a run of success such as few other coaches had ever experienced. Since 1944, his Army teams had won fifty-seven of sixty-three games and lost only two times. And since their 27–7 loss to Notre Dame on November 8, 1947, the Cadets had gone twenty-eight games without a defeat. As Blaik ruefully recalled years later, "We were sitting on top." But on a chilly day in Philadelphia, the underdog Midshipmen spoiled what would have been Blaik's sixth undefeated season at West Point, up-setting the Black Knights 14–2. Navy held Army to five first downs and 137 total yards in a game that was never close. It was one of the lowest moments of Blaik's career, until the events of 1951 overshad-owed everything.

Such was the outsized importance of the Cadets' annual meeting

* Malavasi would later rise to fame as the head coach of the Los Angeles Rams, whom he led to the Super Bowl in the 1979 season.

with Navy that Blaik would assign one coach to scout nobody else but the Midshipmen for an entire season. In 1958, that duty belonged to B Squad coach Barney Gill. Even more than his responsibilities at the head of the practice team, scouting Navy was the most important job Blaik entrusted to the affable Gill, who performed myriad unofficial duties of a more social nature on behalf of Army football. Blaik regularly dispatched Gill to New York every Monday during the 1958 season to meet with the media at Toots Shor's, where he answered questions about the team and discussed the Cadets' upcoming opponent. "Those things were always open bar," recalls Gill, "and by the time we sat down for lunch after an hour or two, everybody was shitfaced."

It was with good reason that Gill, a man who liked a drink as much as the next, abstained from the booze at Toots Shor's. After meeting the press, he and Joe Cahill, West Point's director of sports publicity, would stop at the Waldorf Towers to deliver a color copy of the previous week's game film to General MacArthur. The old soldier lived in splendor high above Park Avenue in suite 37A, surrounded by mementos from his years in the Far East. MacArthur, thin and frail at seventy-eight, would meet Gill in the hall wearing a pair of flapping slippers and a cadet bathrobe, still stitched with the varsity A he had earned for baseball in 1902—he had famously worn his original cadet-issue robe through three wars, even the night before the Inchon landing, and it had become so frayed that the Corps of Cadets presented him with a replacement a few years after he took up permanent residence in the towers in 1951.* After receiving the canister of film from Gill, the general would hand it over to his Asian butler, who would then thread it through a projector while MacArthur and his guests took their seats in the spacious living room. Before the movie began, Jean MacArthur, the general's wife, would bring the men a tray of cookies and coffee. For the next two hours, MacArthur would watch the game intently, rarely taking his eyes off the screen. "He knew every damn player by name," says

---

* MacArthur's casual style caught on among the Corps of Cadets at West Point in the fifties, when the unofficial evening study uniform included a bathrobe and a pipe.

Gill, "and when somebody went in the game that he didn't recognize, he saw it right away and he'd ask, 'Who was that?'"

Gill, a former star running back at Virginia, was as respected a football mind as any other member of Blaik's staff, having coached winning teams at a number of his duty stations—this was in the day when every Army post had its own football team, usually stocked with a number of former collegiate players, and intraservice rivalries were especially keen. Gill was a young captain coaching football for the 82nd Airborne at Fort Bragg, North Carolina, when Blaik picked him for the Army staff. Blaik's assistants typically handled scouting duties on a rotating schedule and delivered their reports on the Cadets' upcoming opponents at the eleven o'clock staff meeting Blaik held in the conference room every Sunday morning. On November 16, the morning after Army's victory over Villanova, Gill kept his report simple. The Midshipmen, he said, were comparable in size and speed to Army but much deeper. They had finished with a respectable 6–2 record despite a horrible run of injuries that had forced them to start a junior at left end named Tom Albershart, who had begun the season as a fourth-string fullback. Along the interior line, a knee injury had limited hulking tackle Bob Reifsnyder to less than thirty minutes of playing time all season. An All-America and the winner of the Maxwell Award as the nation's best player in 1957, the senior was, at 240 pounds, the biggest player in the history of the Naval Academy, as well as one of the fastest men on the team. Reifsnyder was not expected to play much against the Cadets, and his absence became most apparent, Gill noted, when Navy was on defense. The Midshipmen were fast enough to track down ball carriers who tried to run outside, but they were susceptible to rushes up the middle. Offensively, Navy was extraordinarily well balanced, having gained 1,341 yards both running and passing. Junior quarterback Joe Tranchini was one of the top passers in the East, and halfback Joe Bellino was both a talented receiver and a breakaway runner. The five-foot-eight, 182-pound sophomore led the Midshipmen in receptions and had averaged better than fifty yards on his four kickoff returns.

Long before the NFL began taking two weeks off before the Super Bowl, Army and Navy had been giving themselves a fortnight to prepare for their annual clash. Not only did it allow the pregame hype to build, but it also encouraged the respective coaching staffs to conceive new game plans and trick plays. In 1957, the Midshipmen had confounded the Cadets with a jitterbugging defense, lining up in one set—a 4-4, say—and then jumping to another, perhaps a 6-2, or a Gap-8, with defenders positioned in the spaces between players on the offensive line. From hard experience, Blaik was sure that Navy would again roll out a whole battery of fancy gimmicks. Eddie Erdelatz, his sideline counterpart, was devoted to the element of surprise. A laid-back, wildly inventive former line assistant with the San Francisco 49ers, Erdelatz had been in his first season as the head coach at Annapolis when the Midshipmen had stunned Army's mighty 1950 squad. For the better part of the next seven years, he had continued to get the better of Blaik and the Cadets, winning five times and losing only twice, with the 1956 game ending in a 7–7 draw. Blaik wrote off Army's losses in 1951 and '52 to the lasting effects of the cheating scandal, but the press, who hailed the Navy coach as an offensive wizard, nevertheless frequently mentioned Erdelatz's record of success against the Cadets. Before Erdelatz arrived, after all, the Midshipmen had beaten Blaik's team just once in seven years.

The orphaned son of a San Francisco saloonkeeper, Erdelatz was in almost every way the inverse of his buttoned-up rival. With his lineman's bulk, ruddy complexion, and habitually cheerful expression, he appeared capable of presiding over a taproom of his very own, and he took a relaxed and easygoing approach to running his team. Erdelatz had been only thirty-seven when he took over in Annapolis, and he quickly established himself as a players' coach. "I told the guys when I came here," he said to *Sports Illustrated* in 1954, "that I was gonna coach the way I wanted to be coached when I was playing." The Midshipmen adored him. His practices, held on a riverside field called the Flats, were high-spirited and upbeat. And before it became fashionable in college football to break out new uniforms in an effort to inspire players, Erdelatz had made it a regular practice. For the Army game in 1957, he outfitted Navy in powder blue jerseys with light gold numerals. "He had a way of surprising us," says Joe Tranchini. "Nobody ever knew. You'd just walk into the locker room on game day and find a new jersey hanging in your locker." On the Sunday trips back to Annapolis following road games, Erdelatz usually stopped in Baltimore to take the Midshipmen to a Colts game, after which he would order the team bus to halt at a roadside market where he could buy beer for his boys to drink on the way home. "The guys loved him," says Tranchini. "I never played for a better coach."

The Midshipmen, with a 6–2 record, were not as formidable as they had been the year before, when they had gone 9–1–1 and drubbed Rice 20–7 in the Cotton Bowl. But they were still dangerous. Navy had begun the season ranked number seven by the AP, two spots ahead of the Cadets, and won its first three games, including a 20–14 upset of fourteenth-ranked Michigan in Ann Arbor on October 11. The victory over the Wolverines had been highlighted by the pinpoint passing of Tranchini—who was ten-of-thirteen for 171 yards and two touchdowns—and the sparkling play of Bellino, who kept the Midshipmen's fourth-quarter drive to the winning touchdown alive by turning a short reception into a twenty-one-yard gain with an unscripted lateral to trailing fullback Buddy Wellborn.

But Navy had followed that victory up with a shocking defeat at the hands of Tulane, who upset the sixth-ranked Midshipmen 14–6. The scouting report on the Green Wave had been that Richie Petitbon, their talented senior quarterback, would throw the ball frequently. Instead, Petitbon ran behind his big linemen and gashed Navy for eighty-eight rushing yards and two touchdowns—as a team, Tulane ran for 214 yards. Blaik saw in the Green Wave's victory the best way to beat Navy: on the ground, running straight ahead.

The buildup to the Navy game at West Point began on the Monday following the win over Villanova. That night at dinner, the corps cheered each Army player as he hustled into the mess hall late from practice. Soon homemade banners began to appear inside the cadet areas, hanging from windows and emblazoned with beseeching messages: K-I SAYS BEAT NAVY! and, more ambitiously, JOUST THAT KNAVEY GOAT! By the following Monday, November 24, passions had intensified to a fever pitch. Unlike at West Point today, there was no Thanksgiving leave for the Corps of Cadets, which remained at West Point through the weekend. As a result, the holiday was something of an afterthought, a footnote to the week's real significance—the Army-Navy game on November 29.

For five exhilarating days, life at the academy became gleefully chaotic. Some professors, most of whom were active-duty officers and alumni of the academy, spent part of their classes discussing the upcoming contest; a few devoted an entire period to it. On the Wednesday before the game, newsreel cameras appeared in front of the barracks to record the corps marching to lunch and then followed the cadets inside the mess hall to document the annual midweek pep rally. Cheers and fight songs began spontaneously, or were led by the Rabble Rousers, the academy's all-male cheer squad. The Army mules were ridden through the maze of tables (followed by a squad of shovel-wielding cadets, of course). Radio broadcaster Mel Allen, a confidant of Blaik's, wished the team well from the poop deck, the balcony above the entrance from which announcements were read to the corps during meals. It was hardly anarchy, but it was as close to it as things could get at West Point.

The challenge for Blaik through all the commotion was to keep his players, who could not avoid the pregame hype unless they were at practice, focused on preparation for the game. He threw himself into film study, picking at and obsessing over every detail. Even with his team favored by seven points over Navy, he was not going to take anything for granted.

But his devotion to film study—his never-ending search for the hidden keys to victory—had backfired before. In 1957, Blaik was certain he had discovered the secret to beating the Midshipmen's defense: If the Navy defensive tackle's heel was off the ground, he and the rest of the internal linemen would be slanting to the right. If the tackle kept his heel down, the defensive line would slant to the left. Blaik also instructed his players to watch the positioning of the quarterback when the Midshipmen were on defense, a supposed key to recognizing either two-deep or three-deep coverage. Rather than giving his players an edge, however, Blaik had simply given them too many extra details to think about. The information on the defensive tackle and the deep safety was supposed to be relayed throughout the Cadets' offense by a system of signals. "A combination of circumstances—and the cheering of 100,000 fans must certainly have been one of them—was responsible for Army's 'busting' signals about five times" said Steve Belichick, who was then in his third year as the top scout at Annapolis. "Someone on the team would not get the play change, and consequently did the wrong thing. This caused either a mix-up in the backfield action or a missed assignment by at least one of the linemen. These errors undoubtedly caused the players to have a loss of confidence in the check-off system, which might well have affected the outcome of the game."*

Bill Rowe puts it more succinctly, "We were just guessing on almost every play instead of getting after them."

Now, though, the film that Blaik was studying was Navy's loss to Tulane in 1958. And what it showed was unmistakable—the Midshipmen were vulnerable against a power running game. In a letter to MacArthur that week, he laid out his offensive game plan: "We have eliminated all unnecessary plays from our running game and will attack with a few plays selected after considerable study of the Navy personnel and defenses. We expect to hit fast to offset the Navy moving defenses. We have eliminated lateral movement in favor of direct and slanting power." Blaik intended to beat the Midshipmen straight up, and he instructed his players not to worry about how Navy might line up, or how its defenders might adjust before the snap. Army's offense was going to be based around north-south

---

* Steve Belichick is, of course, the late father of Super-Bowl winning coach Bill Belichick, of the New England Patriots. Steve's typical game-day station was in the press box, high above the field, where he would survey the action with field glasses and take copious notes. Erdelatz took to referring to Belichick as "my Upstairs Coach." He remained on the staff at Navy until 1989, and his 1962 book, *Football Scouting Methods*, is considered a seminal work.

running plays, including a new one in which all of the offensive linemen blocked straight ahead except for Bob Novogratz, the weak-side guard, who would step back and pull to the line's strong side. It was the job of Anderson, Dawkins, and Walters to get behind Novogratz and follow. Blaik drilled the play endlessly.

A few subtle wrinkles were also added to the attack. Whenever the wide side of the field was to the left, Army would line up in the Bazooka formation—with the line unbalanced to the right side—but split Carpenter wide to the left. Tom Harp also drew up a new scheme that sent Anderson in motion toward the Lonely End. But such adjustments were mostly cosmetic. All season, Carpenter had functioned marvelously as a decoy. With the Midshipmen vulnerable in the interior of their defensive line, Blaik again planned to use the Lonely End as a distraction. He was going to win this game inside, where no other Army back was as formidable as Bob Anderson.

The crescendo of Navy Week came on Thanksgiving Day, when no classes were scheduled. In the morning, most members of the corps gathered on the Plain to watch the traditional football game between the Goats and the Engineers—the lower half of the Second Class versus the upper half. First played in 1905, the Goat-Engineer game had been conceived as a holiday diversion. A playful list of rules for the first contest included a directive that the Engineers were not allowed to cross the Goats' 10-yard line. "Anyone crossing it will be given a 5 and 10," it read, "i.e., will be thrown back with $\Sigma mr2$ of 5 f/s and will serve 10 days in the hospital." Loosely translated, this flash of engineering humor meant that offenders, no matter their size, would be repulsed forcefully at a rate of five feet per second.*

According to the report on the 1958 game in *The New York Times,* the Goats ran their offense from the Lonely End formation. This,

---

* Normally, a "5 and 10" referred to five demerits and ten hours of punishment, which cadets usually served by marching silently for ten hours, while carrying a rifle and wearing full-dress uniform, from one side of Central Area to the other.

however, may have been the invention of an overenthusiastic academy public relations officer, because the Goats' quarterback, Bob Miser, scratched out most of the team's plays in the huddle. A lacrosse star for Army, Miser was regarded as the best attackman in the country and had helped the cadets to a national title the previous spring. In the first quarter, he got loose for a fourteen-yard touchdown run, then bulled over for the two-point conversion. The Engineers, running out of a conventional T formation, were unable to score even once. The only points they put on the scoreboard came in the fourth quarter, when one of their backs was tackled in the end zone for a safety. Final score: Goats 10, Engineers 0. According to academy lore, a Goats victory presaged a Navy defeat on Saturday. But as the *Times* noted, "Unfortunately for the cadets, it has not always been true that 'as the Goats go, so goes the Army' in the service game . . . Last year the game ended in a 0–0 tie; Navy took the big game 14–0."

After the game, the corps filed into the mess hall for their Thanksgiving meal, then returned to the barracks to relax before reconvening on the Plain for the traditional pep rally and bonfire. In keeping with the week's freewheeling spirit, many cadets invited dates and wore civilian clothes, and most of the Army players joined the fun. With class the next day, however, the festivities did not run late.

During the break between classes on Friday morning, a sprawling, gray-clad crowd of cadets gathered around the team motorcoaches parked on Thayer Road. Atop them, cheerleaders led yells and songs, while the academy's marching band prepared to escort the buses to the main gate. The scene was a repeat of the Notre Dame sendoff, only this time it included an M48 Patton tank at the rear of the procession. Several hundred cadets jogged along with the slow-moving caravan for over half a mile before breaking into a sprint over the last four hundred yards as the buses picked up speed and motored out the main gate and into Highland Falls. "It was thrilling," recalls Pete Dawkins. "I don't think there was any question about the solidarity between the corps and the team. I think there was kind of a golden moment there, where the corps and the team bonded and felt as if they were one."

Rather than taking Blaik and his team directly to Philadelphia, the buses instead stopped at Penn Station in Newark, New Jersey. The Army coach was deeply conservative, and the Cadets' rail trip to Philadelphia was another of his long-established traditions. On board, his friends in the press—Red Smith, Stanley Woodward, and Joe Williams among them—could secure exclusive interviews with coaches and players. "The same buses that dropped you off at the Newark train station would be waiting for you in Philadelphia to get off the train," says Bill Carpenter. "Anytime we went to Philadelphia it was the same drill."

According to another of Blaik's immemorial customs, the team lodged in nearby Fort Washington, Pennsylvania, at the Manufacturers' Country Club, despite the fact that the only place for the players to sleep was in the cavernous ballroom on ancient metal cots. "Those were some of the coldest nights of my life," says one former player. "The place was a dump," recalls Carpenter. "The men's room had one toilet and one sink." In the afternoon, Blaik put his players through a short noncontact practice out on the first fairway, where, after dinner, he also took them for their customary pregame walk. With the temperature just under thirty degrees, the Cadets were bundled into their long gray overcoats. As they huffed against the chill, a cloud of steam rose above them and shone in the light of the full moon. Just short of the first green, Blaik stopped and motioned to his boys to gather round. "Heads, heads," he said.

His speech touched on all his usual points: the game plan and his confidence in it; reminders to hit hard and to be aggressive—to, as Blaik liked to say, "tighten your chinstraps"; and his standing order to ignore what people outside the Army program might be saying about the game. Then he paused for several seconds, staring at the icy ground. When he looked up, the players were surprised to see that his eyes were shining. "I would remind you all that you are playing this game not just for yourselves," Blaik said with strain evident in his voice. "You are playing it for West Point. You are playing it for the corps. And you are playing it for the entire United States Army." Blaik then dismissed the players, who turned to head back toward the clubhouse. As they began to move away, he called out to Anderson, saying, "Andy, stay and talk with me for just a minute." Blaik put his hand on the shoulder of his halfback, and the two began to walk back up the fairway together in silence. After several yards, the coach stopped and turned to look Anderson in the eye. "Son," he said, "there's no doubt in my mind who my best back is."

The implication of the statement, of course, was that Blaik was saying that *Anderson* was his best back. And Anderson's realization of this fact shot through him like a current. "I was so excited," he says. "I was so charged up. He didn't say I was his best back—he didn't commit himself—but that's the way I took it. Isn't that awful?"

Awful maybe, but definitely understandable. Anderson had played all season in the shadow of Dawkins, and Blaik was well aware that the postseason honors for Army's captain had already begun to roll in. Earlier in the week, Dawkins had won the Maxwell Award as college football's player of the year, and he had been one of only two service academy players—Air Force tackle Brock Strom was the other—to be named to the Associated Press All-America team. Dawkins was also, of course, the favorite to win the Heisman Trophy as the nation's most outstanding player. Anderson had gone the whole season without speaking a word of protest over his diminished offensive role, and Blaik likewise had never said a word about it to Anderson. But on the eve of the biggest game of the best season Army had enjoyed in many years, Blaik had said the words that his halfback had longed to hear.

Still on the fairway, Blaik then gave Anderson the same instructions he had given him the year before, when, as a sophomore, he had made his collegiate debut against Nebraska: "Tomorrow, I want you to hold your head up high, lift your knees up high, and run like a stallion." Then he turned, and the two walked together back to the clubhouse in silence. It was a difficult walk for Anderson—who had suddenly been overcome by the urge to run. "Blaik could inspire you without fire and brimstone pep talks," Anderson says. "He didn't need any of that. This day and age, to say that you loved a man . . . I certainly had the greatest love and respect for him."

Early on Saturday morning, the Corps of Cadets marched en masse to the West Point train depot—nestled along the river's edge at the bottom of a steep cliff—and boarded passenger cars bound for Philadelphia. The Pennsylvania Railroad serviced Municipal Stadium on Army-Navy day with special trains that brought passengers to the field's main entrance gate, and the cadets would go straight from West Point to the game.

The rain clouds that hung over Philadelphia on Friday had lifted overnight, and the weather was clear and sunny, though bitterly cold. Morning temperatures hovered in the twenties and were not expected to climb much above thirty degrees by kickoff at one thirty. Despite the cold, the stands filled with more than one hundred thousand shivering fans—the biggest college football crowd of the year. Most of them had arrived well before noon in order to witness the arrival of the Corps of Cadets and the Brigade of Midshipmen, both of which paraded on the field. Lending a dose of glamour to the assembled throng were Prince Ranier and Princess Grace, Monaco's royal couple, who were in town to visit the princess's family. Also on hand was former Army assistant coach Vince Lombardi, then in his fifth season as the offensive coordinator for the New York Giants. The Giants were playing the Philadelphia Eagles at Yankee Stadium on Sunday, and Lombardi would be leaving immediately after the game to return to New York.

As the visiting team, the Corps of Cadets, clad in high-collared dress gray uniforms under heavy long gray overcoats, had marched into Municipal Stadium first, lining up by company on the field facing the press box. A Rabble Rouser strategically positioned in the upper sweeps of the grandstand—clearly visible to everybody arrayed on the field below—then led the corps through several of the academy's traditional cheers, including the Rocket Yell, a call nearly as old as football itself at West Point:

(Whistle)—BOOM!—Ah!
YOO-smay Rah! Rah!

YOO-smay Rah! Rah!
HOO-rah! HOO-rah!
Ar-MAY Rah!
TEAM! TEAM! TEAM!*

Red Blaik and his team had arrived shortly before the Corps of Cadets had taken the field. The atmosphere on the ride to the stadium was edgy and quiet, and as the bus rolled south on Broad Street toward the stadium, Blaik decided it was up to him to help break the tension. "Hey, Rowe," he said, turning around in his seat at the front of the bus. "What do you see?"

The Army center, after swallowing the lump that had risen in his throat, responded with a series of calls that was answered by the rest of the team, "I see the crowd!"

"I see the stadium!"

"I see victory!"

The Navy players arrived to find that coach Eddie Erdelatz had once again chosen special uniforms for the day. Along with their usual gold pants and dark blue jerseys with gold numerals, the Midshipmen would be wearing blue helmets that matched their jerseys rather than their standard gold headgear. The look was a hit with the players. "Those were great," says Tranchini of the new helmets. "We thought we looked like the Chicago Bears."

Army won the opening coin toss and elected to receive. The kickoff from Navy's Buddy Wellborn sailed high along the right sideline. Pete Dawkins caught the ball on the run at the Cadets' 12-yard line and started upfield, cutting to the inside to avoid a pileup of bodies at the 27. Rather than cradling the ball in his right, or outside, arm, Dawkins was instead holding it in the crook of his left arm. As he tried to turn back upfield, he collided with Rowe, who was angling

---

* The yell is a classic of the sis-boom-bah variety and makes use of the acronymic pronunciation of the initials USMA.

to the outside to block a Navy defender. Rowe's right shoulder slammed into Dawkins's left arm and knocked the ball into the air as the halfback haplessly tried to corral it. The Midshipmen's George Fritzinger fell on the ball at the Army 35-yard line.

After a false-start penalty and a rush that lost a yard, Joe Tranchini dropped back on second down and looked to his right. With Rowe and Bill Carpenter bearing down on him, Tranchini turned to his left and whipped a quick jump pass to Joe Bellino, who had released into the flat after chip-blocking Ed Bagdonas. Bellino turned upfield and scooted forward for an eight-yard gain. Tranchini's third-down pass fell incomplete, and the Midshipmen faced fourth-and-eight from the Army 33.

Now Erdelatz got his chance to confound the Cadets. Navy broke the huddle and set up in a formation their coach had dubbed "Convoy Left." Tranchini and two halfbacks lined up behind the center, two guards and a left tackle, with three Midshipmen lined up abreast along the line of scrimmage about ten yards left of the ball, and one more split wide to the right two yards behind the line. Navy's off-kilter alignment forced Army to shift its defense to compensate for Navy's overload on the left side. On the snap, Tranchini turned to his left and then spun back the other way—away from the overload—dashing around the right side, where there was plenty of open room. He gained eleven yards, good for a first down at the Army 22.

The trick play delighted the Navy fans, and with Municipal Stadium in a roaring tumult the Midshipmen began a steady advance. Bellino ran for three yards, and fullback Dick Dagampat did the same. Then Tranchini, rolling to his right on third down, hit end John Kanuch over the middle for thirteen yards to the Black Knights' 3-yard line. Erdelatz's boys then lined up in a power formation, with seven blockers abreast along the line of scrimmage and two wingbacks stationed just off the outside hips of both ends. It almost looked as if they were in field-goal formation. Bellino, the lone back, took a handoff from Tranchini and burrowed over left tackle for the first touchdown of the game. Less than three minutes had expired. Had the square-toed attachment not come loose on

Buddy Wellborn's right shoe during the extra-point attempt, Navy would have led by seven. Instead, the Midshipmen settled for a quick 6–0 lead.

From his seat up in the press box, Dale Hall, Army's defensive backfield coach, hunched over the notes he had scribbled during Navy's opening drive and ran through the sequence of plays that ended with Bellino's touchdown. Though Blaik would later deride the Midshipmen's scheme as a "strange mélange of flankers, double-flankers, double reverses, laterals off double reverses, and even something that looked like the old and hoary Minnesota shift," the fact is that the cumulative effect of all the shenanigans had been to throw the Cadets badly out of step. Now Hall got on the telephone and called Blaik on the sideline. The remedy he proposed was to stick with the game plan and not to get distracted by Erdelatz's trick plays and fancy formations. Navy, said Hall, was showing a lot of movement and a lot of different offensive looks, but its scheme was still the same, a run-pass option system built around Bellino and Tranchini: six-yards-and-a-cloud-of-dust, as it was referred to at Annapolis. The Cadets would be better off countering the Midshipmen's offense with the sort of straightforward aggression that had been the hallmark of the Army defense all season.

Harry Walters had been as confused as anybody by Navy's misdirection. And on Bellino's touchdown plunge, the Black Knights' Monster back had reacted tentatively. For two weeks his coaches had told him not to dive low to tackle Bellino, whose thick, powerful legs were almost impossible to wrap up. The best way to bring him down, the coaches had said, was to hit him high, hang on, and wait for help. Walters had been sure that Bellino would get the ball, but rather than shooting through a gap in the line and attacking the play aggressively, Walters waited for the ball carrier to come to him. His only contact with Bellino came in the end zone, when Walters fell on top of him after the touchdown had already been scored. Now, on the sideline before the Midshipmen were to kick off, he seethed silently, vowing to himself that he would not be so passive the next time.

Army's first drive of the game lasted only three plays, and Caldwell was forced to punt. Starting from its own 41-yard line after a short return by Dagampat, Navy found the going much more difficult against the Cadets' reorganized defense. Tranchini handed the ball off to Bellino on first down—a counter play to the right—and as the halfback hit the line he attempted to hurdle over the scrum. From his knees, Monk Hilliard grabbed at Bellino's right leg, and Bob Novogratz, coming from behind the play, hit the halfback chest-high and knocked the ball straight up into the air. It fell right into Novogratz's hands, and Army had the ball, and the momentum, at the Navy 44.

From there, Blaik's offense set to its grinding work, pounding the ball with Anderson and Dawkins on three consecutive runs down to the 32. On the next play, with Army in the Lonely End set and Dawkins lined up as a wingback, Caldwell dropped straight back, faked a handoff to Walters, and zipped a pass to Don Usry over the middle for a seventeen-yard gain. Seated next to Dale Hall in the press box, Tom Harp was surprised at how wide-open Usry had been. The Midshipmen were arrayed in a 5-2 defensive alignment, with five down linemen and two linebackers, and with quarterback Joe Tranchini, in his defensive role as a cornerback, playing Carpenter man-to-man. The rest of the Navy defensive backs were playing umbrella coverage, with a pair of deep safeties. The alignment showed that the Midshipmen's priorities were on stopping the run and preventing the deep pass. And Harp saw right away that the area in front of the deep safeties would be unguarded. Usry was likely to be open all day long.

But Army did not get another chance to look his way. Two plays after the completion to Usry, Caldwell and Walters failed to connect on a handoff at the 11-yard line and the ball fell to the ground—a miscue that was practically a carbon copy of the one that had ended the Cadets' first drive of the season on the goal line against South Carolina. Navy end Tom Albershart recovered the fumble.

Back on offense, the Midshipmen advanced to their 41 behind Bellino and Tranchini. As the first quarter entered its final minute, Erdelatz sent his second-string offense into the game. Blaik responded by doing the same. Almost immediately, the vast disparity between the depth of the two teams' rosters began to show. Quarterback Jim Maxfield and halfback Roland Brandquist led Navy down inside the Army 20-yard line, making a march of better than forty yards look almost easy. After Maxfield sprinted six yards to the 16, Blaik sent his first team back in. Erdelatz did the same.

Navy, after a short gain on third down, came to the line facing fourth-and-two at the Cadets' 3. The Midshipmen set themselves in the same short-yardage blocking formation they had used on Bellino's touchdown run, and Harry Walters saw his chance. "I knew Bellino was going to run that same play again," says Walters. "So I blitzed." Standing at the line of scrimmage on the left side of the Army line, Walters charged into the backfield through a gap on the snap of the ball and angled toward Bellino. He shed a grasping block from Brandquist and took aim at the halfback's legs. Bellino tried to power through the tackle, but Walters held doggedly to Bellino's left leg as his teammates came swarming in. The play lost two yards, and Army took over on its own 5, still trailing 6–0.

Army again failed to capitalize on the change in momentum. After the Black Knights drove over forty yards into Navy territory, Caldwell threw an interception at the Midshipmen's 32-yard line. Navy, its bag of tricks now empty, punted the ball back after failing to advance beyond ten yards in three plays. The game seemed to be settling into a stalemate.

Throughout most of the first half, Anderson had been the workhorse of the Cadets' offense. He had not broken any long runs, but he was proving good for about four yards just about every time he carried the ball. On orders from Tom Harp, Joe Caldwell also began to look for Don Usry on Army's next possession. On first down, Caldwell hit the tight end for a seventeen-yard gain to the Navy 47. Then Caldwell found Anderson in the left flat for a completion that took the ball down to the 36. After sending Dawkins into the line for three yards, Caldwell threw to Usry again, down to the 15.

Usry's three catches in the first half had gone for fifty-two yards. All season, he had been a footnote in the story of the Lonely End. Now, in the biggest game of the year, he found himself at the center of the attack.

With less than two minutes to go until halftime, Caldwell handed the ball off to Anderson, who stumbled five yards on a quick trap play down to the 10. Anderson carried for two more on the next play, and on third-and-three from the 8 he tore inside to the Navy 2-yard line. Vince Lombardi, from his vantage point in the grandstand—which happened to be right in front of Anderson's parents—was standing and shouting, "Give the ball to Anderson! Give the ball to Anderson!" On the next play, that's just what Caldwell did. Anderson's fourth straight carry of the drive went for an Army touchdown. Just thirty-three seconds remained in the half when Harry Walters booted the extra point. The Cadets went to the locker room leading 7–6.

Shortly after kickoff, the temperature on the field had climbed to thirty-four degrees, but it soon began a slow and steady descent back into the twenties. "Reluctant to quit a slugging match which they had traveled many miles to watch, customers nevertheless started making their numbed way toward the exits when the first half ended, longing for a warm hotel room with the guy across the courtyard beating his wife," wrote a disgruntled Red Smith, who seems to have suffered from the cold himself.*

Joe Tranchini was not concerned with the weather. As the Navy quarterback took the field for the start of the second half, he was instead worried that the Midshipmen had no fresh battery of trick plays to spring upon the Cadets. "As well as it had all been working, we may have gotten a little overexcited in the first half," he says. The game had begun perfectly for Navy, but all of Erdelatz's legerdemain—

---

* Smith wrote about the icy chill in Philadelphia quite a bit. He also noted, "Perhaps never before had so many shivered in such acute misery on so pretty a day at a struggle so fiercely contested between teams so superbly matched."

his "ancient weapons," as Blaik referred to them—could not hide the fact that Army was the superior team. At the line of scrimmage, the Cadets had begun to overpower the Midshipmen, who sorely missed the injured Bob Reifsnyder. Navy had rushed for seventy-seven yards in the first half, most of it before the midway point of the second quarter. In the second half, the Midshipmen endured a dispiriting string of three-and-outs. Army, meanwhile, behind the powerful running of Anderson, kept converting on third and fourth downs. "They were just barely making it," says Buddy Wellborn. "But they kept making it."

Much to Blaik's consternation, the Cadets' sloppy play—they had turned the ball over three times in the first half, twice on fumbles—continued into the third quarter. Army's first possession of the second half began on the Midshipmen's 41-yard line, the result of a muffed Navy punt that traveled only five yards. The Cadets moved the ball to the 18, but linebacker Jim Dunn picked off a Joe Caldwell pass and returned it to the Navy 31, where he fumbled. A hustling Bob Novogratz fell on the ball for his second fumble recovery of the game. Army then drove to the Midshipmen's 4-yard line, where Dawkins fumbled the ball away again. The Cadets had been dominating play since midway through the second quarter, but they only had a one-point lead to show for it.

After another Navy punt, Army had the ball on its 37-yard line late in the third quarter. On first down, Dawkins went in motion toward Carpenter, who was split wide to the left. Caldwell, after a quick play-action fake to Anderson, zipped the ball to Dawkins, who was all alone in the flat when he caught the ball at the Cadets' 42. He sprinted upfield, slipped an arm tackle from a defensive back at the Midshipmen's 47, and dashed down the sideline to the 34, where Brandquist finally knocked him out of bounds. Anderson carried inside for five yards on the next play. Dawkins did the same for three, and then for nine. Inside the final minute of the third quarter, Anderson carried for five more to put the ball on Navy's 9-yard line. By the time the third quarter ended, Army had advanced to the 2, and on the first play of the fourth, Anderson plunged into the end zone for his second touchdown. Walters kicked the extra point, and Army led 14–6.

Still, the Midshipmen refused to succumb to what now seemed to be their inevitable defeat, and the Cadets' lead remained at eight points—a deficit that could be erased by a touchdown and a two-point conversion. Starting from his own 28 with less than two minutes left in the game, Joe Tranchini went to the air, throwing a screen to Bellino along the left sideline that picked up eleven yards. On the next play, Tranchini again dropped back to pass, looking to his right, where Buddy Wellborn had sprinted into the flat. Monk Hilliard was out in the flat as well, and when he saw Trancini plant his feet to throw, he stopped his rush at about the 34-yard line and prepared to jump. A pump-fake by Tranchini would have taken Hilliard out of the play, but with the clock ticking down the Navy quarterback turned the ball loose. Hilliard timed his leap perfectly. Tranchini's pass struck the tackle square on the palm of his right hand and bounced high and to Hilliard's rear. Wellborn, who had frozen at the 36 when he saw Hilliard tip the pass, jumped for the ball, but it sailed over his head and past his outstretched left arm. Don Usry, who had been shadowing Wellborn, caught the ball on the 38 at a dead run. He sprinted into the end zone, casually flipping the ball behind him as he crossed the goal line. Bob Anderson, who was trailing the play, caught the ball and flung it into the crowd as he ran to embrace Usry. Army led 20–6.

To put the game out of reach, Blaik ordered the Cadets to go for two. Running from the Lonely End formation for the last time in 1958, Dawkins took a pitch from Caldwell, rolled to his left, and tossed to a wide-open Anderson for the extra points and a 22–6 lead. The completion was only the third of the season for Dawkins, his first since the victory over Notre Dame. Anderson, in contrast, had connected on ten of his fifteen passes on the year for four touchdowns. Much had been made of the great passing threat posed by both backs, but the truth was something far different, owing not only to Anderson's superlative throwing skills but also to the fact that Dawkins may have been the best receiver in the country. He had caught sixteen passes that fall for 494 yards, averaging just under thirty-one yards a reception. Writing in the *Times,* Arthur Daley noted that there was something symbolic about Dawkins throwing the final pass of his career to Anderson: " 'My football career is over, mister,' [Dawkins] seemed to say. 'You carry on henceforth.' "

Back in the Army locker room, after the players had been borne off the field on the shoulders of their fellow cadets, Blaik and his boys had a brief moment to celebrate together. A sense of elation suffused the cramped space. Less than a decade after he had promised MacArthur that he would not leave under fire, Blaik had restored Army to the mountaintop. His boys, he said, "who were brightened with unusual color and favored with good fortune," had "brought Army football back to the national pre-eminence it enjoyed before the tragedy of 1951." That tragedy, if it could never be expunged from the record books, had now at least been pushed aside.

Joe Cahill, upon reaching the locker room, handed Blaik a slip of paper. Waiting outside the room in a stadium tunnel were the gentlemen of the press. Blaik glanced at the paper and saw that it was a congratulatory telegram from General MacArthur. He asked Cahill to hold off the reporters for a few minutes. Then he called his players together, cleared his throat, and read a message that left both coaches and players swelling with pride:

IN THE LONG HISTORY OF WEST POINT ATHLETICS THERE HAS NEVER BEEN A GREATER TRIUMPH. IT HAS BROUGHT PRIDE AND HAPPINESS AND ADMIRATION TO MILLIONS OF ARMY ROOTERS THROUGHOUT THE WORLD. TELL CAPTAIN DAWKINS AND HIS INDOMITABLE TEAM THEY HAVE WRITTEN THEIR NAMES IN GOLDEN LETTERS ON THE TABLETS OF FOOTBALL FAME. FOR YOU, MY DEAR OLD FRIEND, IT MARKS ONE OF THE MOST GLORIOUS MOMENTS OF YOUR PEERLESS CAREER. THERE IS NO SUBSTITUTE FOR VICTORY.

Chapter 12

FAREWELL

In recognition of his powerful performance in the victory over Navy, Bob Anderson, who had carried the ball a season-high twenty-nine times for eighty-nine yards and two touchdowns, was named the game's outstanding player. That Anderson was the Cadets' best all-around halfback was not an impression that was limited to the Army locker room, and after the game, reporters swarmed him with questions, many of which sought to elicit an expression of disappointment about the supporting role he had played to Pete Dawkins in 1958. But the self-effacing Anderson steadfastly refused to be baited, and he fielded the questions with polite humility.

"Are you disappointed that you aren't All-America this year?"

"No, sir. This is a team effort, sir. I'm proud to be a member of this team, sir."

"How do you compare yourself to Dawkins?"

"He got the [Maxwell] Trophy, didn't he, sir? Pete Dawkins is the greatest back in the country, sir."

The *Times*'s Arthur Daley responded, "That, however, is only one man's opinion. The strong belief here is that Anderson is No. 1 . . . The Army-Navy game merely produced more evidence."

But while Anderson never sought the spotlight, the truth was that he *did* miss the extra attention. He had been thrilled the year before when he got to appear on *The Ed Sullivan Show* as a member of the 1957 Associated Press All-America team. And it bothered him that Dawkins was the Heisman Trophy favorite even though he had rushed for fewer yards. "We were all happy for Pete, and if somebody was going to win it, we wanted somebody on our team to win it," says Anderson. "But I think a lot of the hype . . . I mean, he wore stars on his collar. He was president of his class. I was a ragtag kid from Cocoa, Florida."

Anderson actually did receive first-team All-America recognition later in December, from the Football Writers Association of America, who also honored Dawkins and LSU halfback Billy Cannon. "I had another year to go," says Anderson. "I thought maybe I'd be a three-time All-America." After an undefeated season, anything seemed possible.

A bus took Anderson and his jubilant teammates from Municipal Stadium to the Benjamin Franklin Hotel in downtown Philadelphia. Many of the players spent the evening visiting with friends and family, though some celebrated on their own at the hotel. Making his way back from dinner, team manager John Bryer saw a handful of players in a hallway sharing beers and improvising a beach party with the sand from an upended ashtray. On the train back to West Point the next morning, the team's underclassmen officially began the 1959 season by electing their team captain. Bill Carpenter won the vote as Dawkins's successor in a landslide—the country's most mysterious player inheriting command from its most glamorous. On December 1, the AP released its final college football poll of the season. Army was ranked number three, behind national champion LSU—the only major team in the country with a perfect record—and number-two Iowa. The ranking was the highest for the Cadets since 1950, when they had finished second behind Oklahoma. "If the West Point eleven was not the best of 1958," wrote Allison Danzig in *The New York Times,* "certainly none was gamer or showed more of the poise and fortitude of a champion than did the Black Knights in the closing performance of their first undefeated season since 1949." And the *Times*'s editorial page gushed, in an unsigned piece, that the Lonely End had "fired the imagination of the entire country. Holding aloof from the huddle, presumably getting the signals by radar or through someone's twitching an ear, Cadet Carpenter came as close to being the nation's dreamboat as is good for an Army man to be."

Blaik was not worrying about the rankings during the trip back to West Point. Without a bowl game to prepare for—undefeated Air Force, ranked number six, had gladly accepted the Cotton Bowl invitation that Army had declined—his thoughts turned to his future. For much of the season he had been toying with the idea of retirement, but now he would have to make a decision. Blaik's first order of business would be to re-sign each of his coaches for the 1959 season—a sound move in the event he decided to retire, since the administration was likely to hold to the tradition that West Point's coach be a West Point man. That meant his successor would almost certainly be Dale Hall, and Blaik felt it would be best for Hall to work with men he knew and liked. In his role as athletic director, Blaik signed all of his assistants to new contracts in the first week of December, before they departed on their pre-Christmas recruiting trips.

He and Merle then departed for the sands of Key Biscayne. The Blaiks did not make an appearance at New York City's Downtown Athletic Club on the evening of December 10 to see Pete Dawkins accept the Heisman Trophy. But on December 17, they made a side trip to Richmond, Virginia, where Blaik received the city's Sportsmen's Club Award. Otherwise, his only other contact with the outside world came during a series of lengthy telephone conversations with Victor Emanuel, the president and chairman of the board of the Aviation Corporation, popularly known as AVCO.

Emanuel and Blaik knew each other well. They had grown up together in the Riverdale neighborhood of Dayton, Ohio, on the banks of the Great Miami River. Though they had gone to separate high schools—Blaik attended Steele High, a fabulous Gothic structure on the southeast corner of Monument and Main streets, while Emanuel, a Catholic whose father was a wealthy utilities man and the owner of the Dayton Street Railway Company, went to the nearby

St. Mary's Institute—their bond had been forged by a broad sweep of shared childhood experiences. No event had made a bigger impression on either boy than the Great Dayton Flood, which, on March 25, 1913, submerged the city beneath up to twenty feet of water and killed nearly four hundred people. Both Blaik and Emanuel had been forced to evacuate their homes with their families. The Army coach liked to refer to the flood and its aftermath as "my introduction to catastrophe."

The Dayton of Blaik's youth was a bustling hub of technical and industrial innovation. Orville and Wilbur Wright still lived on the city's west side and had a small bicycle shop on Third Street. Among the residents of Riverdale was Hugh Chalmers, who would later become vice president of the National Cash Register Company (NCR) before leaving town for Detroit to start the Chalmers Motor Car Company. And two doors down from the Emanuel house was the workshop of the brilliant, colorful inventor Charles F. Kettering, a former researcher at NCR—he had designed the world's first electric cash register—who had left the company to found the Dayton Engineering Laboratories Company (DELCO) with his friend Edward Deeds. In his autobiography, Blaik recounted how he used to peek into Deeds's garage, "one of those old, two-story converted stables," to watch Kettering at work on his revolutionary electronic automobile ignition system.

Emanuel, who was a year younger than Blaik, graduated from Cornell in 1919 with a bachelor of arts degree after having served as a naval aviator during World War I. Olive skinned and stocky, he kept his black hair permanently slicked back and carried himself with an air of sophistication. He returned to Dayton after college to work for his ailing father, and soon swung his first big business deal when he and a partner bought out his father's interest in the family utility business. Renaming the operation the National Electric Power Company, Emanuel undertook an ambitious expansion, snapping up smaller utilities in rapid succession. In 1926, he and his partner sold National Electric Power to investor Samuel Insull for an estimated thirteen million dollars. Emanuel, who was just twenty-eight years old, promptly retired to a lavish estate in the English countryside. Along with his wife, Dorothy, he leased Rockingham Castle, an eleventh-century Norman fortress that had been built on the orders of William the Conqueror. Emanuel maintained a stable of 125 horses, one of which he entered in the Grand National, became master of the Woodland Pytchley Hounds, went fox hunting with the Prince of Wales, and spent lavishly to restore his ancient residence. He and Dorothy also became famous for hosting extravagant parties, once importing three hundred guests from the United States. The English press dubbed Emanuel "the King of Glory."

But he had not retired completely from the world of business. Emanuel hobnobbed with London's top bankers and continued to play the stock market, and two years after his arrival in England, he had increased his net worth to some forty million dollars. Along with his friend the Belgian business magnate Alfred Loewenstein—who at the time was the third-richest man in the world—Emanuel hatched a plan to take over nearly every utility company in the United States. Before the scheme could be put into effect, however, Loewenstein died mysteriously when he jumped or fell from a plane into the English Channel.* Emanuel, after finding new partners, went ahead and put up a stake of sixty million dollars to acquire the Standard Gas & Electric System and formed the U.S. Electric Power Corporation (USEPCO) as a holding company. Almost overnight, Emanuel's utility empire stretched over twenty states and was worth over a billion dollars. But the stock market crash of 1929 wiped out both USEPCO's paper empire and Emanuel's fortune, though he and his partners kept control of Standard Gas. Emanuel's stake in the utility helped him get through eight lean years until, in 1937, he acquired the sprawling Cord Corporation, of which AVCO was a subsidiary. He nurtured this supplemental holding until AVCO was big enough to swallow up its parent companies and then grew the

* Emanuel always maintained that his friend had fallen to his death, not jumped. Loewenstein had apparently mistaken the entrance door of the aircraft—a small Fokker F.VII trimotor—for the door to the washroom. This was not the most notorious accident involving a Fokker. Three years after Loewenstein's death, Notre Dame coach Knute Rockne was killed when the TWA Fokker F.10 in which he was flying crashed into a Kansas wheat field after the wings separated in flight.

business into a profitable manufacturer of aircraft and aviation components. AVCO boomed during the Second World War, and Emanuel later expanded the corporation into commercial production, making everything from refrigerators to farm equipment and becoming a pioneer in the building of industrial conglomerates.

Known as VE in the corporate hallways of AVCO, Emanuel shed his former flamboyance, though he maintained a taste for double-breasted pinstripe suits and large flowered ties. He rarely submitted to interviews with the press and never permitted his picture to be taken. In a cover story on Emanuel and AVCO in 1946, *Time* magazine noted, "Most newspaper morgues have only one formal photo of him." The war years had introduced Emanuel to the backrooms of Washington, D.C., and he was widely regarded as one of the most politically well-connected men in the country, counting among his friends Ohio senator Robert Taft—son of President and Chief Justice William Howard Taft—who had launched unsuccessful bids for the Republican presidential nomination in both 1940 and 1948.

Emanuel's political ties and Blaik's friendship with MacArthur put the two childhood friends squarely in the middle of the action during the 1952 Republican National Convention. That summer, Senator Taft, a stalwart of the party's conservative wing, was locked in a bitter primary fight with Dwight Eisenhower, the choice of Republican moderates, and the nomination was still undecided when the convention opened in Chicago in July. MacArthur, whose own aspirations for the nomination had seemed to vanish earlier in the year, was a Taft supporter, and he was the senator's probable choice for a running mate in the event he won the nomination. The general still had plenty of clout in the Republican Party. He had campaigned aggressively, and bitterly, against Harry Truman after the president had ordered him home in the spring of 1951, railing against massive American aid to Europe and ridiculing the prolonged Korean truce talks. MacArthur's vengeful crusade against the president had been a factor in Truman's decision not to seek reelection in 1952, and the general's keynote address to the convention on July 7 was one of the most politically charged events of the summer.

But for one of the few times in his professional life, MacArthur's oratory was not up to the occasion. In the words of biographer William Manchester, "It was probably the worst speech of his career—banal, strident in content, wretchedly delivered, a bungling of his chance to become a dark horse." An onlooker who saw the speech said, "One could feel the electricity gradually running out of the room." A humbled MacArthur returned home to New York to await the convention's verdict, taking no calls from any of his political allies, including Taft. The night after MacArthur's speech, Taft lost several key delegates to Eisenhower. The senator abandoned hope for himself but was optimistic that, with proper maneuvering, MacArthur could still defeat Eisenhower. The negotiations on MacArthur's behalf were frantic, stretching late into the evening, and there are several conflicting accounts of the proceedings. One version holds that Emanuel called Red Blaik from Chicago and told him to stand by until two in the morning. Since nobody had been able to reach MacArthur on the telephone, Blaik was to await word from the convention and be ready to go in person to the Waldorf and ask MacArthur to call Taft. Manchester quotes Blaik: "The call from Victor never came; the Eisenhower delegates overcame the more conservative elements in the Republican party, and I was not commissioned to inform MacArthur of the sudden switch in his favor."

Blaik never did warm to Eisenhower, whom he regarded as inarticulate and an inferior officer to "the brilliant MacArthur." (Eisenhower had served as an aide to MacArthur when the latter had been chief of staff.) "[Ike] had absorbed enough from the General to give him an articulate flare which during the last decade has done so much to pave his way," Blaik wrote to a friend in 1952 before petulantly adding, "The war in Europe was not won by brilliant strategy, but rather by the relentless weight of superior arms and sound field leadership."

Through the next six years, Blaik remained in close contact with Emanuel, who telephoned the coach regularly during the 1958 season. During these calls, Emanuel frequently took the opportunity to offer Blaik a job, reminding him that AVCO would be happy to have a man with his interpersonal skills and business background. Though there's certainly some merit to this evaluation—Blaik was beloved by most of the people under his command, particularly his assistants and players—it's also true that many people with whom he dealt at West Point despised him. It had been Davidson's estimation, when the two men were assistant coaches together, that Blaik was self-centered and did not have any use for people who could not help him get ahead in the world. Blaik's business experience, as well, was more than thirty years out of date. But he saw no flaws in Emanuel's reasoning. More importantly, he was finally prepared to listen to his friend. "The temptation to accept had been strong because of the problems that faced me during my last few years at the academy," Blaik wrote later. "I had not wanted to leave, however, until I felt I had restored Army football, at least within the restrictions that surround it. That time had come, I felt, after our 22–6 victory over Navy provided a soul-satisfying climax to the Lonely End campaign."

Blaik was not the only person who had begun to consider the possibility of his retirement. Within days of Army's victory over the Midshipmen, a report in the *New York Journal-American* by sports editor Max Kase, who had won a Pulitzer Prize in 1952 for his exposure of bribery and corruption in college basketball, predicted that Blaik would resign. Blaik, on vacation in Key Biscayne, hadn't fully made up his mind, and he denied Kase's report in a carefully worded statement to *The New York Times*. "I have no intention as of now of leaving West Point," he said. "It would be wrong to suggest that I might never leave. Every year I have been offered splendid opportunities in football and otherwise. However, my present contract has two years to run."

Blaik waited to make his final decision until after the holidays. On Sunday, January 11, 1959, he had his older son, Bill, draft his letter of resignation. The coach took it to work with him the next morning and read it over several times while making notes. Late in the afternoon, he called in Harriet Demarest, his secretary at West Point since his first day on the job in 1941. She knew nothing of Blaik's plans, and as he dictated the final draft of the letter from behind his desk, he could see the expression on her face change from happy expectation to shocked sadness. He did not wait for her to comment. "When you've finished it and I've signed it," he told her, "put it in an envelope, seal it, and lock it away until tomorrow morning. I want one more night to sleep on it."

First thing the next morning, Blaik summoned director of sports publicity Joe Cahill to his office. Blaik told Cahill that he was going to tender his resignation and that he wanted a press release prepared for later in the day. Cahill, who had been at Blaik's side since 1943, was stunned. "I guess I was a little stunned myself," Blaik would later say. The two men spent some time trading stories of the old days, until finally Cahill said, "What time are you figuring on delivering the letter?"

Blaik rose from behind his desk, picked up his familiar fedora and overcoat, and said, "Now's as good a time as any, Joe."

He walked out of the gym and headed across the Plain. The day was overcast and bitterly cold, with temperatures just above ten degrees. "I had never realized," Blaik later said, "that it was such a long walk." Turning south on Thayer Road, he continued into the keep of West Point's towering Headquarters Building. Davidson was not in. Blaik left his letter with the general's secretary and returned to the gymnasium.

Much like Blaik himself, the letter to Davidson was direct and formal. It is also abrupt. Nowhere in it do the words "thank you" appear.

January 12, 1959

Dear Gar,

It is not easy to terminate years of association with cadets and the Military Academy, so the task of writing this letter is a sad one.

My resignation as football coach and Director of Athletics is submitted herewith to take effect on February 15th.

Since I have several years of accumulated leave I hope it will be acceptable to be relieved of all duties at once, so that Merle and I may take a short vacation after which we will return to complete

*our moving arrangements. Every effort will be made to vacate
our quarters prior to March 1st.*

*It is my earnest desire that my service terminate without cer-
emony or special recognition and that as Superintendent you will
accord me this request.*

With best wishes,
Sincerely,
Red Blaik

Just as he had done in 1933 when he left West Point for Dartmouth, Blaik caught Davidson by surprise. After reading the letter,
Davidson first phoned Blaik to acknowledge its receipt. Then he
called a meeting of the athletic board, setting in motion the process
that would determine successors for Blaik as both football coach
and director of athletics.

With no work to do, Blaik went home for lunch and then left for
New York with Merle and Bill; Bob, an assistant coach at the University of Miami, was out on the recruiting trail for coach Andy
Gustafson. The Blaiks went to dinner with their old friends Willis
and Elizabeth McDonald. Willis McDonald was a vice president
at the New York Trust Company, and he had had been roommates
with Blaik at the academy before serving with him in the cavalry at
Fort Bliss, Texas. It was during their cavalry days that Blaik had introduced McDonald to his future wife. While Blaik and his family
were relaxing in the McDonalds' Manhattan apartment, news of his
resignation from West Point came over the radio. According to Blaik,
it was the first his wife had ever heard of it. "Although she had suspected I might do it, she wasn't sure," he wrote. "So she was stunned
and, I think a little sad and happy, mostly happy."

Blaik's retirement was one of the top stories in the country the
next morning, alongside the recent arrival in Havana of a triumphant Fidel Castro. Throughout the next week, countless encomi-
ums hailed Blaik for his enormous influence on college football, and
stacks of letters wishing him well overwhelmed Joe Cahill's press
office. "It was with feelings considerably stronger than astonishment
that I learned last evening of your resignation," wrote Dwight Eisen-

hower to Blaik on January 14. "It is high time you thought of yourself—and you have already given more of yourself for the sake of your deeply felt loyalties than have most people." Ike went on to mention the speculation that Blaik's departure stemmed from a disagreement over the academy's bowl-game policy, a possibility to which the president gave no weight. Those who loathe the modern bowl system can take heart in the knowledge that Ike was no fan either. "For my part," he wrote to Blaik, "I have never even turned on the television or the radio to keep track of a bowl game. My interest is in the contests of the season."

Blaik left college football in a blaze of glory. His Lonely End attack had led the nation in passing offense and tied for second in scoring offense, with 29.3 points per game. The Army defense, which allowed just two rushing touchdowns all season, had been nearly as good, ranking third in total defense and fourth in scoring defense, allowing just 5.4 points per game. Though the tie against Pitt had ultimately cost the Cadets the national title, they were named winners of the Lambert Trophy as the top college football team in the East. It was the seventh time Army had won the honor, but the first since the 1953 team had begun Blaik's drive for redemption and vindication—a drive that had now ended with a team that had proven itself to be as dynamic and resilient as any he had ever coached.

"Should it be inconceivable that a man my age would finally want to leave?" he asked rhetorically in a postretirement discussion with *Sports Illustrated*. "Now if we had had a losing season, then I would stay. It would be against my nature to pull out . . . I just felt it was time to leave."

While Blaik was being hailed as a legend of the game, his players were well into their second month of being showered with individual honors in numbers not seen at West Point since the glory days of the 1940s. In addition to Dawkins's Maxwell and Heisman trophies, Bob Novogratz won the Knute Rockne Award—given by the Touchdown Club of Washington, D.C.—as college football's outstanding lineman.* The Football Writers Association of America also named Novogratz, who three days after the win over Navy had been selected by the Baltimore Colts in the twenty-fourth round of the NFL draft, a first-team All-America, giving Army a total of three players to be so honored. Only Notre Dame and Ohio State had as many All-Americas as the Cadets in 1958.

Blaik's announcement had blindsided his players. None of them had any inkling he might step down. Bob Anderson was stunned at first, then angry—"It pissed me off," he says. *What about next year?* But no one had much time to contemplate the possible consequences of Blaik's departure, or to worry much about who might take his place. The daily rigors of cadet life saw to that. A handful of the first classmen had also been exceedingly busy. On December 27, the night before the Baltimore Colts beat the New York Giants in sudden-death overtime to win the NFL title, Bob Novogratz played in the East-West Shrine Game in San Francisco. In early January, Pete Dawkins led a four-man West Point contingent—which also included Monk Hilliard, Bill Rowe, and Harry Walters—to Miami to play in the North-South Shrine Game.

As the most decorated college football player of 1958, Dawkins was required to attend a seemingly endless cycle of awards banquets. In addition to the ceremonies for the Maxwell and Heisman trophies, he was honored by the Army Athletic Association, the People to People Sports Foundation, and in late January by the B'nai B'rith Association, for "upholding high principles in athletics." B'nai B'rith had also honored Johnny Unitas, the Baltimore Colts quarterback, at that dinner. The night before, Unitas had been at the Touchdown Club of Washington, D.C., with Cleveland Browns running back Jim Brown, Iowa quarterback Randy Duncan, and Bob Novogratz, for the Knute Rockne Awards ceremony. During the dinner, Brown took a moment to admire Novogratz's trophy—a wooden square base topped by a lineman in a three-point stance—and said, "I dig your trophy, man." Novogratz had brought his parents to the banquet, and after the meal was over, he was surprised to see his

---

* The award has since been discontinued.

father, whose command of English was not strong, engaged in a friendly conversation with Vice President Richard Nixon. (Frank Novogratz, a lifelong Democrat, cast his vote for Nixon for president in 1960. When his appalled family asked him why he did not vote for John Kennedy, he said, "I never met Kennedy!")

Back at West Point, the focus was on finding a new football coach, and the athletic board turned a scrutinizing eye on defensive backfield coach Dale Hall. He was young, having turned thirty-four a few months before the season began; he knew the Army players and coaches, as well as the Lonely End offense; and like Blaik, he was an academy graduate. Hall wanted the job, and there was little doubt that it was his to lose. But some members of the board had reservations. Hall, with his open face and pronounced overbite, was a country boy from Pittsburg, Kansas, who spoke with a twang in his voice and who possessed none of Red Blaik's polish. "Dale was a brilliant son of a bitch," says Barney Gill. "And he was quiet, very dignified. We were close friends. But he would go to New York to a goddamned cocktail party wearing one of those big goddamned parkas with the goddamned fur collar."

The athletic board screened forty candidates, including LSU coach Paul Dietzel, who had twice been an assistant under Blaik, first in 1948 and again in 1953 and '54, and who was known to covet the job. Dietzel may have been ambitious, but he was also wary. "My wife and I had long ago decided that West Point was where we would ultimately like to be," he told a reporter several years later. "It's a wonderful place to raise a family. But I turned the job down. I wasn't about to follow Blaik. Blaik is a legend. It is not healthy to succeed a legend." The board also considered Blaik's current offensive backfield coach, Tom Harp, who was the favorite among most of his fellow assistants. Harp had not only been instrumental in the development of the Lonely End attack, but he had also played a major role in the dramatic transformation of Pete Dawkins from a hapless left-handed quarterback into college football's most decorated player.

Harp, too, wanted the job. He had gone to Blaik's office a few days after his retirement and asked if the new head coach would be a West

Pointer. Blaik told Harp that such a background "probably would be an advantage." Harp went back to his office and thought about it for a few minutes. Then he called a meeting with every assistant coach except Hall. "We all knew that Dale had applied right away," says Harp. "We were close friends, and we wanted to keep the thing going. I never pursued it, and we decided that we would all support Dale."

But as the days stretched on, the athletic board, now under the direction of Lieutenant Colonel Fran Roberts, refused to make a decision. Roberts had been running the day-to-day operations of the department for several years as Blaik's graduate manager of athletics, and he knew Hall as well as any other board member. Harp and his fellow assistants, who had assumed that Hall was the obvious choice to succeed Blaik, began to get nervous that somebody would be brought in from the outside—in which case some of them did not want to stay. Kentucky coach Blanton Collier had noticed the hesitation at West Point, too, and called Harp to offer him a spot on his staff in Lexington. The offer intrigued Harp, but he did not want to renege on the deal he had struck with the other Army assistants. Impatient for an answer, he went to see Roberts in his office and asked point-blank, "Are you going to hire Dale Hall or aren't you?"

"We're not quite ready to make a decision yet, Tom," said Roberts. "Give us the weekend to think about it and we'll announce something on Monday."

As it turned out, Roberts and the athletic board didn't need so much time. On Saturday, January 31, the academy announced that Dale Hall was Army's new head football coach. Harp turned down the offer from Kentucky. Not long after, Collier hired Don Shula to fill the position he had offered to Harp.

The man responsible for bringing Red Blaik to West Point in 1941 had been the superintendent, Brigadier General Robert L. Eichelberger. The two men first met during Blaik's years as an Army assistant, when Eichelberger, then a lieutenant colonel, had been the academy's adjutant general, a job that required him to deal with most of the administrative affairs of the athletic department. A graduate of

West Point's Class of 1909—George S. Patton was a classmate—Eichelberger was a career infantry officer and a passionate fan of Army football. As the AG, he cultivated a chummy relationship with the Cadets' coaching staff and made all the road trips with the team. In 1932, Eichelberger advocated for Blaik to get the head coaching job over Gar Davidson.

The handsome, lanky son of a lawyer from Urbana, Ohio, Eichelberger had spent two years at Ohio State before attending West Point. Relatively untroubled by the academy's rigorous academic demands, he pursued the social side of cadet life with zeal and was an ardent supporter of the football team. After graduation, he served first in Panama and then later, with MacArthur, along the U.S.–Mexico border. Eichelberger missed combat in Europe during World War I but served from 1918 to 1920 in Siberia as an intelligence officer for the American Expeditionary Force, observing the Japanese intervention in the region. He was popular with soldiers, who bestowed on him the affectionate nickname "Uncle Bob" in recognition of his approachable nature, as well as for his tendency to talk of military affairs in football terms. A 1945 *Time* magazine profile, written on the occasion of his postwar appointment as the commander of the Tokyo area—he had served at the right hand of MacArthur throughout the war in the Pacific—noted that he "does not believe in generals who buck the middle of the opponent's line; instead, he favors the end run, the cleverly concealed multiple pass, even on occasion a well-executed shoestring play."

On November 16, 1940, Eichelberger had been on hand at Philadelphia's Franklin Field to watch Army take on Pennsylvania. The Black Knights lost to the Quakers that day 48–0, at the time the worst defeat in academy history. Two days later, on his first day as superintendent at West Point, an appalled Eichelberger called a meeting of the athletic board. "I was impressed Saturday by the way the cadets cheered our team right to the end," he said in his opening remarks. "It looks as if we are developing the finest bunch of losers in the world." He then announced that he intended to hire Blaik away from Dartmouth. As the chastened board members left his office, Eichelberger began typing a private letter to Blaik, telling him, "If you have not signed a new contract don't sign any until you have talked to me first."

On the eve of the 1940 Army-Navy game, Blaik met with Eichelberger in the general's suite at the Benjamin Franklin Hotel. Blaik wanted to take the West Point job, but he had three demands: that he be allowed to bring his entire coaching staff from Dartmouth; that the academy's height and weight restrictions—which, as written, dictated that a tall candidate had to be underweight to gain admission—be revised; and that a home be built on academy grounds to replace the one that he and his family would be leaving behind in Hanover, New Hampshire. When Blaik and his wife visited West Point a few weeks later, Eichelberger and his wife, Emma, took them on a walk around Lusk Reservoir. The general led the group to a wooded ridge, just beyond the reservoir's south wall, and turned to face Michie Stadium. "I have always thought," he told Blaik, "that this would be God's chosen place to live." Eichelberger promised to build a home on the site to Blaik's specifications. Upon accepting the job on December 22, Blaik sent Eichelberger plans for a redbrick Colonial like the one he was leaving behind. That home has served ever since as the quarters of Army's head football coach.

The evening after his resignation became official, on February 16, 1958, Blaik—he and Merle were living in a New York hotel while they shopped for an apartment—headed to Leone's to meet Eichelberger, to whom he always referred as "Uncle Bobby." When Blaik arrived at the restaurant, Gene Leone met him at the door and told him that Eichelberger was already inside. Leone then escorted Blaik to the wine cellar, where Uncle Bobby was waiting with about twenty of Blaik's friends and colleagues, including MacArthur and his longtime aide, Major General Courtney Whitney; Tim Cohane and Stanley Woodward, Blaik's confidantes in the New York press; Lieutenant General Blackshear M. "Babe" Bryan, who had preceded Gar Davidson as superintendent at West Point; Victor Emanuel; Biff Jones, the coach who brought Blaik to West Point 1927; and every member of the current Army coaching staff. There were no women. "I was a senior at Miami when MacArthur got fired by Truman, and I sat at my desk and cried like a baby," says Bill Gunlock, who still marvels at the formidable guest list. "Less than ten years later, I'm sitting in the wine cellar at Leone's with General MacArthur on one side and General Whitney on the other, and we're watching highlight film."

After the screening was over, Gene Leone handed out specially printed menus, which billed the party as the "Bull Pond Banquet for BIG BROTHER"—Woodward had given Blaik the nickname during the 1958 Bull Pond retreat—and listed the location of the feast as "The Lonely End Inn." The bill of fare was:

Antipasto Novogratz

———

Fish Cakes à la Notre Dame

———

Half Baked Goat garnished with Sauce Erdelatz

———

Chuckles Axmurder Salad

———

Dawkins Parfait

———

Hot Cocoa Anderson with Whipped Linebackers

———

Iced Hemlock. Cashew Nuts. Opium

"Thank goodness," said Blaik later, "there was an optional dinner on request."

The wine cellar at Leone's, with its low ceiling and bare stone walls, was not an especially big room, and as the night wore on the sound of laughter and sentimental conversation fairly filled it. The party did not run late. MacArthur was seventy-eight years old, and the fastidious Blaik was perpetually sober. No one lingered. But as the celebration broke up, there was a general feeling among the celebrants that it had been a singular evening, and as the men made their way to the stairs, Gene Leone put the sentiment into words, telling them all that it had been the finest party in the history of the restaurant.

And now it was over. The revelers went their separate ways and vanished into the New York night. When they were gone, the 1958 season went with them for good. All that remained was the memory, and the sense that something special had happened.

EPILOGUE

BOB ANDERSON'S SENSE OF FOREBODING about the 1959 season turned out to be prescient. Army entered the year as a consensus top-ten pick, ranked number five by the AP, and Anderson was the favorite to win the Heisman Trophy. On opening day, with Red Blaik in attendance—his first game ever as a spectator at Michie Stadium—the Cadets whipped Boston College 44–8. Dale Hall and the coaching staff had tweaked the Lonely End position to have Bill Carpenter occasionally line up as a flanking halfback, and Joe Caldwell found him for four touchdown passes as Army's aerial game soared for 314 yards. It was a performance that seemed to presage another season of greatness, but things soon began to go horribly wrong for the Cadets. In the first half of a stunning 20–14 loss at Illinois the next week, Anderson tore cartilage in his knee as he was drifting back to catch a punt, the first injury in what became a horrible run of casualties. Don Usry rolled an ankle against the Fighting Illini and would shuttle in and out of the lineup for the rest of the year; Steve Waldrop went down for the season with a torn anterior cruciate ligament the next week in the opening quarter of a 17–11 loss to Penn State, Army's first loss at Michie Stadium since 1955; and Don Bonko's season was also cut short with knee problems.

Such a streak of misfortune would be hard for any team to withstand, but for undermanned Army it was devastating. After the loss to the Fighting Illini, it was as though the Cadets never stopped exhaling. Army beat overmatched Duke and Colorado State the next two weeks, then narrowly escaped foggy, drizzly Yankee Stadium with a 13–13 tie against Air Force in the first meeting between the two academies. In a courageous performance, Anderson, who had eschewed season-ending surgery on his knee, scored both of Army's touchdowns against the Falcons, the last on a soaring one-yard dive over the goal line. "Tom Harp and Dale Hall had come to me," says Anderson, "and said, 'Bobby you need an operation on your knee, but we need you in uniform. It's your decision, but we need you in uniform. We have a bunch of young guys.' I didn't want to be operated on right away, anyway."

Hall rested his starters in the next game, as the Black Knights beat Villanova 14–0 while preparing to visit Oklahoma on November 14. Carpenter played against the Sooners with a dislocated shoulder, which he kept strapped down to prevent him from raising it too high. He nevertheless grabbed six passes for sixty-seven yards and ran back four kickoffs for sixty-five more. But he could not prevent Oklahoma from winning 28–20. Carpenter's grit certainly impressed the Sooners. "I remember that game vividly," he says, "because Bud Wilkinson came into the locker room after the game—never seen that happen, before or after. And he really gave a better speech to the football team than Dale Hall did. He said, 'We thought it was gonna be a walkover, but you guys hit us harder than we've ever been hit before.' And then he went around and talked to everybody on the team, whispered in their ear, patted them on the back. Which I thought was just super."

But there were no moral victories to be found in the 43–12 drubbing the Cadets suffered at the hands of Navy two weeks later. Joe Bellino, showcasing the form that would win him the Heisman Trophy in 1960, ran for 113 yards and three touchdowns as the Midshipmen rolled up 405 yards of total offense. Red Blaik did not mince words in his evaluation of the 1959 season, which had fulfilled all of his dark prophecies about what would happen if the academy continued to strictly limit the number of football recruits. "It would be naïve . . . to impute the entire blame [for the poor season] to injuries and the consequent fumbling and overemphasis on passing," he wrote in his autobiography. "It is also a fact that the devaluation of football's importance, inherent in the 'equality for all sports' philosophy, contributed to what happened, even though the players themselves might not be aware of it."

For most of the next ten years, Army football held its own. From 1960 to 1969, the Cadets went 60–37–3, but they never again challenged for a national championship, and they made their last appearance of the decade in the AP college football poll in 1962. Dale Hall lasted only three years at West Point despite an overall record of 16–11–2. His greatest sin was his failure to beat Navy in three attempts. ("If you didn't beat Navy," says Barney Gill, "they'd hang you up by the balls.") The man hired to replace Hall was none other than Paul Dietzel, the young, charismatic LSU coach, who so coveted the Army job that he had left Baton Rouge with four years remaining on his contract. Blaik had once called his former assistant "the world's greatest recruiter," and Dietzel's migration to West Point was accompanied by a tremendous amount of hype—the scrimmage that concluded his first spring practice was attended by more than three thousand people, among them General Douglas MacArthur. Though Dietzel, who was known as Pepsodent Paul for his near-constant smile, proclaimed that he would need four years to rebuild the program, there seemed to be little doubt that the glory days had returned to the banks of the Hudson. "The prospect of losing," Dietzel said, "does not concern me."

But after two modestly successful seasons, the Black Knights stumbled to a 4–6 record in 1964, their first losing season since the dark days of 1951. When they sank to 4–5–1 in 1965, Dietzel, who beat Navy only once in four tries, fled West Point for South Carolina. "One thing I had never realized was how much the situation at West Point had changed since 1955," he wrote in *Sports Illustrated*. "There were two things that I felt were the hardest blows at the academy. First, the number of years a boy has to serve after graduation had been raised [from three] to five. Second, the pros were throwing around so much money that blue-chip athletes were forced to think about that first."

Dietzel was right. The talent required to compete against the best teams in college football was no longer at West Point. Army won just four of fifteen games against ranked competition from 1960 to 1969 as the National Football League continued to grow in importance, seemingly with each passing Sunday. In the fall of 1958, networks were still negotiating broadcast deals worth hundreds of thousands of dollars with individual pro teams. But the Colts' victory over the Giants in sudden-death overtime in the 1958 NFL championship game soon changed that. A record television audience of forty-five million had tuned in for the game—which was played twenty-nine days after Army's 22–6 victory over Navy. The championship game broadcast did more than anything else to convince executives in the league, and on Madison Avenue, that pro football could be a profitable television feature.

One of those NFL execs was Pete Rozelle. Shortly after the owners elected him commissioner in 1960, the thirty-four-year-old former public relations man set about securing a television deal for the entire league. In 1962, after overcoming daunting legal hurdles, he secured a broadcast agreement with CBS worth $4.65 million per year, with the revenue to be shared equally among the league's fourteen franchises. Two years later, CBS re-upped with the NFL for $14 million annually, a deal that spurred NBC to outbid ABC for broadcast rights to the fledgling American Football League to the tune of $36 million for five years. By decade's end, broadcast rights for the NFL were worth $46.25 million, and the league was in a major bidding war over players with the AFL. *Sports Illustrated*'s John Underwood, who in 1958 worked for Joe Cahill in the Army sports publicity office, summed up Army's problem thus: "Since Joe Namath got $400,000 to sign with the New York Jets [in 1965], every high school quarterback with half a pound of talent dreams of getting his share." Underwood also noted, "Formal declaration or no, the U.S. is at war," before adding that in 1958 "the chances were that a West Pointer would not find himself being shot at immediately after graduation."

The man that West Point chose to replace Dietzel and face these challenges was Tom Cahill, the amiable coach of the plebe team. In 1966, Cahill steered Dietzel's recruits to a surprising 8–2 record and earned National Coach of the Year honors. In his first four seasons on the sideline, he won twenty-seven of forty games and beat Navy three times. But in 1970—the year of both the AFL-NFL merger and the debut of *Monday Night Football* on ABC—the Cadets could no longer resist the rising tide. Army finished 1–9–1 that season, the Cadets' worst record since they went 1–7–1 in 1940, the year before General Eichelberger hired Red Blaik. The academy fired Cahill after Army finished 0–10 in 1973, but the football program at West Point remained underwater for the better part of the next ten years. From 1970 to 1983, the Cadets won only 48 of 151 games and had just three winning seasons. Only when second-year coach Jim Young installed the wishbone offense in 1984 did Army end this long stretch of futility. By then, the standard of success was far different than it had been for Red Blaik. Young was hailed as a savior because his record in eight years at West Point was 51–39–1. Blaik, in contrast, lost only thirty-three games in eighteen years.

And what became of Blaik's Lonely End? The formation did inspire imitation, and, as discussed earlier, Army did use it again in 1959. Tom Harp even took it to Cornell after the school hired him as head coach in 1961. But the Lonely End never again duplicated the smashing success of its debut season at West Point. In part, this was due to the Black Knights' personnel, especially Bob Anderson, who proved to be a marvelous passer whenever he ran Blaik's favorite action pass, the halfback option.

But the main reason for the sharp decline in the effectiveness of the Lonely End was the simple fact that—as happens in football all the time—defenses adjusted to the tactic. Before Blaik's far flanker, the standard four-man defensive backfield rotated players in one of two directions: either forward to the line of scrimmage or laterally into pass coverage, depending on the offensive formation and the flow of the play. A spread end split as much as twenty yards wide nullified this since it was impossible to both put a man on the far flanker and maintain the integrity of the defensive secondary. With Carpenter split wide, a rotating "four-spoke" defensive backfield could not both contain sweeps and counter the dual run-pass threat presented by Anderson and Dawkins.

The defensive adjustment to this dilemma was to "invert" a safety, dropping him down to the flat zone, i.e., the dead area between the offensive line and the Lonely End. From the flat, the safety could both provide run support on sweeps and defend against the pass. This inverted coverage was something wholly new to defensive football and is the enduring legacy of the Lonely End. Every time Pittsburgh Steelers strong safety Troy Polamalu creeps forward from his position deep in the secondary and stations himself in the flat—something strong safeties throughout the NFL seem to do dozens of times every game—it is a tribute to Red Blaik's far flanker.

The late Homer Smith, who died at the age of seventy-nine on April 10, 2011, was one of college football's most brilliantly creative minds. A former offensive coordinator for Alabama and UCLA, as well as a former head coach at West Point, he was also an author and a noted football historian. "With the lonesome end, the wide receiver could release and that would—until the defenses adjusted—drive two defenders back," said Smith in July of 2010. "You can imagine how that opened up the running game. That's one offensive player taking away two defenders.

"I was manning the phones on the sideline in a game when I was the freshman coach at Stanford in 1958, and someone we were playing, I forget who it was, was using the inverted rotation. We didn't know what the heck was going on; at least the coaches didn't, and I sure didn't. It was that new, that surprising. It's kind of an obscure defensive development, but defenses didn't know how to have inside safetymen rotate to the line of scrimmage until the lonesome end came along, and then they started doing it."

There is more to Red Blaik's legacy at West Point than the Lonely End, of course. Over the years there have been several attempts to honor him at the academy, almost all of which have culminated in bad feelings and further dredging up of the catastrophe of 1951. The acrimony reached its height in 1986, when there was a move to name the academy's newest athletic facility for Army's most successful football coach. Built adjacent to Michie Stadium, just beyond the south end zone, the building was to contain a new hockey arena and basketball court and would serve as the headquarters for the bulk of West Point's indoor sports. The academy's new superintendent, Lieutenant General Dave R. Palmer, had been warned by the outgoing superintendent, Lieutenant General Willard W. Scott Jr., that naming the new building for Blaik would be a major problem. This fact was driven home to Palmer in September, when he received a letter from none other than Garrison H. Davidson, who opposed naming anything for his old rival. "My blood boils and I see red," wrote the eighty-two-year-old former superintendent, "when my mind drifts to the possibility of a draft dodger memorialized at West Point."

Palmer was in a very tough spot. He decided that before the academy did anything, it needed to have a policy on the naming of athletic facilities. Palmer formed a committee, which eventually settled on a recommendation that any facility in which cadets compete would follow the process that had been behind the naming of Michie Stadium—named in 1924 for Dennis Mahan Michie, the cadet who had first introduced football to the academy in 1890, and who had been killed in action eight years later during the Spanish-American War. This meant that any name used would have to be of a West Point graduate who had been a renowned athlete and who had died in battle in the prime of life, a requirement that disqualified Blaik from all further consideration. In June 1987, Palmer signed a memorandum establishing the committee's recommendation as official policy, and the new building was named for Don Holleder, Army's end-turned-quarterback from 1956, who had been cut down by enemy fire in Vietnam in 1967.

But Palmer's policy did not end the matter. On May 6, 1989, Red Blaik died at his home in Colorado Springs. Soon after, a coterie of his supporters, including his son Bob and Harry Walters, began to push for the academy to rename Michie Stadium for the coach. But rather than challenge West Point's new naming policy, the group, which was well connected within the Republican Party, appealed directly to the White House, where they believed Blaik would get favorable treatment. First Lady Barbara Bush was one of the daughters of Marvin Pierce, who had roomed with Blaik when the two had been students at Miami. And President George H. W. Bush had nominated Blaik for the Presidential Medal of Freedom, which the coach received from Ronald Reagan in 1986. Former presidents Richard Nixon and Gerald Ford made official appeals to Bush on Blaik's behalf.

Instead of acting on the request, however, the White House forwarded it to the Department of the Army, which contacted Palmer. Not long after, the superintendent began to hear from Blaik's detractors. Among them was General Andrew Goodpaster, a 1939 graduate of West Point and the former Supreme Allied Commander of the North Atlantic Treaty Organization. The scholarly Goodpaster was so highly regarded in the Army that he had been coaxed out of retirement in 1977 to become the superintendent at the academy in the wake of the 1976 cheating scandal. But the mild-mannered general's opposition to the stadium issue took Palmer aback. "I have never gone against my president," he told the superintendent, "but if the White House goes along with that request, I will hold a press conference and tell everybody everything I know about Red Blaik."

Palmer, desperate to find a compromise, called Bob Blaik and proposed to name the building that housed the department of athletics for his father. But the offer was rebuffed, and Blaik's son, according to Palmer, "cut off communications." The White House, having learned of the controversy, assigned presidential adviser Andrew Card to find a suitable way out of the mess. In a meeting with Card, Palmer explained the situation, saying of Blaik's supporters, "They are going around me [to the president] because they know that we have policies in place to keep this from happening." He also predicted that if the stadium was renamed for Blaik, "there will be a firestorm."

The controversy got passed around the Department of the Army from one desk to another over the next year, until it eventually was overtaken by more pressing concerns. The issue lingered, however, until the fall of 1999, when the field at Michie Stadium was finally named for Blaik. But the compromise did not do away with the deep divisions among the academy's graduates. "People who are tied to the honor system will never, ever give up about Blaik and football—ever," says Harry Walters. "West Point is not a religion. Some graduates believe it's a religion. It's not. It's a national, federal place where we train military officers to fight and win our wars. Nothing more. Nothing less."

Five years after the dedication of Blaik Field at Michie Stadium, another dispute arose when the coach's acolytes attempted to erect an eight-foot bronze statue of Blaik at West Point. The pose itself is unobjectionable. It is of Blaik the coach: kneeling and looking out on some imaginary scrimmage, his right hand hanging to the ground and resting on a football, his head topped by his familiar Army baseball cap. But the likeness sits on a five-sided black granite pedestal, with each side bearing a plaque upon which are engraved the names of every man who lettered for Blaik at West Point, including the names of his "ninety scapegoats." Once again, the academy's deepest wound was ripped open. Among the voices speaking out adamantly against the statue was Pete Vann, the quarterback of the Cadets' redemptive 1953 team. Vann said a statue that honored only Blaik would be fine, but he refused to allow his name to be put on anything that also honored men who had been kicked out in the cheating scandal of 1951.

The statue of Blaik now stands at the College Football Hall of Fame in South Bend, Indiana.

The record of achievement for the players from Red Blaik's, and West Point's, last undefeated football team is remarkable. Pete Dawkins, who graduated tenth in the Class of 1959, earned a Rhodes Scholarship—one of six in his class to do so—and studied for three years at Oxford before beginning his career as an infantry officer. Tackle Ed Bagdonas competed for the United States in the hammer throw at the 1960 Olympic Games in Rome, placing nineteenth. Fullback Harry Walters served in the administration of President Ronald Reagan, working first as the assistant secretary of the army for manpower and reserve affairs until, in 1983, the president appointed him as the administrator of veterans affairs. Reserve guard Al Vanderbush returned to West Point in 1990 to become the director of athletics, a job he held for nine years. Of the thirty-eight players on the roster, ten reached the rank of colonel before their retirement from the army. Three of those men wore general's stars: Dawkins retired in 1983 as a brigadier general; Bill Carpenter left the service in 1992 as a lieutenant general; and reserve guard George Joulwan, who was a sophomore in 1958, retired in 1997 with four stars. His last job in the army was as the Supreme Allied Commander, Europe.

Dawkins has never stopped living a life of remarkable achievement—though he never fulfilled all the lofty expectations that were a result of his singular cadet career. He played rugby during his time in England and left a lasting mark on the game by popularizing the overarm throw. He later worked as an adviser in Vietnam, taught at West Point, earned a Ph.D. at Princeton, and served as a White House Fellow. After several senior command assignments, he retired in 1983 from a position in the Pentagon as the army's deputy director of strategy, plans, and policy. If there was a disappointment in Dawkins's military career, it was that he never reached the lofty heights that were predicted for him. In the regular army, his reputation as a "water walker" sometimes worked against him. When, at the age of thirty-six in 1974, he became the first man in his class to reach the rank of colonel, the *Army Times* ran a story on his imminent promotion under the headline STAR FOR DAWKINS BEFORE 40? Later that year, his wife, Judi, lamented to the *Washington Post,* "Well, if you are going to hang somebody, that's about as good a way in the Army as any—to say something like that in a publication that most Army officers read. They're going to say, 'Well, I'll make darn sure that doesn't happen.'"

Once Dawkins became a civilian, he enjoyed a four-year run of success as a partner at Lehman Brothers in New York. He left finance in 1988 to run as a Republican for the United States Senate in New Jersey. Facing incumbent Frank R. Lautenberg, he lost a bruising campaign in which he was painted as a carpetbagger who would only use his Senate seat as a springboard for an eventual run at the White House. Two of Lautenberg's key political operatives were James Carville and Paul Begala, who four years later would make their own successful run at the White House with Bill Clinton. Dawkins returned to Wall Street, eventually rising to be vice chairman of the Citigroup Private Bank. He recently launched a new commodities hedge fund.

Like thousands of other West Point graduates, the men of 1958 also served their country in battle. Twenty-one players served at least one tour in Vietnam, and thirteen served there twice. The team's most famous combat veteran was Carpenter, who wound up getting sent to war after he resisted orders to play for the base football team at Fort Campbell, Kentucky. Carpenter was wounded twice during his first tour in Vietnam. During his second, he distinguished himself in one of the most memorable engagements of the entire war. On June 9, 1966, with his company being overrun by a North Vietnamese infantry regiment on a ridgeline in the bamboo jungle outside the village of Dak To, Carpenter called in a napalm strike on his own position. The napalm canisters detonated when they struck the treetops, providing protective cover to the troopers immediately below and unleashing a horrible hot fury on all who surrounded them. The explosion bought Carpenter enough time to gather his wounded and wait for reinforcements. Not one of his soldiers perished in the napalm strike, and his company lost only eight men in the entire engagement. For his actions that day, Carpenter was awarded the Distinguished Service Cross, the American military's second-highest award for valor in combat. The engagement received extensive publicity back in the United States and added to the mystique that had attached to Carpenter during his days as Red Blaik's Lonely End.

The war was harder on some other members of the 1958 team. Charlie Lytle, the strong-side guard on Army's offensive line, earned the Silver Star, the nation's third-highest honor for combat valor, during his first tour in Vietnam. During his second, he was wounded when he stepped on an enemy land mine. Lytle retired due to disability in 1973, after doctors diagnosed him with post-traumatic stress disorder as a result of his combat experiences. "He was always still really sweet [after Vietnam]," says his ex-wife, Bobbie. "He was just checked out. I took care of him for nine years and then he went home to live with his family." Lytle, who was known as Jolly Cholly during his days at West Point, worked for a time as an accountant for the state of Ohio, and he was a volunteer football coach at the high school in his hometown of Lancaster, but he never really found his way back to the man he used to be. Lytle and Bobbie had two girls, Mary, who is forty-three, and Tiffany, now forty-one. He never remarried, and he died suddenly in 1996 of an abdominal aortic aneurism. He was buried at Arlington National Cemetery.

Fullback Don Bonko, the only member of the 1958 Black Knights to be killed in action, is also buried at Arlington. An artillery officer, he went to Vietnam with the 1st Infantry Division in 1965. Although the division headquarters were in Phu Loi—a village about twenty-five miles north of Saigon—Bonko was housed four or five miles outside of town in an encampment maintained by the 145th Aviation Battalion. For daily staff meetings, Bonko and his fellow expatriate officers used to shuttle back and forth to division headquarters in jeeps, driving through an open, unguarded area. On November 26, 1965, less than two months after his arrival in the country, a small unit of Viet Cong ambushed his jeep as he was returning to his quarters from Phu Loi. Bonko had been driving, and he was struck below the shoulder blade by a round that entered the jeep through the rear and ricocheted upward off the metal frame of his seat. The round burrowed deep into his chest cavity, and he died of his wound soon after. He was twenty-eight and left behind a wife, Marge, who was six months pregnant with the couple's second daughter.

The end of the war in Vietnam was not the end of war's impact on the '58 team. On February 27, 1991, First Lieutenant Donaldson Preston Tillar III—a 1988 West Point graduate and the son of Army guard Don Tillar, one of the heroes of the 1958 victory over Rice—

was killed when the UH-60 Black Hawk helicopter in which he was flying was shot down over Iraq during Operation Desert Storm.

On September 17, 2011, ten members of the 1958 Army football team—the last undefeated Army football team—returned to West Point. The occasion was the induction of Bob Novogratz into the Army Sports Hall of Fame. He is the fifth member of the 1958 team to be so honored, joining Red Blaik, Bob Anderson, Bill Carpenter, and Pete Dawkins. Novogratz is so far the only one of the five not to also be enshrined at the College Football Hall of Fame, though a diligent collection of his teammates have been working to change that. The '58 cheering section for Novogratz consisted of Anderson, Dawkins, team manager John Bryer, quarterback Frank Gibson, assistant coach Bill Gunlock, halfback Jim Kennedy, end Chuck Millick, end Jack Morrison, center Bill Rowe, and guard Al Vanderbush. Morrison, who in the fifty-three years since the autumn of 1958 has taken on the dual roles of team social director and official keeper-of-the faith, had laid out an entire program for the weekend.

From his home in South Carolina, Morrison organizes team reunions, big and small, every five years—a tradition that began in 1983, after the team had been invited back to West Point to be honored on the twenty-fifth anniversary of their undefeated season. Attendance at the get-togethers is usually pretty good, though Bill Carpenter has mostly stayed away, remaining the Lonely End to this day. He did return to West Point in 2009 for his own Hall of Fame induction, driving all the way from his home in Whitefish, Montana, on rural highways for an experience that was, as he called it, "more real."

After his graduation in 1959, Morrison spent five years in the air force, flying B-47 bombers with the Strategic Air Command. From there, he went to work in advertising on Madison Avenue in New York City, spending fourteen years at the influential firm McCann Erickson, where he rose to be a senior vice president. In 1981, he moved to Atlanta and joined Coca-Cola, which had been one of his major clients at McCann Erickson, to run the company's corporate advertising department. He retired in 1993 and eventually opened a restaurant, which he sold four years later. "There was a period of time when I was with Coke that I was doing so much traveling that I'd pretty much lost track of what was going on with the '58 team," he says. "You might as well say I dropped out."

But he had been keeping in touch with several of his classmates, including Monk Hilliard, Charlie Lytle, Bill Rowe, and Harry Walters. Many of the team's early reunions revolved around these players and their wives. When new Army athletic director Rick Greenspan fired head coach Bob Sutton in 1999 and replaced him with Todd Berry, Morrison began to get more involved. He did not think Berry, who had been a successful coach at Division I-AA Illinois State, was a good fit for the Cadets, primarily because the coach planned to convert Army's wishbone offense into a spread passing attack that would require the sort of skilled players that had been spurning the academy for years. "I didn't care for a lot of the things that Greenspan was implementing," says Morrison. "And I predicted that Berry was going to be a disaster."

Morrison was right, and West Point spent most of the next decade trying to dig its football program out of a very deep hole. The result of Berry's four-year tenure was untrammeled ignominy and the beginning of a nine-year slump in which the Cadets sank to the depths of college football—in 2003 they became the first team in major college history to finish 0–13. Morrison started a Web site, supportarmyfootball.com, that he used to advocate for Berry's termination, and he began sending weekly e-mails about the state of the team to a distribution list that grew quickly. From that, he says, "I somehow became the team secretary."

The '58 reunions for many years were ad hoc affairs, and the organizing responsibilities got passed around to several former players. "But the last two or three reunions," says Morrison, "I finally said, 'Hell, once you do one, it's so much easier to do the next than having somebody else start over from scratch.'" Occasionally, when the team meets at West Point, they journey together to the cemetery to visit the grave of Red Blaik. His headstone, a tall piece of polished black granite in the shape of a football, rests on a patch of ground between the Old Cadet Chapel and the river, on the cemetery's south side. Blaik remains a divisive figure in West Point history, but Morrison and his teammates still revere their coach, whom they give all the credit for their remarkable success.

There was no time for such a visit the weekend of Novogratz's Hall of Fame induction, which also included the dedication of a room given over to the commemoration of the 1958 team at the Thayer Hotel, the academy's on-post lodgings. Morrison had spent months securing photographs and mementos to decorate the walls of the suite, and, after a breakfast reception on the ground floor, he and his teammates gathered in a small reception hall to witness the room's formal dedication. From there, the party moved to the Plain for the pregame parade, and later to Michie Stadium to watch the Cadets take on Northwestern.

Army football still struggles for wins and relevance. Coach Rich Ellerson, who was hired in 2009, and whose brother John had captained the Army team for Paul Dietzel in 1962, has brought the triple option back, restoring a measure of success to the program, though as of this writing he has yet to beat either Air Force or Navy. The Cadets finished 7–6 in 2010, their first winning season since 1996, and capped the season by beating Southern Methodist University 16–14 in the Armed Forces Bowl. On this day, the Wildcats were six-point favorites over Army, but the Cadets pulled out a 21–14 upset that sent everybody home happy.

It was a beautiful late-summer day, and spirits at the reunion were high. Bill Gunlock, now eighty-three, was horsing around with the linemen he had coached so many years ago, going so far as to get down in a three-point stance opposite Bill Rowe and demonstrate proper blocking technique. And later, Dawkins—whose gift for extemporaneous public speaking is prodigious—addressed his former teammates. "We had the good fortune to play during a golden age for college football," he said. "The connection that developed between this team and the Corps of Cadets was amazing. Those Friday night pep rallies—that spirit was spontaneous, and it was very genuine. There was just kind of an exuberance, and a shared sense of connection."

Dawkins's sentiment was close to something that Gene Mikelonis—the brilliant halfback whose injured knee prevented him from starring for the 1958 team—had said a few months earlier. "The one thing that sports does is it bonds you," he said. "You're thrown together with a group of people who you realize have the same aspirations, the same fears, the same goals as you do. You watch them struggle and you watch them sail. And you do it all together."

THE A SQUAD

Red Blaik: Four years after he left West Point, Blaik was called upon by President John F. Kennedy to go to Birmingham, Alabama, along with former secretary of the army Kenneth Royall, to help restore peace in the community following the bombing of a black church that killed four children. It was a tough mission that achieved, at best, mixed results. Blaik clashed with police commissioner Bull Connor, whom he described as "the symbol of the uncompromising redneck," as well as with Martin Luther King, who he felt tried to sabotage the proceedings. "I felt strongly that King could not abide progress made in his absence," wrote Blaik, "and felt he must force the issue and thus be credited as the leader behind the scenes." Blaik and Royall never submitted their final report to the president, who was assassinated on November 22, 1963. Blaik remained friends with Robert Kennedy, and the two frequently visited with each other in their respective New York offices, sometimes bandying about the idea of purchasing a professional football team. Blaik remained in New York at AVCO until he retired for good in 1969. He and Merle moved soon after to Southern California, where Blaik was a regular at La Quinta Country Club. Merle died in 1984, and Blaik moved to Colorado Springs to be close to his son Bob, who, like his older brother, Bill, had become successful in the oil business. In 1986,

President Ronald Reagan awarded Red Blaik the Presidential Medal of Freedom. He died on May 6, 1989.

Bob Anderson: He had no desire to devote the rest of his life to the army after he graduated from West Point in 1960. "I looked at Bill Carpenter and said, 'That's the way you're supposed to be if you're going to be a military man,'" he says, "and I did not feel that. I certainly wanted to defend my country if necessary, but I had no preconceptions of making it a career." The New York Giants drafted Anderson in the ninth round of that year's NFL draft, but his military commitment kept him from joining the team immediately. An infantry lieutenant, he was assigned to the 101st Airborne Division at Fort Campbell, Kentucky. From there he went to Ranger School at Fort Benning, Georgia, where he tore the anterior cruciate ligament in the same knee he had hurt against Illinois in 1959, an injury that effectively ended his army career. He made the Giants' roster in 1963 but only saw action in one game, when he rushed once for a loss of two yards. He soon went to work for Xerox, where he was in sales for eight years before he left to go full-time into the restaurant business. In 1965, with New York Yankees utility infielder Phil Linz, he opened a sports bar called Mr. Laffs on Manhattan's Upper East Side, an area that was then brimming with swinging singles bars because of its proximity to the notorious Stew Zoo, an apartment building at 345 East Sixty-fifth Street, where 90 percent of the tenants were airline stewardesses. Anderson left the restaurant business in the early 1980s and went back to work for Xerox for a time before joining the New Jersey Turnpike Authority. Never married, he retired in 2010 and moved with his girlfriend—a former stewardess whom he met at Mr. Laffs in the early 1970s—to West Melbourne, Florida. There, he is able to help take care of his mother, Mary, who turned one hundred years old on September 1, 2011.

Ed Bagdonas: The Cadets' tackle embarked on a twenty-one-year career in the army after graduating in 1959. But before fully dedicating himself to the military, Bagdonas qualified for the 1960 Olympic team in the hammer throw, placing third in the event at the Olympic trials in Palo Alto with a heave of 62.76 meters. At the Olympic Games in Rome, he finished nineteenth. An armor officer, he served two tours in Vietnam and retired in 1980 as a lieutenant colonel. In January 1985, after a day of chopping wood at his home in Bedford, Massachusetts, he suffered a heart attack. Bagdonas spent the next two months in the hospital while doctors tried in vain to stabilize his heartbeat. He died after he suffered a second heart attack on March 29, 1985, leaving behind a wife, Elizabeth, and two sons, Edward and Andrew. Elizabeth Bagdonas, who still lives in Bedford, is not a football fan, but she remembers being fascinated by the Lonely End when she used to visit Ed at West Point on football weekends. "There was so much style to it," she says. "There was a real glow. That team made everybody proud." Her husband, she says, did not have much growing up, and the academy was "his big huge chance to get an education. And he got it and took that as far as he could. But the athletics at West Point, and going to Rome—it was really the high point of his life."

Joe Caldwell: The Army quarterback entered the Corps of Engineers after graduation in 1960 and served with the 82nd Airborne Division for two years before returning to West Point as an assistant under new coach Paul Dietzel for a year. In 1964, Caldwell took his wife, Genevieve, or Gigi, and their two-year-old son, Daniel, to the University of Illinois, where Joe began working toward his master's degree in civil engineering. In late November, while on a weekend trip with his family to visit friends in Lansing, Michigan, he was seriously injured in a two-car accident in which he was thrown from the backseat and struck his head on a curb. He lay unconscious in the hospital for nearly forty-eight hours—through the Cadets' 11–8 win over Navy the next day, their first victory in the series since 1958—before succumbing to his injuries and dying on November 29, 1964. Gigi moved with Daniel to Paris, where friends took them in. She soon set up her own household, taught herself to speak French, and began working towards a master's degree in architecture and interior design. After she finished school, Gigi moved with Daniel back to Miami and began a successful career in interior design. She continued in her career until she succumbed to carcinoid cancer on February 27, 2007. Daniel now lives in Fort Lauderdale. An oil painter, he has his own studio filled with his contemporary impressionist paintings. He and his wife, Liz, have three children.

Bill Carpenter: The Lonely End earned All-America honors in 1959, when he caught forty-three passes for 591 yards. In the spring of 1960, he was named to the All-America lacrosse team—this only a year after he had first picked up a stick. After graduation, he dedicated his thirty-two-year military career to being a troop commander. His interests were out in the field with his soldiers, not in a staff room at the Pentagon, where he served only one tour despite rising to the rank of major general. He retired after earning his third star in 1992 and moved with his wife, Toni, to Whitefish, Montana, where the couple built a log home on a hill in the woods and christened it, appropriately, the Lonesome End. (Carpenter is adamant that he prefers "lonesome" to "lonely.") By this time, the couple's three sons—Bill Jr., forty-nine; Ken (a 1986 graduate of Air Force), forty-seven; and Steve, forty-six—were out on their own. In September 2011, Toni died after a long fight with cancer. "West Point taught you how to learn in the classroom," says Carpenter. "But the things I learned there that had the most value were out on the athletic field."

Pete Dawkins: He and his wife, Judi, have one daughter, Noël, who runs her own business communications company in New York. Their son, Sean, died suddenly of a flaw in his heart valve at the age of forty-two on March 23, 2007.

Monk Hilliard: He graduated sixth from the bottom in the Class of 1959 but nevertheless went on to a successful twenty-two-year army career. Hilliard served two tours in Vietnam, the first as an airplane pilot, the second as the commander of an attack helicopter company. He was twice awarded the Distinguished Flying Cross and rose to the rank of lieutenant colonel before he retired in 1981. He settled in Carlisle, Pennsylvania, and became the director of training for the Pennsylvania Emergency Management Agency, for which he worked until he retired in 1998. In the summer of 2011, Hilliard was diagnosed with bladder cancer and underwent grueling chemotherapy that finally ended in early December. He and his wife, Betsy, have three daughters. The Hilliards still live in Carlisle, not far from Bill Rowe, Monk's old teammate. The two families remain close, in large part because Betsy's sister, Butch, is married to Rowe.

Charlie Lytle: (see epilogue)

Bob Novogratz: His Army career spanned thirty years after his graduation in 1959 and also included a pair of tours in Vietnam. An infantry officer, Novogratz specialized in logistics, contracting, and international programs. He rose to the rank of colonel, and his final active-duty tours were as the head of army contracting in Europe and as an assistant to the secretary of the army. After he left the service, he became a consultant on international defense issues, retiring for good in 2008. Novogratz and his wife, Barbara, raised seven children, and he spent many years as a youth football, wrestling, and soccer coach. He also taught high school religion classes for twenty years. The seven Novogratz siblings are an eclectic, often highly successful bunch. Jacqueline, the oldest at fifty, is the founder and chief executive of the Acumen Fund, a nonprofit venture capital enterprise with the goal of creating "a world beyond poverty"; she is also the bestselling author of *The Blue Sweater: Bridging the Gap Between Rich and Poor in an Interconnected World*. Forty-eight-year-old Bob and his wife, Cortney, have their own successful design business in New York City and, along with their seven kids, were featured in the Bravo program *9 by Design*. Michael, who is forty-seven, is a principal at the hedge fund Fortress Investment Group. Forty-year-old Elizabeth is a freelance writer. John, who is thirty-eight, is the head of marketing and investor relations at the Millennium Partners hedge fund. Amy, who is thirty-six, is the director of the TED prize, which is awarded annually at the Technology, Entertainment, and Design Conference. Matthew, the baby at thirty-three, works in foreign exchange sales at RBC Capital Markets in New York.

Bill Rowe: The Cadets' fiery center spent four years in the army as an artillery officer after his graduation in 1959. Rowe spent his final year on active duty at West Point as an assistant football coach. He then spent one year as an assistant coach at Manlius before returning to the academy to join Paul Dietzel's staff in 1964. Rowe stayed at West Point for two years—"long enough to beat Roger Staubach in 1964," he says—before moving on with Dietzel to South Carolina, where he worked as the defensive coordinator for eight years. From there he went to Florida State, where he was the assistant athletic director until 1976. It was during that time that he was in the running for the head coaching job at the military academy, which had just parted ways with Tom Cahill. Rowe, however, lost out on the job to Homer Smith. He left Tallahassee in 1976 and returned with his wife, Butch, to his hometown of Carlisle, Pennsylvania. There the couple raised their four children, and also started their own successful antiques business.

Don Usry: Army's Friendly End entered the air force after his graduation from West Point in 1960. After a year of pilot training, Usry's first permanent duty station was in Tripoli, Libya, where he was flying F-100 jet fighters. In 1966, he was assigned to fly F-100s in Vietnam. It was during this time that he was the subject of a documentary program on ABC called *War in the Skies*, which was narrated by the actor Jimmy Stewart. The documentary followed Usry from his home in Homestead, Florida, to Tuy Hoa, Vietnam. He came home in 1967 and returned to Texas, where he earned a master's of science in math from Southern Methodist University. In 1969, he was assigned to the math department at the Air Force Academy. In addition to his teaching duties, he also served as a plebe coach and an advance scout for the varsity football team. On October 25, 1969, Major Usry was in Palo Alto, California, to scout the game between Stanford and UCLA. Air Force would be playing the Cardinals, who were led by a junior quarterback named Jim Plunkett, in three weeks. Usry, much like Doc Blanchard had done during his days as Red Blaik's chief recruiter, had flown himself to California in a T-33 jet trainer. That night, he was at the controls of the plane for the return flight to Colorado Springs. Sitting behind him was Captain Marty Bezyak, who was also a coach and scout for the Falcons. With the weather in Colorado Springs deteriorating rapidly—fog was rolling in, and the visibility was extremely low—Usry attempted to land without the use of his instruments. He crashed about a half mile short of the runway; the plane exploded upon impact and killed both men instantly. Don Usry left behind a wife, Maggie, and two children, Don, who's now forty-eight, and Sharon, who was born severely handicapped with spina bifida and died in 1983 at the age of sixteen. Maggie remarried a year after her husband's death. A retired schoolteacher, she's now seventy-two and lives in Monroe, Louisiana, not far from the city of Shreveport, where her son, a 1986 graduate of Air Force who is a business manager for an oil and gas company, now lives.

Harry Walters: He served four years in the army before joining the Kimberly-Clark Corporation, first in Neenah, Wisconsin, and later in New York City. Walters stayed in the paper business and, in 1977, rose to be the president and chief executive officer of the Potsdam Paper Corporation. After he left his position at the White House in 1986, he took charge of the Great Lakes Carbon Corporation, but not before he watched President Reagan award the Presidential Medal of Freedom to Red Blaik. In 1991, President George H. W. Bush named Walters president and CEO of the Desert Storm Homecoming Foundation. Walters has founded two 501(c)(3) organizations to benefit veterans. He and his wife, Illa, live in Williamsburg, Virginia. The couple have two children.

KEY RESERVES

Glen Adams: He went into the artillery after graduation in 1961 and was stationed in Germany, where his commanders' endless demands that he play for the base football team ultimately convinced him to leave the army three years later. Adams returned to Texas and earned his J.D. at the University of Texas in 1967. He went into private practice for four years before becoming general counsel for Ross Perot's Electronic Data Systems Corporation. Adams remained in the world of business for the rest of his career, eventually moving into bankruptcy law in 1985. He also served on several boards of directors before finally retiring to Southern California in 1996. Adams's first wife died shortly after the birth of his first daughter, Kimberly, in 1964. A second marriage produced two more daughters, Kathryn, who is forty-three, and Melissa, who is forty-two. Adams and his third wife, Jeri, to whom he has been married since 1983, live in Rancho Santa Fe, California. "West Point," he says, "was the best thing that ever happened to me."

Don Bonko: (see epilogue)

Al Vanderbush: The captain of the 1961 Army football team returned to the academy for the first time one year after his graduation to serve as an assistant coach for the plebe team. He returned in

1971 for a three-year assignment in the office of the dean and came back again in 1984 as the deputy director of athletics. Between Vanderbush's tours at West Point, he served overseas as an infantry officer in Korea and Vietnam, as well as in Alaska and Hawaii. He retired from active duty in 1990, when the academy named him as the athletic director. He now lives just outside West Point, in the town of Highland Falls, New York, and is a regular at the West Point golf course. He and his wife, Carin, a silver medalist in the 100-meter backstroke at the 1956 Melbourne Olympics, have two sons.

Steve Waldrop: After graduating in 1960, he spent most of his time on active duty working as the commander of the Nike Missile Base in Denton, Texas. Waldrop resigned from the army in 1963 and spent several years working as an organizer for the state Republican Party. He moved east in 1969 to work for Polaroid as a manufacturing manager. Staying in the Boston area, in 1974 he joined Prime Computer Company, where he worked in purchasing. He moved back to Texas in 1979 and went into business for himself. In 1996, he founded Integrated Web Solutions, a company centered around the design and development of corporate Web sites. Waldrop still runs the business out of his home in Kingwood, Texas. "I'm one of those old codgers who doesn't know a lot about HTML, but I know what to do with it," he says. He and his wife, Sarah, have two sons.

ACKNOWLEDGMENTS

Writing a book can be a solitary pursuit, a fact I discovered early on in this project. But as I also learned, it can be a wonderfully communal one, and I was blessed with abundant support from some very patient and helpful people during my retelling of this tale. Some of them are friends and family, but many more came into my life because of my work on this book. And I owe every one of them a great debt.

Thanks first of all to my agents, Adam Korn and Brian DeFiore. When I first met Adam in the early fall of 2009, I had only an idea, and an extremely fuzzy one at that. He was enthusiastic about it from the very start, and I'm still not sure I would have gotten this thing off the ground if not for his advice and encouragement—he recognized the value in it even before I did. After he left DeFiore and Company, Brian DeFiore saw the project through to completion.

I'm also grateful to my editor at Thomas Dunne Books, Rob Kirkpatrick, who has provided, among other things, wise counsel, the book's title, and a much-needed extension on my deadline—and I'm not sure it's possible for me to say which one of those represents his most valuable contribution to this book. My thanks also go to Nicole Sohl, who helped me put this whole project together.

I am particularly beholden to production editor Rafal Gibek and to copy editor India Cooper, who gave my manuscript a careful reading and contributed countless helpful notes that did much to make this book better. (I would also like to remind them that my undergraduate degree was in Engineering, not in English.)

My first interview was with Bob Novogratz in the fall of 2008, when I was just beginning to kick this idea around. I think he was a little puzzled about what I was up to, but he was infinitely patient and very insightful. At the time, I thought it would be best to focus on the amazing collection of players at West Point in 1958. Bob was the first one to tell me that the key to the whole season was Red Blaik. It was a point that would be echoed and reechoed by his teammates over the next three years. And it was invaluable in helping me to find a structure in my story. Thank you, Bob.

My first sit-down interview with a former Army player was with Al Vanderbush, and he provided me not only with chips and salsa to snack on but also with a handful of resources that proved invaluable. Among them was the highlight reel for the 1958 season, as well as a book about, among other things, the life of Don Usry. Written and self-published by a former accountant from Fort Worth, Texas, named Dennis Meals, *Men on a Flying Trapeze* painted a complete and touching portrait of the Cadets' Friendly End. I also received a raft of artifacts from former assistant coach Bill Gunlock, including the complete game film of the Army–South Carolina contest and a copy of the menu for Red Blaik's farewell feast at Leone's. More importantly, Bill bequeathed to me a set of mint-condition 1958 playbooks. My analysis of the 1951 cheating scandal was helped greatly not only by Bill McWilliams's fine book, *A Return to Glory*, but also by the author's thorough personal knowledge of the whole affair. Bill is a member of West Point's Class of 1955, and there are very few who know more about this painful incident, or who understand it better. Thank you for the guidance and friendship.

Outside of the film in my possession, footage of the 1958 team was extremely scarce. Luckily, former Fighting Irish halfback Norm Odyniec sent me a copy of Notre Dame's 1958 highlight film, which helped me to re-create the Cadets' first important victory of the season.

A large chunk of my research took place at West Point, either in the Athletic Communications Office or in the USMA Archives. In Athletic Communications, I was helped greatly by senior executive associate athletic director Bob Beretta, who has been at the academy for twenty-five years and knows everything about everything. I also received a great deal of support from his staff, especially Mady Salvani, the assistant director of athletic communications. She was a hero at finding photographs, press clippings, game programs, and statistics. Mady has been at West Point for forty years and, I'm pretty sure, could actually produce Red Blaik's fedora if I requested it. At the archives, Suzanne Christoff and her staff (Susan M. Lintelmann, Casey Madrick, and Alicia M. Mauldin-Ware) kept me buried in a treasure trove of primary documents and long-lost newspaper clippings for an entire month.

Many of the players and coaches from Army's 1958 team generously shared their recollections of that season with me. And some went the extra mile to help. Bill Carpenter hosted me at his home in Whitefish, Montana. Bill Gunlock flew to New York from his home in Dayton, Ohio—and barely made it back ahead of a major snowstorm. (He also made the mistake of volunteering to carry my son out of a restaurant one evening. The boy was only one at the time, but he already had the build of a future offensive lineman. Sorry, Bill, but I did try to warn you.) And several former players and coaches answered multiple phone calls to provide counsel and direction. Among the gentlemen I bothered most often: Glen Adams, John Bryer, Pete Dawkins, Bill Gunlock, Tom Harp, Frank Lauterbur, Jack Morrison, Bill Rowe, Steve Waldrop, Harry Walters, and Russ Waters. Thanks to you all. I also received a tremendous amount of help from former B Squad coach Barney Gill, who passed away at the age of 84 on April 17, 2012. Barney was funny, insightful, and extraordinarily generous with his time throughout my work on this book. He was a fan of both Red Blaik and Army football, and he was also beloved by just about every player on the 1958 team. He will be missed.

I received a great deal of assistance from the men who faced Army that fall on the fields of friendly strife. From South Carolina, Weemie Baskin, King Dixon, and Dwight Keith provided an outsider's perspective on the Lonely End's debut. Of additional help were Steve Garban, of Penn State; Terry Brennan and Chuck Puntillo, of Notre Dame; Jim Zanos, of Pittsburgh (as well as Beano Cook, who was the Pitt sports information director from 1956 to 1966); Bill Bucek and Alvin Hartman, of Rice; and Wayne Hardin, Joe Tranchini, and Buddy Wellborn, of Navy.

One of the most valuable interviews I conducted for this project was with Tom Davidson, the second oldest of Gar Davidson's three sons, and the loving keeper of his father's legacy. Tom painted a very vivid portrait of his dad. He also provided greatly needed perspective on Gar Davidson's opinions about football, the military academy, and the issue of honor, as well as his long and often contentious relationship with Red Blaik. Despite their differences, both men will certainly live on as two of the most unique and important figures in West Point's long history. Thank you, Tom.

Many other relatives of players now departed also contributed to this project. I owe a debt of gratitude to Elizabeth Bagdonas, Daniel Caldwell, John Caldwell, Bobbie Lytle, Tiffany Lytle, and Don Usry II. I also greatly appreciate the help of former Army fullback Al Rushatz, who got his break in the starting lineup in 1959 when Don Bonko went down with a knee injury. Once their playing careers ended, the two men served together in Vietnam. Colonel Rushatz's memories of his friend and former teammate came in handy where the rest of my research had come up empty. I was also assisted in my investigation into Bonko's time at West Point by Todd Counts, who had been Don's roommate for a time.

I did not take leave from my job as a writer and editor at *Sports Illustrated* to work on this book. So I owe a world of thanks to my boss, Terry McDonell, who made it possible for me to do two things at once. When I did have to take some time off, assistant managing editors Neil Cohen and Hank Hersch went to great lengths to accommodate my requests. The *SI* Library, in the persons of Joy Birdsong and Susan Szeliga, assisted me greatly in my research. And around the office, I found sympathetic ears, helpful advice, and much-needed transcription services from many colleagues, some of whom have been down this road before (I hope I don't forget anybody): Lars Anderson, David Bauer, Mark Bechtel, Stephen Cannella, Richard

Demak, Amanda Doyle, Michael Farber, Mark Godich, Kostya Kennedy, Tim Layden, Sarah Kwak, Gabe Miller, Mark Mravic, Austin Murphy, Rich O'Brien, Rebecca Shore, and Jon Wertheim.

Outside of the office, I received valuable advice, help, moral support, and friendship from my friends and family, including (but not limited to) Rebecca Ascher-Walsh, Gregg Chabot, Eric Chibnik, Kelly Gildea, Bo Keane, Mary Ann Keane, Phil Keane, and Rich Ryan.

This book wouldn't be close to complete without the beautiful photos that appear within. For those, I owe my undying thanks to Claire Bourgeois, who tracked down and secured the rights to every single one of them. Always cheerful and never daunted, she has made this book look much better than I ever dared to hope.

I grew up knowing the story of the 1958 Army football team because my father was a classmate of the seniors on that squad. As a young kid in the 1970s, when the program at West Point was going through an especially unsuccessful period, it was unthinkable to me that the Black Knights had ever been undefeated and highly ranked, and I used to study the pages of my dad's yearbook that had been devoted to that magical season. I'd like to thank my parents, Gary and Nadine Beech, and my sister, Cynthia Lawrence, for everything, and my father especially for pointing me down this long road.

Finally, this book never would have happened without the love, support, and encouragement of my wife, Allison. She lived through every day of this project and dissected and edited much of my book as it took shape—my best reader and best friend. Because of her and our son, Nate, our daughter, Annie, and our dog, Maddy, I never lacked for inspiration or support, and my inkwell never ran dry.

NOTES

1. LINING UP IN THE SNOW

Interviews with Bob Anderson, Barney Gill, Tom Harp, Frank Lauterbur, Jack Morrison, Bob Novogratz, and Al Vanderbush. Red Blaik's first memoir, *You Have to Pay the Price,* was full of details about the coach's early years and also chronicled—from his perspective—the creation of the Lonely End offense. Blaik's mannerisms, personality, and relationship with Douglas MacArthur are discussed extensively in the authoritative biography *When Pride Still Mattered: A Life of Vince Lombardi,* by David Maraniss, as well as *Vince: A Personal Biography of Vince Lombardi,* by Michael O'Brien. Some notes on MacArthur's tenure as superintendent also came from Stephen E. Ambrose's colorful study of the academy, *Duty, Honor, Country: A History of West Point.* Army football received heavy (and quite favorable) coverage in most of the New York–area newspapers, notably *The New York Times,* and Blaik's travails with West Point's admissions policies were widely reported heading into the 1958 campaign. In a *Times* story previewing Dale Hall's debut season at Army the next year, Duffy Daugherty's connection to the Lonely End is made clear.

2. THE PROMISE

West Point's 1951 cheating scandal, as well as its aftermath, has been well chronicled in a variety of places, including in Blaik's own memoir, Maraniss's biography of Lombardi, and Murray Sperber's searing indictment of collegiate athletics, *Onward to Victory: The Crises That Shaped College Sports*. Sperber's work was also a valuable source of information about college basketball's game-fixing episodes, as were several articles that appeared in the pages of *Sports Illustrated* over the years. Another story from the pages of *SI* that provided additional perspective on events at the academy in the summer of '51 was Frank Deford's "Code Breakers." I also turned often to *A Return to Glory: The Untold Story of Honor, Dishonor, and Triumph at the United States Military Academy, 1950–1953*, by Bill McWilliams (USMA '55), a book of epic sweep and scope that nevertheless pays great attention to the both the details of the cheating scandal and the resurrection of the Army football program. Interviews with the author were also helpful in keeping my own work moving in the right direction. The results of the academy's investigation into the cheating ring are detailed in the report of the Collins Board; the recommendations for fixing the problem are contained in the report of the Bartlett Board. Both are available, along with the personal correspondence of Colonel Blaik, in the USMA Archives. The incident was also widely covered by the newspapers of the day.

3. THE SOLDIER'S SON

Impressions of spring practices under Red Blaik came from various interviews with players and coaches, including Bill Carpenter, Tom Harp, Harry Walters, and Russ Waters. Many of the same interviews highlighted the personality of Chuck Gottfried. Bill Carpenter has been the subject of countless newspaper and magazine stories, none more complete than William Nack's brilliant *Sports Illustrated* profile from 1993, on the occasion of Carpenter's retirement from the army. These stories, along with my own interviews, helped to recount his remarkable journey to West Point. Doc Blanchard has also been the subject of numerous profiles, but few of them mention his time as the plebe football coach at West Point. Luckily, every awestruck cadet who ever played for Blanchard, particularly Bill Rowe and Harry Walters, remembers him well. All details of Blaik's adjustments to the offensive and defensive schemes during the spring came from assistant coaches Bill Gunlock, Tom Harp, and Frank Lauterbur, as well as from Blaik's autobiography.

4. OLD ENEMIES

Blaik wrote extensively about his struggle to find a competent quarterback in his autobiography, where he also retold the heroic story of Don Holleder. John Caldwell remembered Holleder's visit to Miami and told me all about his brother, Joe. Additional information on Joe Caldwell came from an interview with his son, Daniel, as well as from research in the self-published memoir of Genevieve Caldwell, Joe's wife. His exploits at Miami High were recounted by his teammate Jack Westbrook. Blaik's conflict with Gar Davidson is laid out in several places: in Blaik's own autobiography; in the book *On, Brave Old Army Team: The Cheating Scandal That Rocked the Nation*, by James Blackwell; in contemporaneous newspaper stories; and in the extensive resources of the archives at the United States Military Academy. Here you can see, spelled out in great detail, Blaik's breakdown of the numbers for General MacArthur, as well as the official paperwork from General Davidson responding to Blaik's requests. Some details were also provided by Davidson's son Tom, who has lovingly compiled extensive resources about his father's career and his family's history. Background on Blaik's excursions to Bull Pond came from Maraniss's biography of Lombardi, Blaik's autobiography, and interviews with his assistant coaches. Blaik's encounter with Andy Gustafson comes from his own book, and the system of signals for the Lonely End came from interviews with Bob Anderson, Bill Carpenter,

Pete Dawkins, and Bill Gunlock, who provided the original list typed up for the coaching staff. Gunlock also recounted portions of MacArthur's address to the team in advance of the Syracuse scrimmage, as did Pete Dawkins.

5. LONESOME GEORGE

Interviews with John Bryer, Bill Carpenter, Bill Gunlock, Tom Harp, Jack Morrison, Bill Rowe, and Harry Walters provided details about game days at West Point and the hours before the opening game against South Carolina. Interviews with Weemie Baskin, King Dixon, Alex Hawkins, and Dwight Keith—all members of the 1958 Gamecocks football team—provided the viewpoint of Army's opposition. A copy of the game film helped fill in many details not provided in the official record of the game or in contemporaneous newspaper reports. Barney Gill provided a colorful retelling of his appearance at the Toots Shor's press conference following the victory. Former Penn State linebacker Steve Garban recounted his experiences during the Nittany Lions' 26–0 defeat.

6. JUGGERNAUT

Interviews with Bob Anderson, Bill Gunlock, Tom Harp, Jack Morrison, Bob Novogratz, and Harry Walters. Red Blaik documented his laundry-room encounter with Joe Byrne in his autobiography. Some details of the 1946 Army–Notre Dame game came from Blaik's own account, as well as from Murray Sperber's *Onward to Victory*. Additional interviews with Terry Brennan, Norm Odyniec, and Chuck Puntillo. Norm Odyniec also contributed a highlight reel from the game that helped provide a complete account of the struggle between Notre Dame and Army.

7. MR. WONDERFUL

Interviews with Bob Anderson, John Bryer, Pete Dawkins, Bill Gunlock, Frank Lauterbur, Peter Stromberg, John Underwood, Steve Waldrop, and Harry Walters.

8. THE END OF PERFECTION

Interviews with Bob Anderson, John Bryer, Bill Carpenter, Pete Dawkins, Barney Gill, Tom Harp, Monk Hilliard, Jack Morrison, Bob Novogratz, Bill Rowe, Al Vanderbush, Steve Waldrop, and Harry Walters. Further interviews with Pittsburgh mule thieves Herbie Dodell and Harvey Wimmer, as well as with Panthers end Jim Zanos and Beano Cook, who was the sports information director at Pitt in 1958.

9. THE CRUCIBLE

Interviews with Glen Adams, John Bryer, Bill Carpenter, Pete Dawkins, Bill Gunlock, Monk Hilliard, Bob Novogratz, Don Tillar, Don Usry, and Al Vanderbush. The perspective of the Rice Owls was provided by interviews with Bill Bucek and Alvin Hartman. It is a fascinating twist to the story of this Army team that Usry, and not Carpenter or Dawkins—both of whom were nationally famous as collegians and went on to prominent military careers—is the one player who has so far been the subject of a book-length biographical sketch. In 2006, Dennis Meals, a former accountant from Fort Worth, self-published an exhaustive hardcover oral history on the life of Usry and a high school teammate named Thurman "Bulldog" Dennis. Both men had died in 1969. (Dennis, a self-destructive misfit, choked on his own vomit in an alcoholic stupor.) Titled *Men on a Flying Trapeze* in reference to a halfback-option play that Dennis and Usry had run with great success in high school, the earnest, sprawling tome covers 644 pages, and Meals proves himself a remarkably thorough and resourceful reporter by filling them all with wonderful detail. He spoke to just about everyone with any connection to Usry, including extended family, friends, and former teammates. And many of the photographs that illustrate his story are primary documents—in many cases handwritten letters and personal notes, as well as official papers from schools, athletic associations, the Department of Defense, and law enforcement. Taken all together, it paints a detailed, insightful and often unsparing portrait of Army's Friendly End.

10. GOLDEN DAYS

Interviews with Bob Anderson, Bill Carpenter, Pete Dawkins, Barney Gill, Tom Harp, Monk Hilliard, Gene Mikelonis, Bill Rowe, and Peter Stromberg. The story of the rapid rise of Air Force football was detailed for me in interviews with former assistant coach Jim Bowman and former All-America Brock Strom. Stephen Ambrose's excellent history of West Point, *Duty, Honor, Country,* provided some much-needed detail about life at the academy. Some of the details of the closed-circuit broadcast of the Army-Rice game came from a 2003 story written by former cadet Bill Mogan (USMA, '62) for *Assembly,* the academy's alumni magazine.

11. NO SUBSTITUTE FOR VICTORY

Interviews with Bob Anderson, Bill Carpenter, Pete Dawkins, Barney Gill, Bill Gunlock, Tom Harp, Monk Hilliard, Rob Miser, Jack Morrison, Bill Rowe, and Harry Walters. Wayne Hardin, Joe Tranchini, and Buddy Wellborn provided Navy's perspective on the game and also contributed some valuable details about Eddie Erdelatz.

12. FAREWELL

Interviews with Bob Anderson, John Bryer, Pete Dawkins, Barney Gill, Bill Gunlock, Tom Harp, Bob Novogratz, and Harry Walters. Red Blaik provided a detailed rundown on his decision to retire in his autobiography, which also outlines the basics of his history with Victor Emanuel. A *Time* magazine cover story on Emanuel in October 1946 titled "Everything, Inc." provided a more thorough biographical sketch of the AVCO CEO. The machinations on behalf of General MacArthur at the 1952 Republican National Convention are detailed in William Manchester's biography of MacArthur, *American Caesar*. Additionally, several valuable primary resources came from the archives at the United States Military Academy.

BIBLIOGRAPHY

Ambrose, Stephen E. *Duty, Honor, Country: A History of West Point.* Baltimore: Johns Hopkins Press, 1966.

Belichick, Steve. *Football Scouting Methods.* New York: Ronald Press, 1962.

Blaik, Earl "Red." *The Red Blaik Story.* New Rochelle, NY: Arlington House, 1974.

———. *You Have to Pay the Price.* New York: Holt, Rinehart & Winston, 1960.

Bowden, Mark. *The Best Game Ever.* New York: Atlantic Monthly Press, 2008.

Boyles, Bob, and Paul Guido. *The USA Today College Football Encyclopedia.* New York: Skyhorse, 2009.

Caldwell, Genevieve. *God Stories: Five Generations of Floridians: Short Stories, Essays and Thoughts. . . .* Miami: Centennial Press, 2009.

Carroll, Bob, Michael Gershman, David Neff, and John Thorn, eds. *Total Football.* New York: HarperCollins, 1997.

Cavanaugh, Jack. *The Gipper: George Gipp, Knute Rockne, and the Dramatic Rise of Notre Dame Football.* New York: Skyhorse, 2010.

Clary, Jack. *Army vs. Navy: Seventy Years of Football Rivalry.* New York: Ronald Press, 1965.

Cromartie, Bill. *Army Navy Football: The Greatest Rivalry in All of Sports.* Atlanta: Gridiron Publishers, 1996.

Halberstam, David. *The Coldest Winter: America and the Korean War.* New York: Hyperion, 2007.

———. *The Fifties.* New York: Villard, 1993.

Jackson, Kenneth T., ed. *The Encyclopedia of New York City.* New Haven: Yale University Press, 1995.

Layden, Tim. *Blood, Sweat and Chalk—The Ultimate Football Playbook: How the Great Coaches Built Today's Game.* New York: Sports Illustrated Books, 2010.

Manchester, William. *American Caesar: Douglas MacArthur, 1880–1964.* Boston: Little, Brown, 1978.

Maraniss, David. *When Pride Still Mattered: A Life of Vince Lombardi.* New York: Simon & Schuster, 1999.

McWilliams, Bill. *A Return to Glory: The Untold Story of Honor, Dishonor, and Triumph at the United States Military Academy, 1950–1953.* Lynchburg, VA: Warwick House, 2000.

Meals, Dennis. *Men on a Flying Trapeze: Bulldog Dennis and Don Usry.* Fort Worth: Privately printed, 2006.

O'Brien, Michael. *Vince: A Personal Biography of Vince Lombardi.* New York: Morrow, 1987.

Schoor, Gene. *100 Years of Army-Navy Football: A Pictorial History of America's Most Colorful and Competitive Sports Rivalry.* New York: Holt, 1989.

———, ed. *The Army-Navy Game: A Treasury of the Football Classic.* New York: Dodd, Mead, 1967.

Sperber, Murray. *Onward to Victory: The Crises That Shaped College Sports.* New York: Holt, 1998.

Weyand, Alexander M. *Football Immortals.* New York: Macmillan, 1962.

INDEX